MEETING THE INVISIBLE MAN

Saddled With Darwin

MEETING THE INVISIBLE MAN
SECRETS AND MAGIC IN WEST AFRICA

Toby Green

Weidenfeld & Nicolson
LONDON

First published in Great Britain in 2001
by Weidenfeld & Nicolson

© 2001 Toby Green

A CIP catalogue record for this book
is available from the British Library.

ISBN 0 297 64615 X

Typeset by Deltatype Ltd, Birkenhead, Wirral

Set in Minion $11\frac{1}{4}$ on $14\frac{1}{2}$

Printed in Great Britain
by Butler & Tanner Ltd, Frome and London

Weidenfeld & Nicolson
The Orion Publishing Group Ltd
Orion House
5 Upper Saint Martin's Lane
London, WC2H 9EA

'My God! My God! But why deprive me of my pagan senses which cry out?'

Léopold Sédar Senghor

'Something with all the appearance of an epidemic of blindness has broken out, provisionally known as the white sickness.'

José Saramago

For Alice, Eileen and Hetty,
in testament to their bravery,
and to that of the peoples of Senegal,
Guinea-Conakry and Guinea-Bissau

AUTHOR'S NOTE

The official name of the country that I have called Guinea-Conakry in this book is *La République de la Guinée* – Guinea. However, in West Africa the country is widely known as Guinea-Conakry, in order to avoid confusion with Guinea-Bissau. This seems the clearest way of writing about the two countries, and so I have used the name Guinea-Conakry throughout.

Contents

Illustrations

Sections of Illustrations appear between pages 146 and 147. All photographs come from the author's collection.

Dawn at Chelekoto, Guinea-Conakry
Looking south from Gorée, near Dakar
The Ouésséguélé river plain, Fouta Djalon mountains, Guinea-Conakry
Bushels of rice drying in a hut, Chelekoto, Guinea-Conakry
The scars of gunfire from the civil war, Bissau
Old Portuguese cannons on the River Cacheu, Cacheu, Guinea-Bissau
Sharing food from the communal bowl, Bissau
El Hadji and child, the Casamance, Senegal
Oumi Ndiaye
Newborn babies, the Casamance, Senegal
The griot plays the kora, Balimé, Senegal
Ablai's mother, Chelekoto, Guinea-Conakry
Owe, the author's 'daughter' and El Hadji's 'wife', Kabakunda, Guinea-Bissau
Children, Jeta Island, Guinea-Bissau
Community prayers at the end of Ramadan
El Hadji pours the tea
Pounding millet, the Casamance, Senegal
Talla Seydi's hut, Kabakunda, Guinea-Bissau
February's Carnival, Bissau
A Marabout buries a charm, the Casamance, Senegal
Sacred stone in the Fouta Djalon, Guinea-Conakry
The strips of black cat skin, used for the gris-gris for invisibility
Bushfires at dawn, Diaobé, Senegal
Maraboutic tablets with secret verses from the Qu'ran, Guinea-Bissau
A gris-gris hangs at the threshold of a restaurant to entice the clientele, Guinea-Conakry
Fetish house for the worship of ancestral spirits, Jeta Island, Guinea-Bissau
Four pictures demonstrating the success of protective charms on chickens
Two pictures illustrating the result of an invulnerability charm

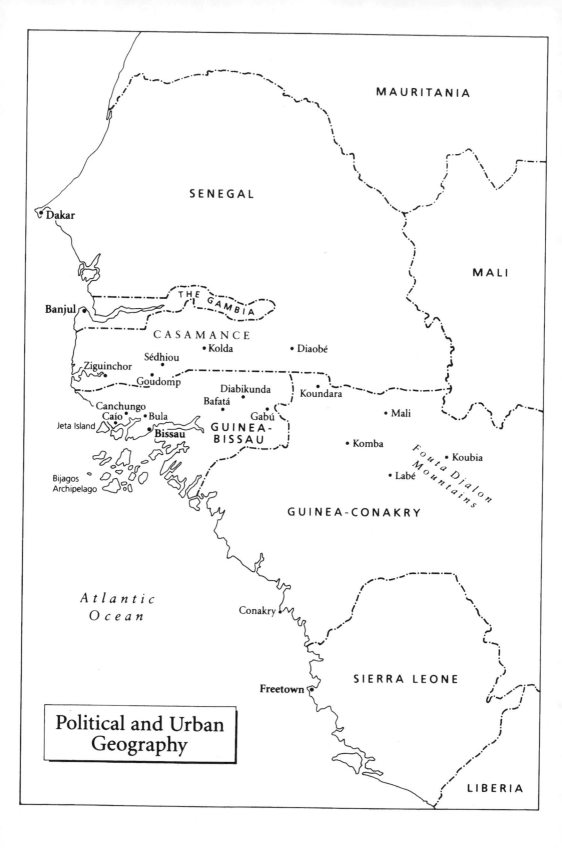

MAURITANIA

SENEGAL

• Dakar

MALI

THE GAMBIA

Banjul

CASAMANCE

• Kolda   • Diaobé

Sédhiou

Ziguinchor

Goudomp

Diabikunda   • Koundara

Bafatá

Canchungo   Gabú   • Mali

Caío   • Bula

Jeta Island   GUINEA-
BISSAU

Bissau   • Komba   • Koubia

Fouta Djalon
Mountains

• Labé

Bijagos
Archipelago

GUINEA-CONAKRY

Atlantic
Ocean

Conakry •

SIERRA LEONE

Freetown •

Political and Urban
Geography

LIBERIA

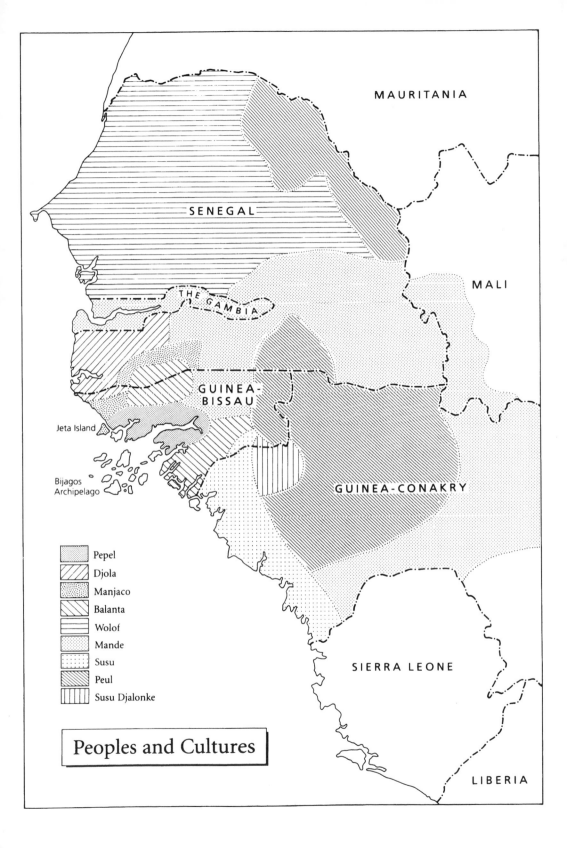

MAURITANIA

SENEGAL

MALI

THE GAMBIA

GUINEA-BISSAU

Jeta Island

Bijagos
Archipelago

GUINEA-CONAKRY

SIERRA LEONE

LIBERIA

Pepel
Djola
Manjaco
Balanta
Wolof
Mande
Susu
Peul
Susu Djalonke

Peoples and Cultures

Prologue

In the summer of 1995, I looked at a map of Africa with my Australian friend Evan. We both wanted to visit a country that would give us an experience as different as possible from any that we had had before. But, as we looked at all the many places before us, we became increasingly confused. We tried to imagine ourselves in the jungles of the Congo Basin or in the ancient city of Timbuktu, but could not do so without a sense of unease which neither of us could pin down. Gradually our eyes turned further west, and our attention leaked to the humid swamplands of the Atlantic coast, past Côte d'Ivoire and Liberia and Sierra Leone and Guinea-Conakry.

'Guinea-Bissau,' we both said, and, for some reason, I began to relax.

The countries of the Congo Basin were always in and out of the news and Timbuktu was a legend. But Guinea-Bissau was a country about which neither of us knew anything, and it was for precisely this reason that we decided to visit it. Being a bloody-minded person, I tended to believe the opposite of what I was told, and so when I realised that no books, newspapers or television programmes reported anything from this distant part of the world, I agreed with Evan that it had to be one of the most fascinating places on earth. Perhaps, I hoped, my time there might begin to reveal the invisible source of the unease that I had felt when I had first turned my attention to the map of Africa.

And so in December 1995 we flew to The Gambia. We bought Chinese bicycles and made our way south through the Casamance. Five days after we departed from Banjul, we entered Guinea-Bissau. There we lodged in a foul room in Ingore with neither lights nor windows, and mattresses that were so infested with bedbugs that, even when we smeared them with insect repellent, it was impossible to sleep. We were still bleary-eyed when we left for Bissau in the morning. The asphalt road swept through groves of palms and cashews and then past salt flats which shone in the sun. But as the heat intensified the road began to burn, and our bicycles developed flat inner tubes. We had no spare parts, and so walked for an hour towards pulsing mirages, which eventually transformed themselves into the small town of Bula.

In Bula we soon found the only workshop. Tyres and spare parts lay beneath the shade of a mango tree, next to the disembowelled hulks of what had formerly been cars. One of the mechanics tried to understand my instructions, but I quickly realised that there was little common ground between his Kriolu and my Portuguese. As we struggled with this linguistic impasse, a slight man wearing a spotless white T-shirt sidled up and spoke to me in French.

'You speak French!' I exclaimed.

'*Mais oui. Je suis Sénégalais.*'

I was thrilled.

'What's your name?' he asked me.

'Toby.'

'I am El Hadji.'

We shook hands warmly, and I introduced him to Evan. Then I explained the problem with the bicycles, and he translated to the mechanic.

'But it's going to be too late for you to continue to Bissau tonight,' he said.

'Where can we stay in Bula?' I asked him.

'You can stay with me.'

I looked at El Hadji for a moment. He was thin. His eyes were wide and dark. Like many West African men, his head was shaved. He had rings on both hands. When he smiled, his whole face lit up with an expression of untrammelled joy. He seemed like a person that we could trust, and we accepted his offer with thanks.

We went with him to his rooms, and stowed our things away safely before dusk. When darkness came we sat drinking tea on the veranda and getting to know one another. There was no moon, and the stars were so bright that they hurt my eyes as I listened to El Hadji telling us his story. Although his grandmother had been from Guinea-Bissau, he

2

had been born and brought up in the Casamance. However, he had come to his grandmother's country because he had thought that work might be easier to find. Eventually he had reached Bula, where he had been able to earn a living.

Our conversation was frequently interrupted by the spitting embers, and the evening was filled by the shadows of people and the flickering of their lanterns which tried to penetrate the furthest corners of the compounds of huts where everyone lived. At one point I turned from El Hadji and stared at the sky, and the utterly alien feeling of being in one of the remotest countries in Africa almost overwhelmed me. My eyes spun, and El Hadji watched me with quiet understanding for a moment.

'It's beautiful to explore the world,' he said.

We ended up spending a week with him. Since Evan spoke only a little French, El Hadji and I were forced into a closer relationship than might have been expected. On arriving in Banjul, Evan and I had wanted to see as many different places as possible, and the idea of spending a week in one small and unremarkable town would have been difficult to entertain. Certainly, we did little of note in Bula, passing whole days drinking tea and strolling from compound to compound, meeting El Hadji's friends. But it was on those apparently banal walks that I began to see just how different this place was from anything that I knew, and I was grateful that El Hadji had encouraged us to stay there.

This thought began to take shape one evening in Bula's market. Night had fallen, and El Hadji had just finished the evening prayer. We were walking by the narrow lines of stalls where people sold oranges and groundnuts and piles of tins. We hoped to find an eatery where we could dine on spaghetti and sauce. The night was dark and the air was filled with the shadows of people and bats, which vanished before they could be seen. But, although we were hungry, we never managed to proceed very far, because El Hadji was constantly stopped by friends.

'El Hadji!'

'El Hadji . . .'

The men clapped him on the back, while the women spoke more voluptuously.

3

'El Hadji,' I said, after we had stopped for what seemed to be the twentieth time, 'how do you know all these people?'

'It is my work,' he said. 'I have to know everyone.'

He was a photographer, taking pictures of people at special occasions and having the films developed in Bissau. Nevertheless, the explanation was not entirely satisfactory. El Hadji must have sensed the doubts that Evan and I felt, because he leant over and whispered to me.

'In Canchungo there is a woman with very strong powers,' he said.

'Powers?'

'She knows a secret that makes you very popular with everyone,' he said, smiling broadly.

This was not the first time that he had referred to magic. On other evenings he had talked about the mystical powers of people in this part of the world. He was a devout Muslim, and prayed rigidly five times a day. But this did not stop him from believing that some people could transform themselves into hyenas when they wished to harm others. In West Africa, he said, there were powerful mystics, the Marabouts, who could perform all sorts of extraordinary feats. Some of them could become invisible, and others possessed the secret of invulnerability.

'Is the woman in Canchungo a Marabout?' I asked.

'She has powers,' was all that he would say.

El Hadji led Evan and me past rivers of people, dimly illuminated by the growling light of the lanterns. Behind the stalls stood a row of low, shabby concrete buildings, and we were on the point of entering one of them when El Hadji was stopped yet again.

'El Hadji!'

A young man took our friend by the arm, and spoke to him rapidly in Kriolu.

'So,' said El Hadji, turning to me when their conversation had subsided, 'this friend can tell you about Marabouts.'

'What about them?' I asked.

'The real Marabouts are near Guinea-Conakry,' the young man said. 'I always used to doubt their powers, because I had never seen one.'

'You have never been to see a Marabout?'

'Not until recently,' he said. 'But then I went to that region a few months ago, and a friend took me to see one. I told the Marabout that I did not believe in his invisibility, and he smiled, and then disappeared from in front of my eyes. All I could see was a small light near the top of the room. Then I heard the Marabout speak.'

'What did he say?' I asked.

'He asked me if I could see him,' said El Hadji's friend. 'But all I saw was this one light.'

El Hadji chuckled with delight at the story. His friend stared at us with a soft gleam in his eyes, which for an instant made the night sparkle, as if the Marabout's wisdom had still been with him.

When El Hadji's friend told me this I did not dismiss him as deluded. In spite of my extraordinarily logical education, all I could wonder was whether these people did not perhaps possess a sort of understanding which was so alien to our own as to belong to a different world entirely.

Once we had eaten, we made our way slowly back towards El Hadji's rooms. The air was heavy and musical with the gentle burr of crickets. Although each house betrayed a weak light of some sort, there was a definite sense of impenetrability. Since the moon was waning it had not yet risen, and the whole town was clutched by a veil of darkness which I did not know how to pierce.

Evan and I slept on El Hadji's bed, as we had been doing since our arrival. Our new friend had insisted on this, for he said that he found the concrete floor comfortable enough. In the morning, we discussed whether or not we should leave, but El Hadji raised his hands in protest.

'No,' he said, 'you must stay one more day.'

'What will we do?' I asked.

'We will go to Canchungo to visit the old woman, and see if she can make the potion for you.'

So we squeezed ourselves into the back of an overloaded pick-up truck and jolted along the road towards that neighbouring town. The air was hot, and the vehicle was crammed full of people and their bundles and their animals, whose excrement clung to the floor of the truck and made me feel sick. The leaves of the cashew trees were thick and knobbly, they seemed to yellow like time in the heat, although perhaps the nature of the colour that I saw was more imaginary than real, since I know that they were green.

In Canchungo, El Hadji led us to a distant compound set around kola and mango trees, where an old lady sat on colourful and neatly woven prayer mats on the veranda. Her husband had died a few months before, and she was dressed in white, the colour of mourning. Her flesh had concertinaed across her chest, and her hands were hard and riddled with knotted veins. Her face had sunk into her neck, and was half concealed by the headscarf that she wore.

She welcomed El Hadji with the affection of a relative, and Evan and I then exchanged greetings with her.

'Welcome,' she said slowly, in Kriolu.

Her son beckoned us to follow him, and we entered a dark concrete room where we squatted against the back wall. Then the old lady came in and sat on a stool. El Hadji explained that we would like her to make the potion for us. She nodded and then washed her hands with water from a plastic tub.

'You must write down your names,' she said, drawing out a dusty piece of paper from the folds of her dress.

When we had done this, she began to prepare herself. She rose and went out on the veranda, where she muttered incantations in a language that I did not understand. Then she scooped clean water into glass bottles with her hands, and treated it with perfume, dyes and incense. A sweet smell wafted over the compound. She dropped seven grains of rice into the potion for luck and blessed each container with our names. Then she returned to the room with the bottles and handed them to us, before sitting next to her son and talking to him about the work that she had done.

'Use this wisely,' her son told us. 'Whenever you want a particular job to go well for you, wash yourself in this potion before you leave the house. Wash your arms, your face, your scalp, and then your chest and your legs. If you do so, you will meet only with success.'

We paid them the sum that had been agreed, and then walked off through Canchungo. El Hadji was looking happy again, for he had procured his own bottle, and expected to be successful for a good while to come because of it. Canchungo was so unremarkable that in many ways it seemed very natural to be there, even though we had just obtained magic potions for ourselves.

'Toby,' El Hadji said to me after a while, 'when you use this potion it will work. Everyone will like you in Europe. Everyone will want to work with you.' He smiled. 'Even this matter of invisibility exists too. There are Marabouts who can make you disappear.'

'Are there many of them?'

The region was full of such wise people according to El Hadji. Back in the Casamance there were many Marabouts. They abounded here in Guinea-Bissau as well, while the people of Guinea-Conakry were also famous for their magic.

'Magic really exists?'

'Everything exists.'

I looked into my new friend's eyes, and saw there the fire of absolute certainty. In my own environment, I would have been thoroughly sceptical of El Hadji's claims, but now I felt my scepticism waning. This man had so little, but he was willing to share whatever he had. When Evan and I gave him our bicycles to sell in Bula's market, he scrupulously handed over the proceeds, which must have seemed like a fortune to him. Of course we gave him a gift before we left, but, nevertheless, as we jolted off southwards and left Bula behind us, I realised that I had made a real friend.

Our pick-up swept over the tarmac into the swelling heat that was, even at that early hour, gathering above the land. As we went, I thought back to the tracks near Bula, where we had walked with El Hadji in the late afternoons. There we had passed through palm groves, crossed over seething columns of driver ants and heard drumming from distant villages which filled the air as if these sounds had been the guardians of some untold drama.

'Come back and see for yourself,' El Hadji had said on our last morning, talking about the Marabouts.

As we accelerated into the hot air, I decided that one day I should do just that.

PART I

'Witchcraft is an imaginary offence
because it is impossible'

In Dakar, I had the strange sensation that I was slowly becoming invisible. This nonsensical feeling settled over me almost as soon as I entered the foyer of the airport, where a harsh and artificial light was reflected in the whites of the floor and the eyes of the many people who wanted to greet me. The glare was so bright that it threatened to overshadow my pallid skin, making me as transparent as the tension which preoccupied my thoughts.

As I walked out into the throng, however, I soon realised that I was seen by everyone. Many people came towards me. Some of them made persistent efforts to get my attention, but I did my best to ignore them. Passengers had piled up their things like sandbags against the flood of people who continually flowed through, and I picked my way through the breakwaters until at last I reached a space of comparative calm. There I stopped and stared at the sea of faces which reflected my gaze like a mirror. Now I saw black and they saw white, but perhaps we both saw the same thing.

Turning from side to side, I swivelled my head as I looked for El Hadji. Four years had passed since we had seen one another, and I worried that I would not recognise him. After writing a letter, I had called from home, and explained that I was coming over. Between the crackles and hiatuses in the diabolical phone connection our conversation had been punctuated by real gaps, as we had tried to bridge the chasm that separated us.

'I am arriving in December,' I had said. 'I will stay for four months.'

'I will help you.'

'The Marabouts,' I had said.

'Of course.'

'Is that all right?' I had asked him.

'What do you mean?'

'I don't want to interfere with your work.'

He laughed.

'No, no,' he had said. 'I'm at ease.'

I waited anxiously amid the crowds of people in the airport concourse. I crossed my arms over my chest and squeezed my legs tightly around my bag. My entire body was tense, and betrayed its unease almost without my being aware of it. But the people near me seemed to move so languidly that my own nervousness was laughable. Several men whispered in my ear as I stood waiting. Did I want a place to stay in Dakar, or a guide with whom to explore Senegal? I told them that I did not, and waited with my hands clasping my money belt.

Then a stocky young man came forward. He looked me up and down before he spoke.

'*Excusez-moi,*' he said.

'Yes,' I replied with impatience, trying to fend off another unwanted 'friend'.

'Are you Toby?'

I looked at the man again, but I did not recognise him.

'Yes.'

'I am El Hadji's brother Bouabacar,' he told me. 'El Hadji is over there.'

He gestured towards the window at the edge of the concourse.

'Come with me,' he said.

I followed him warily, and we broke through to the edge of the mass. There, leaning against the tinted glass door, was my friend, waving to me with joy. He was wearing a Manchester United football shirt.

'I wanted you to feel at home,' he said, stroking the blood-red colour.

We embraced. Then we laughed at the thought of all the time that had passed since we had last met. El Hadji insisted on carrying my bag, and we walked off through the car park in the darkness.

'I wouldn't have recognised you,' he said, as we went.

'Why not?'

He turned to face me, his eyes shining with glee.

'This beard,' he said, pulling at the tufts on my chin. 'This belly,' he said, smacking my stomach. 'No, it's a different person!'

He laughed, and strolled out onto the main road, where he hailed a taxi. El Hadji was different as well, I realised. His slight frame had swollen with the years so that now his chest strained the flimsy polyester of his T-shirt. His drawn, oval face had rounded, so that his cheeks were fleshy. But his wide eyes and mischievous chuckle were unchanged.

'My family are in for a shock,' he said, laughing again, as he put my bag into the boot of the taxi. 'I've shown them photos of you, but now they'll see that you're completely different. A fat old man.'

He clearly thought that such ribbing would rekindle our friendship. I had forgotten that El Hadji was ten years older than me, and had definite opinions about how things ought to be done. With the authority of age, he did not expect me to contradict him. The initial elation of our meeting gradually began to subside.

The taxi moved off along the motorway towards the city. There was no moon, and Dakar skulked in the darkness. Even at this late hour horses were hauling carts along the hard shoulder. We passed Chinese restaurants and craft shops and public telephone offices. Some of the buildings were painted with slogans betraying Senegal's principal obsession: *alhamdoulilah, Dieu merci,* I thank God.

We swept up onto a flyover and then floated down towards the lights ahead. The embankment flashed with countless small wood fires, but they were eclipsed by the powerful white lights high above the city. For a moment my eyes lost themselves in this harsh aura and my thoughts drifted off into their own world, so that the actual details of the impoverished shacks and the creaking traffic and the expanse of low-rise constructions escaped me. But then we turned off the highway, and the sudden confrontation with a bad road forced me to take in my surroundings.

We made our way through a large building site. The concrete and the cement mixers and even some of the tools had been abandoned for the night, and lay disconsolately by the roadside. But soon these were behind us, and I forgot them. We turned into the quiet streets where El

Hadji's brother Tidiane lived. These homes were fronted with the purples and reds of flowering bougainvillaea and hibiscus. At this late hour, the neighbourhood was largely empty, as this was a backwater for diplomats and government functionaries, and the children were kept indoors.

'Welcome,' said El Hadji, breaking the uncomfortable silence that had settled over us soon after we had left the airport.

I stepped out of the car and breathed in the sweet night air. Even though this was a large metropolitan city, the ceaseless humming was less pervasive than it was in London. Already I felt a slackening of my knots.

'Come on,' said El Hadji, following Bouabacar into the house.

My friend ushered me in, past the patio to a narrow tiled corridor. He turned into the first room on the right, the sitting room. Here there was a white three-piece suite, a glass table covered with a lace mat, and several naive prints of pastoral scenes from Europe, all illuminated by a naked light bulb.

We sat together on the spotless couch, wondering where we should begin. I looked at El Hadji and thought of Bula. Two large python skins had been pinned above his bed there, I remembered.

'Don't worry,' he had joked when I had looked up at them in alarm. 'The only thing that will harm you here is my pet lion.'

I could still see this humour in his eyes as he surveyed me cautiously. But there was something else there, too, a deeper sense of sadness.

'Toby,' he murmured now, as we faced one another.

N'Deysan, Tidiane's wife, came in bearing a tray with glasses and a bottle of Coca-Cola. A large, gracious woman, she wore a bright yellow dress which spiralled with flowers. She placed the tray on the table and then surveyed me with undisguised interest.

'*Nanga def?* Where are you?' she asked me, posing the traditional Wolof greeting.

'*Mangi fi rek.* I am here.'

'*Ana wa keur gi?* Where are the people of your compound?'

'*Nyunga fa.* They are there,' I said – far, far away.

14

She flashed her eyes at me in approval as she left the room, and returned us to our silence.

'El Hadji,' I said.

'Four years!'

'A long time...'

He grinned. 'How is Evan?'

'Evan is married, and the father of a little girl.'

El Hadji nodded and looked at me with gentle eyes. His gaze was softening, I saw, like butter in the Senegalese heat.

'You're looking good,' I ventured now. 'You were terribly thin when we met. You look stronger now.'

He shook his head. 'You should have seen me when things were going well. I have been ill since then.'

He held up his right hand. Now that I looked carefully, I saw that his little finger was missing. But I had not seen this before.

'It became infected during the rainy season,' said El Hadji. 'It was completely rotten. Pus was dripping off it. The doctor said there was no choice but to amputate.'

'I'm sorry.'

He shrugged. 'There's no point pretending that people are never ill.'

He leant forward and unscrewed the bottle top. There was still a week left before the end of Ramadan, and the fast gave the treat a greater sense of importance than usual. He poured the sugary drink from the bottle and we watched the bubbles froth with fascination. Then I sipped from my glass, and watched him silently. Our reticence began to gnaw at us.

'How long have you been in Dakar?' I asked eventually.

'For six months. I came after I lost my finger.'

He had fled Guinea-Bissau after the civil war had started there in 1998, he said. Of course, it had been the long-running civil war in the Casamance that had pushed him to go to Guinea-Bissau in the first place, but nevertheless he had decided to return home. So he had gone back to Ziguinchor with his wife, Djinaba, and their two daughters, Marém and N'Daye. Then during the mango season he had travelled to

15

the family village to help with the harvest, and his finger had become infected.

'*C'est difficile,*' he said.

But still he smiled.

'And what about England?' he asked me in turn. 'How is it over there?'

'England,' I said slowly, 'well – it seems as if not much has changed.'

El Hadji smiled. 'And you decided to come again! When I got your letter I was so happy. I told everyone, my English friend is coming – but they did not believe me.' He laughed. 'But God is great. The Qu'ran is full of miracles. And there are Marabouts who know those secrets.'

'El Hadji,' I said. 'What about those secrets?'

'The gris-gris.' He smiled.

'Gris-gris?'

'The charms,' he said.

He lay back on the settee and watched me closely.

'We will find them,' he said. 'You need not worry.'

'The gris-gris for invisibility?'

'Invisibility, invulnerability . . . There are so many powerful people here,' he said. '*L'Afrique, c'est mystique.*'

The nature of these charms had nagged at me ever since I had met him, until I had understood that, unless I resolved the question for myself, it would dog me for the rest of my life. But although I had decided to return to West Africa, the prospect had scared me. Even now, I had no idea what I was getting myself into. I stared deep into the eyes of my friend, and he saw the fears and uncertainties that had preyed on me in the days leading up to this moment.

He leant forward, and touched my hand gently.

'You must not fear your fear,' he said.

Then he stood up without warning, and opened the door into the corridor.

'But why are we talking alone! You should meet the others.'

Suddenly I saw that he felt uncomfortable in here. Later on, I realised that this sitting room was never used except for the arrival of important guests. The symbols of plenty were so unreal that they made the family feel awkward, and they preferred to cram together in the living space between the kitchen and the bathroom.

We walked through to this area, where Bouabacar was sitting with Tidiane's young children. They had all waited up to greet me, and now decided that enough time had passed without their having given me a proper inspection. So Lena, Ayeesha and Mohammed clung onto my clothes and closely examined my skin.

'*Tonton tubab*,' said Mohammed, and everyone laughed at my new nickname – 'Uncle Whitey'.

'Look, *tonton tubab*,' said Ayeesha. 'I've made a paper aeroplane!'

She was about to throw it at me when N'Deysan swooped and snatched it away. Lena giggled, but Ayeesha started to cry. N'Deysan chaperoned them out of the room, but the light touch of the children remained with us after they had gone.

Then we settled around the table. N'Deysan brought in a dish of rice, fish and vegetables laced with palm oil, and we all shared the food in silence. There was one tin mug, which El Hadji filled with water so that each of us could drain it in turn. Then, when the meal was over, he suggested that we go outside for a walk.

The night was quiet. The wind hustled the fronds of the palm trees and chased dust-devils along the streets. Pale light filtered through the shutters of the whitewashed villas, illuminating the cloying white sand of the street.

'You know,' El Hadji said, smiling broadly, 'when I got your letter, I thanked God.'

'Why?'

'There is only one divinity, one God,' he said. 'Who created the stars? Who built the planets?'

El Hadji looked up at the stars, which twinkled so brightly that the eternity that separated them from us was impossible to imagine.

'If you find a beautiful building in the street, and you did not see it being built, do you say that it built itself? No, you praise the builders, the architects and the financiers. So why doubt in God?'

He spoke volubly. For two years his troubles had mounted up, but now he felt optimistic once more. Allah, the mysterious, unfathomable and invisible divinity, would work His holy magic.

These thoughts were hard for me to understand, being so alien to the world from which I had just arrived. I knew that the arguments that my friend had just voiced had been discredited by the philosopher David Hume over two centuries before. The intellectual revolution appeared to have replaced the old gods, and technology had now progressed so far that electronic images seemed to possess more power than any objects that they might represent. Sometimes you could believe that the very nature of things was on the point of being subverted.

But as we stood together in the warm Dakar night and renewed our friendship, none of these developments seemed to matter.

'Everything is as it should be,' he said.

'We have a long way to go,' I said.

'The Marabouts! We will find them. Do not worry. Africa has many secrets hidden below the surface.'

I stayed in Tidiane's house for five days. I had imagined that El Hadji and I would leave for the Casamance at once, but the requirements of Ramadan and the importance of the family dictated otherwise. El Hadji did not want to make the journey to Ziguinchor until the month-long daytime fast was almost over. And furthermore, he told me, we could not possibly leave before I had met his family in Dakar.

This was no small undertaking. El Hadji's family, as I soon discovered, seemed to account for most of the population of Senegal. The next three days disappeared into an endless series of journeys around far-flung districts of Dakar, during which we would enter modern apartment blocks and locate his cousins or brothers, who often lived ten to a room and three to a mattress. El Hadji had forty brothers and sisters, and matters were further complicated by the fact that the sons and daughters of his father's brothers were also brothers and sisters to him. So, when you took nephews, nieces, uncles, aunts, cousins and in-laws into account, he had well over three hundred close relatives. What was more, they all seemed to expect a visit. On one afternoon alone, we visited one of El Hadji's father's wives, three of his brothers, his mother's cousin and one of his aunts whom, El Hadji later told me, he had not seen for thirteen years. Yet when we walked in through her front door in the Parcelles neighbourhood, there was no expression of surprise. We did not even stay for long, or say anything apart from the ritual greetings.

On our fourth morning together, we awoke as usual on the mattress that we shared. El Hadji ran through the day's programme. Today we would be taking it easy, since we only had one brother to visit, Aliou, who had invited us for dinner. So with the day before us, I managed to persuade my friend to take me down to the beach at Yof. We crammed into one of the brightly painted public buses, and lurched towards the sea. El Hadji held my hand in his as we went, so that everyone would know that we were friends. His gesture told others that this was not simply a commercial relationship, although naturally money came into it. Of course, I wanted to make a gift to El Hadji at the end of my journey, as a token of thanks and fellowship. But although we had financial discussions, everything was finally based on trust and, at this point, the true nature of our friendship was still unfolding. I had only spent a week with El Hadji before – we now had months ahead of us.

In Yof, the streets were filled with people carrying baskets of fish. Flies swarmed around the offal which sat inert in the morning market. Dogs scuttled through the sandy alleys, past naked children playing in the dust. Some of them ran after me, shouting *tubab*, but others seemed not to notice me at all.

I commented on this to El Hadji; perhaps my vanity was piqued.

'What do you expect?' he said. 'Your beard puts them off. And anyway, there are too many tourists in Dakar now for them to take any notice of you.'

Of course, it was fatuous to suppose that my presence was anything new. For the Europeans sailing down the Saharan coast, this peninsula of Cap Vert had been the beginning of the slow pull eastwards around the Gulf of Guinea, which provided the richest coasts for slaves and gold and ivory. Many Portuguese *lançados* had settled here at the beginning of the sixteenth century, setting up small communities on the Isle of Gorée, and at Rufisque, Portudal and Joal. Like my ancestors, some of these *lançados* had been Sephardic Jews, and for a time Rufisque and Joal had each had a synagogue. For centuries, the people of this peninsula had seen *tubabs* like me coming and going with the slaves, who simply went.

El Hadji led me down to the beach, which was covered in pirogues, piled up like driftwood on the sands. Beyond the boats people hauled bundles of netting and buckets of fish up towards the market. A series of breakers poured in from the dissolving horizon. At the same time, an aeroplane flew overhead, its engines roaring and the echoes reverberating like thunder over the people, so that it was difficult to decide whether it was the noise of the water or of the machine that was the louder, and the more pervasive.

To me the place seemed wild, just as Europeans had imagined Africa as wild from the very beginning. Tear down the jungles, cut up the elephants, and decimate the natives; we can buy up to fifteen Africans, Cadamosto* related of Senegal in 1455, with only one horse. So, while the Europeans took their captives to plantations and mines in the Americas, the Wolof used their horses as part of a fearsome cavalry, setting up the most powerful empire on this part of the West African coast.

And, as I walked with El Hadji along the beach, I noticed a succession of horse-drawn carts passing us, hobbling slavishly with their cumbersome loads of sand. Then, where the shore broke down into the ocean, groups of men stood cleansing themselves in the brine. They soaped themselves into a thick lather, and their skins gleamed like the sea at their feet.

'Look at that,' El Hadji said to me, pointing to those who were washing themselves. 'They're brave.'

'Why?'

'The water is cold,' he said. 'But they know that he who washes in the sea here gets good luck.'

The skyline ahead was dominated by the domes and minarets of the mausoleum of Saidi Limamou Laye, founder of the Layen Islamic

* See Historical Notes, p. 272.

20

brotherhood. When we reached it, the forecourt of the mausoleum was virtually deserted. El Hadji led me up to the fountain which stood in the middle.

'The Lebu people say that there was a time when they were suffering from the worst drought in memory,' he told me. 'But the Marabout came and caused a well to spring up right here.'

'Where did he come from?'

'From the north,' said El Hadji. 'He performed many miracles. One day, he pushed the sea back, and it never returned to its former place.'

And that was why, according to El Hadji, the sea at Yof possessed mystical qualities. Some people came from the most distant parts of Senegal to cure themselves of mental illness.

We walked on for an hour, and turned into the streets of Parcelles. By now it was almost dark, and El Hadji would soon be able to break the fast. The buses lurched past us, their touts hanging out of the back doors. Some of the vehicles had lit up their headlights, which glared in our faces as they passed, picking out the piles of goods for sale at the roadside stalls: pirated football shirts from Europe's most famous teams, enamel eating bowls, plastic kettles for the ritual ablutions performed before prayers, cloth sold by the metre, toiletries, cassettes, spoons, glasses, mugs, hammers, knives, nails, light bulbs and anything else that could be left sitting all day by the verge waiting for buyers, who rarely came.

Dakar was a city of vendors, but not of manufacturers. When I looked at the pale illumination cast by the headlights onto these imported goods, I could only see inexpensive wonders from Eastern Europe, China, Brazil and the Far East. The African goods were almost all from Côte d'Ivoire, and, although the first Europeans, visiting West Africa in the fifteenth century, had been greatly struck by the quality of weaving and ironwork, these products were now almost all made by franchisees of a multinational corporation. Almost coincidentally, just shortly before the arrival of these international interests at the start of the twentieth century, Côte d'Ivoire had also suffered some of the more violent French programmes of pacification. Villages were burnt down, chiefs and their people were killed in large numbers and the heads of the murdered were placed on poles. The natives' insolence came from their accumulated wealth, declared the first Governor, Gabriel Angoulvant, when he came to assess the collateral damage. But when they were deprived of it, he went on, they were led to a more modest attitude, and forced to work.

Yet, notwithstanding the achievements of former empires and the intentions of the colonists, unemployment was now spiralling out of control. Work was problematic at all times, and food was often lacking – during Ramadan things were even more difficult. As we walked through Parcelles there was hunger in the air, with the fast not yet broken. Even though most people would not eat until dark, piles of perishables lay all day alongside the other goods. People's hunger could have been satisfied, the resources were before us. But such an act was taboo, its consequences feared and unknown.

'Where are we going?' I asked El Hadji now.

'We're going to Aliou's flat,' he said.

But just before we turned off the main road, we became caught up in an extraordinary procession. Thousands of men and women marched through the streets bearing food. Some balanced dishes on their heads, others carried plastic bags in their hands, or tucked baguettes wrapped in greaseproof paper under their arms. They all belonged to the Mouride Islamic brotherhood, and were following the orders of their Marabout, who had commanded them to feed the hungry during Ramadan. As they went, the *talibes* drummed out staccato rhythms on their *tamas* and clapped their hands in time to their step. Since the rest of the world would not intervene, only faith, it seemed, would feed the hunger that I sensed all around me.

El Hadji and I stood to one side of the street to allow the crush to pass. My friend shook his head as he watched them.

'Most of them aren't real Muslims at all,' he said. 'Some of them say that their Marabout himself is divine. They don't understand their religion.'

Many of these people themselves seemed to be hungry. They had been fasting for almost a month. Some had sunken cheeks and eyes that stared with feverish desperation. Yet they followed their Marabout's command because, according to Mouridic theology, if they worked for him, he would pray for them and thus gain them entry into paradise.

We turned off the main road and walked through the maze of dusty side streets that characterises Parcelles. Aliou lived on the second floor of a modern apartment block, whose flats were set around an inner courtyard. His wife was watching Egyptian mullahs reading the Qu'ran on television when we arrived. As the clock hands reached four minutes past seven, she brought in a tray of baguettes, butter, sachets of Nescafé, powdered milk and sugar.

'What are you doing?' El Hadji asked me, as I prepared to tuck in.

I looked at him in surprise.

'You haven't been fasting,' he pointed out, putting on a stern expression. I was about to defend myself, but then he burst out laughing and clapped me on the back. We both laughed wholeheart-edly, since jokes about hunger need to be greeted with humour during Ramadan in Africa.

While we ate, neither of us said anything, but when the food was finished I asked El Hadji which Islamic brotherhood he belonged to.

'None of them,' he said. 'I am neither Qadirriya, Tijanniya nor Mouridiya. I am just a Muslim.'

'Why is that?'

'God's word is in the Qu'ran. Nowhere else.'

'So what about the Marabouts?'

El Hadji smiled.

'The Marabouts work with the Qu'ran,' he said.

'They're all Islamic?'

'There are fetishists as well,' he admitted, 'but they only do bad things.'

He stood up and walked over to the balcony, where he began to perform his ablutions. The Muezzin's call to prayer echoed around the neighbourhood, and the general chatter of the streets dwindled with the light.

'The only thing that is required from you,' he called over to me, 'is that you believe in what the Marabouts can do. If you believe in them, anything is possible.'

'Anything?'

'Look at the 1998 World Cup Final,' he told me, voicing a popular Senegalese theory. 'The French got a Marabout to work for them. On the day of the final, Ronaldo came down with a mysterious complaint, which never turned up in any scan or medical examination. Brazil had no chance.'

For most people in most places, this comment would have excited ridicule. But even though I had not yet been in Senegal for a week, Africa was beginning to affect me. Gris-gris and Marabouts had been known since the time of the first European visitors and from long before, and their hold over this part of the world was unquestionable.

'*L'Afrique, c'est mystique*,' El Hadji said again, before he began his prayers.

I turned my attention to the television, which was droning on in the background. Now that the fast had finished, there was a succession of advertisements. While El Hadji prayed, I watched the images come and go. One commercial showed an eddy of milk dissolving into a cup of coffee, which was then gradually transformed into a setting sun. The image on the screen and the light beyond the window vanished simultaneously, and I began to daydream. Time seemed to pass so quickly now, everyone was saying so, and the memories of a moment often fell into oblivion almost as soon as that moment had passed. The noise outside began to die down, but in the distance I could hear rhythmic handclaps. I thought back to the faces of the *talibes*, and saw the prominence of their bones and the righteousness in their eyes. But already I found that the details were fading, and this reminded me that, before leaving for Africa, I had noticed that I often found it impossible to remember what had happened even five minutes earlier. Sometimes, in the evenings, I had wondered whether anything at all had happened during those days.

The light had gone now. A sharp wind hustled through the streets, and I could hear the gentle flapping of washing in the night air. Another programme was being broadcast. The images flickered and changed rapidly. They did not interest me, but I watched them anyway as they swept past my eyes.

After a few minutes, El Hadji returned from the balcony and sat down on the couch.

'Tell me more about the Marabouts,' I said. Believing in invisibility and invulnerability, in djinns and spirits, required a different notion of reality than the empirical ideas that I had learnt back home. Was our visibility really so flimsy that a simple act of magic could destroy it?

According to El Hadji, it was. Like everyone in Senegal, he had his own magical stories. His brother had a friend who could make the charm that rendered a person invulnerable to knife attacks, he knew that it was true. 'I myself,' he told me, 'used to have a charm that protected me from danger at all times, but I gave it to my brother Samba when he entered the army and began to fight the rebels in the Casamance.'

'You must believe,' El Hadji told me.

'I would like to,' I said. 'But it is hard for me. Most people in my country would think I was mad even to consider this.'

'People in Europe think that they no longer need God,' said El Hadji. 'But here, we cannot understand that. My brothers go over to Europe, and when they come back they are changed. I never understand what has happened to them.'

Things were different over there, I said. Time was such a precious commodity, life was swallowed up and there was no space for reflection. And this in turn made us restless and unwilling to confront mysterious legends of magic and spirits. Some people thought that such things lay in the depths of a chasm from which we had only hauled ourselves out with great difficulty.

'In Europe people say that,' El Hadji agreed. 'That is why Toby has come here. The only thing to take care about,' he went on, 'is which Marabout we go to see. We must not visit the bad sorcerers. We must not drink anything if it is offered to us. Some of their potions are poisonous. But if we find the right person you will not believe your eyes. When you go home, everyone will say that you are a liar. That it is impossible.'

Then he smiled and told me that, in years to come, even I would wonder whether the things that I had seen had really taken place.

*

Eventually we left for Ziguinchor, where much of El Hadji's family lived. Koriteh, the festival marking the end of Ramadan, was expected in two or three days' time, and the roads were filled with bush taxis transporting people from Dakar to all corners of Senegal. Everyone moved with an air of urgency, especially the vendors, who needed to find the wherewithal to return home and celebrate the feast. There was a thirst for money in the eyes of the young men who hung through the windows of our car as we crossed the border of The Gambia. One of them thrust a mosque-shaped alarm clock into my face.

'Just 2000 CFA,' he said – about two pounds.

I turned away. He tried to open the car door, and I slammed it shut.

'You white people are bad people,' he said. 'We will not associate with you.'

I said nothing.

'We want nothing to do with you,' he shouted, as our car pulled away and made for the Gambia river, where we waited for the ferry to cross over from the opposite bank. When the boat arrived, its load turned out to be composed mostly of large motorbikes, covered in logos, on which sat proportionately large Europeans who would set out the next morning on the desert race from Dakar to Cairo, a recent replacement for the more famous and equally questionable Paris–Dakar Rally. We watched in silence as the adventurers picked their way through the stalls selling only the basic needs of life, until they roared off on their bikes into the flickering mirages.

Before we reached The Gambia, the country had consisted of baked-hard scrub sprinkled with hundreds of baobab trees. The land billowed in gentle undulations and then paled into the dusty haze. Sometimes you glimpsed a circle of huts beneath a groundnut tree, or saw cattle lumbering through the burning air; but mostly this place had spoken of emptiness. South of the river and the country, however, and back in Senegal, the soil became more fertile. Lush glades swept away on either side of the road into groves of palm trees, and creeks that filled at high tide. Some of the glades were cultivated with rice, but others were set aside for cattle. The green expanse of forest came right down to the roadside, and covered the tarmac with shade.

After eight hours we reached Ziguinchor, which had once been a Portuguese possession. Inertia slumbered in the back streets, where chickens, goats and children all played in the sand, and dogs licked their paws. The air of lassitude was distinct from the atmosphere in Dakar. Here it resided intangibly in the whitewashed walls of the old colonial buildings, and the spread of bougainvillaea that enveloped the town.

El Hadji's family lived in Ndiayekunda, the compound of the Ndiaye family. Ndiayekunda was in a quiet residential area, where nothing much disturbed the calm except for periodic calls to prayer. Our taxi pulled up on the nearest section of paved road, and then we bore our things unhurriedly over fractured rocks, past dried orange peel and coconut shells half buried in the sands.

My friend led me through the rusting iron gates at the entrance to the compound, and we advanced into the welcomes of his brothers and sisters, his mother and her co-wives, his wife, daughters, nephews and nieces.

'Toby,' said Oumi, El Hadji's mother, eyeing me up and down. 'So, you have finally come.'

'*Mangi fi,*' I agreed.

Oumi said something to El Hadji in Wolof, and then she turned and gathered her dress, before shuffling back inside.

'She wants you to come and sit with her for a little,' he murmured. But before I could do so, I had to greet his father's other wives, all of whom had been hard at work when we arrived, pounding millet and chopping vegetables in preparation for dinner. There were many jokes, and everyone laughed when the youngest wife suggested that I take over from her at descaling the huge pile of fish.

'No,' said El Hadji's sister, Sophie, a young, sparky girl, 'he's going to do the ironing for me instead.'

She filled an iron with hot coals and gestured to the teetering pile of washing beside her.

'Don't be silly,' said El Hadji. 'You'd soon complain if he tried to do that. He doesn't even know how to wash himself properly, let alone iron your clothes.'

He led me into the living space, with its cracked walls and curling linoleum, past the television, which seemed permanently to be on, and then brushed through a curtain at the side of the room leading to Oumi's chamber.

Oumi was a large woman, tall, with a dignified and stately face. Her jowls tapered unevenly down to her chin. She was sitting on her bed when I entered, with a wrap hanging loosely around her bosom. She hitched it up, and told me to sit down.

'You're French,' she said.

'English.'

'Yes.'

El Hadji murmured something to his mother, and she smiled.

'He says that you look older than you did when you met in Bula.'

'So does he,' I replied, taking the offensive. She laughed, but El Hadji failed to see the funny side.

'You have got older,' he repeated, ruffled that I should have challenged the privilege of age, which largely consisted in ordering around everyone who was younger than yourself.

'Well, Toby,' said Oumi, 'we are suffering here.'

She gestured at the dust and the meagre furnishings.

'Yes.'

'But we have God.'

'Yes.'

'How are your family?'

'They are well.'

'*Alhamdoulilah.*'

'*Alhamdoulilah.*'

We exchanged greetings for some minutes, but eventually ran into a slurry of silence. I always found it difficult to know how to end these conversations. A moment would come when there was nothing more to be said. The ritual act of the greeting had been performed and the encounter needed to be concluded. But gracefully putting an end to such an event required more care and tact than I was used to.

'Come on,' said El Hadji eventually, after many long and embarrassing pauses, 'I must take you to meet my father now.'

We returned into the yard. The youngest of the co-wives was

despatched to see if the patriarch could be disturbed. Then El Hadji led me into a small antechamber. He took off his sandals and indicated that I should do the same. Then he knocked on his father's bedroom door and opened it. The old man was kneeling on a prayer mat, fingering his rosary. The lower part of his face was whitened with stubble, and his eyes seemed to vanish into their sockets as he stared stoically ahead into the middle distance. He acknowledged my greeting – *salaam malekum, malekum salaam*, peace be on you, and on you also – but his thoughts were not much disturbed from their concentration on God. Everything in Senegal was subordinate to faith, and the unfamiliarity of a society in which the existence of God was never brought into question was so intense that it made me feel uneasy.

Later that evening, El Hadji and I had a longer audience with his father, and we explained my aims. The rest of the world had never believed in Africa's mystical powers, and the whole history of Africa's relationship with Europe was characterised by misunderstandings. Surely it was time for Europe to recognise that such things deserved to be taken seriously, I said, concealing the doubts that I felt.

'I will pray for you,' the old man said. But whenever he looked at me, it seemed as if his mind was elsewhere.

During the next two days, El Hadji and I waited for the new moon which would herald Koriteh. After the festival was concluded, we would be able to begin our investigations. In the meantime, we talked to his brothers and friends beneath a spreading mango tree, a few metres down from Ndiayekunda.

One of El Hadji's brothers – or, as we would say, cousins – was Omar, the son of El Hadji's uncle, who had died recently. Omar had come to Ziguinchor for Koriteh, but he lived in the Ndiayes' native village, Diouparé, where he tended their groves of orange, grapefruit, mango and cashew trees. His face was angular and smooth, and his skin so dark that it shone. His eyes shone along with his skin at the slightest sign of humour, and the right-hand one was so sensitive that it seemed almost permanently to be watering.

'Omar and I have always been close,' El Hadji confided in me. 'We were circumcised together.'

'In our time,' Omar told me one afternoon, 'we still went out into the bush and had our foreskins chopped off with a blunt knife. Then you had to eat the skin yourself. These days, they just go straight off to the clinic.'

'People used to die of tetanus,' El Hadji added.

'If you're lucky,' said Omar, 'you will see a circumcision ceremony near Diouparé.'

The Marabouts only got involved, he explained, if someone became ill during the rites. There were many Marabouts in that area and, when we went there after Koriteh, we would find many miracles. El Hadji had told me that Omar was very knowledgeable where Marabouts were concerned, and now he began to talk about a man called Asis.

'There is no doubt that he can perform miracles,' said Omar. 'With my own eyes I have seen him call down a vulture from the sky when a friend needed one for a ritual. On another occasion, about ten years ago, my uncle had trouble with creditors in Dakar, and I asked Asis to work for him. He produced a gris-gris, and my uncle never saw the creditors again.'

'But what sort of powers does he have?' I asked Omar.

'Oh, he only works with secrets from the Qu'ran,' he said. 'He's a good Muslim.'

El Hadji later told me that there was nothing in the Qu'ran that forbade visiting a Marabout, but that sorcery was a different matter. The Qu'ran recognised the power of sorcerers, but could not countenance a good Muslim seeking them out. El Hadji believed that Marabouts were different, as do almost all Senegalese, attaching gris-gris to their waists and arms with devotion. And yet, as the Khalif of the Tijanniya brotherhood once admitted, gris-gris are not acceptable in orthodox Islam. These Muslim brotherhoods are Sufi in origin, and some have had a presence in West Africa since the eleventh century. The arrival of Islam and of the Marabouts seem to have been simultaneous, and the Marabouts were resident in the courts of the Wolof kings when the Portuguese first arrived in the 1440s. And well before the influence of Islam and this coming of the Europeans, the Phoenicians, Greeks and Romans may all have circumnavigated Africa, before the Dark Ages wiped the slate of history clean and for a while plunged Europe into a sea of limitless forgetting, when few Europeans could speak with authority about Africa and the vision of its emperors.

The Arabs never lost their trade links with Africa, however, so the historian Al-Umari, writing in the 1340s, knew that Mansa Mohammed,* Emperor of Mali, was said to have despatched two naval expeditions into the ocean to the west at the beginning of the fourteenth century, which may have reached the Americas. The emperor equipped the first of these undertakings with 200 ships carrying men and 200 ships carrying gold, water and provisions sufficient for two years, wrote Al-Umari. At length only one ship returned, whose captain told of a river with a violent current which had drawn his associates into it, but which he had decided not to enter. At this, the emperor equipped 2000 ships, 1000 for men and 1000 for provisions, and they too sailed west.

Some historians have cast doubt on the truth of this story, but the fact that Al-Umari recounts it with equanimity suggests that such a thing was at least conceivable. These events took place near the heyday of the empire of Mali, which, at its apogee, stretched from the Niger to Guinea-Bissau, and received tribute from the Jolof empire as well. In 1324, Mansa Musa† embarked on a hadj to Mecca, and left so much gold in Cairo that he caused its price to fall. Arabs often came to this land of riches, and eventually, in the fifteenth century, Europeans renewed their African trade, adding to the external influences that have preponderated over life in West Africa for many centuries. Nevertheless, in some quarters an impression somehow lingers that an 'untouched' African reality still existed before the colonial era and the subsequent upheavals of the independent African states.

Now, in these uncertain times, perhaps nothing is more secure than magic. The number of people claiming to have magical powers soars, together with the number of problems against which those powers need to contend. Religion, gris-gris and magic are the pillars of faith,

* See Historical Notes, p. 273.
† See Historical Notes, p. 273.

31

unshakeable in the face of hunger, war and disease. The question of whether these people are animists who practise Islam or Muslims who practise animism is perhaps a spurious one, since there is no doubt that they believe fervently in their God. Even Saudi Arabians, Omar once claimed, accept that no one is quite as good a Muslim as a Senegalese.

Now, at the end of Ramadan, Ziguinchor was heady with the fast. The days were hot. Piles of oranges and groundnuts lay untouched by the roadside, and people sat listlessly by their wares, waiting for the evening. It was not even possible to quench the thirst and boredom of an afternoon with the ritual of tea. Everyone longed for the sighting of the new moon, but for two nights it refused to appear, skulking beneath the rooftops which stretched out in an orange haze towards dusk. People were subdued, and the old men prayed unceasingly. But one night, El Hadji came in with a broad smile across his face. It had been announced on the radio that the moon had been seen near Louga, so tomorrow would be Koriteh.

The next day, everyone dressed in their best clothes. The sunlight glittered on braid and sequins. In the morning, the men went to the mosque, while the women prepared the feast. A goat had been slaughtered by four of the Ndiaye brothers, and the meat was served into seven bowls which were taken to various parts of the compound to be shared by the family. In the afternoon, people walked slowly around the city, visiting their relatives. El Hadji insisted that I don a flowing white *boubou* before I went with him and his brother Salif, but I did not thank him for this. The children of Ziguinchor were used to seeing *tubabs*, but they had never seen *tubabs* in *boubous* before. They collapsed into helpless fits of giggles when they saw me, before following me resolutely along the crowded streets, under the mango trees and past piles of rusting metal and patched tyres abandoned by the kerb. The old men, by contrast, assumed that I was a convert, and some of them spoke to me in Wolof, believing that I must already have spent several months here.

But El Hadji seemed to be oblivious to my difficulties. We visited his aunts and his cousins before making for the house of an uncle, who lived next to a mosque.

'The mosque was founded by my grandfather,' El Hadji told me, as we left it. 'By my mother's father.'

'It's true,' said Salif, who did not have the same mother. 'If you want tales of miracles, ask El Hadji about his grandfather.'

'Was he from Ziguinchor?'

'No. He was from Mauritania. A Saraholé.'

'Why did he come here?'

'He was on the point of being murdered by the French,' said El Hadji. 'They had lined up the whole village to shoot them. But then . . .'

He turned to face me. His eyes were gleaming with the family triumph.

'What happened?'

El Hadji made a buzzing noise, and rolled his eyes. 'He flew here.'

'What do you mean?'

'Mystically. He was there – and then he came here.'

El Hadji went on to explain that his grandfather had not been the only member of his family to use magic in the air. His uncle, his grandfather's eldest son, was a prominent member of an Islamic organisation in Europe, but had never bothered paying for his airfares until a few years before. Of course, I did not have the same faith in these stories as El Hadji and Salif. Nonetheless, I knew that El Hadji's grandfather must have been an extraordinary man to escape the French programme of pacification under which Mauritania suffered in the early twentieth century. At this time the wars and civil oppression were so brutal that in Taodenni, between 1905 and 1912, the entire population died of starvation.

Later, I discovered that when the fighting finally ended in 1912 the French had captured Oualata in a bloody battle. Oualata had once been the capital of the kingdom of the Saraholés, the people of El Hadji's grandfather.

At Ziguinchor's bus station, El Hadji and I found a charabanc that was making for the village of Balimé, where Asis lived. We agreed the fare with the tout and found our seats as our bags were strapped onto the roof. We both had rucksacks, and their contents expressed our characters succinctly. I had brought medicines and sterile syringes and health manuals, together with some books and a few ragged clothes, while El Hadji had brought his prayer mat, his Qu'ran, a stash of tobacco for his pipe and his smartest garb. I wore a pair of faded shorts and a stained T-shirt, but El Hadji was dressed in a spotless grey Nike T-shirt and sported a bright red Nike baseball cap. I was fearful and messy; El Hadji was faithful and took pains over his appearance.

However, in spite of the strength of his belief, our bus hardly seemed reliable. It had been on its last legs for a good while. It was rusting and patched together, but I felt that the most important thing was not to be put off by the bullet holes in the metalwork. This was nothing unusual, since, looking around, I noticed that most of the buses parked nearby had been sprayed with gunfire. To judge from the condition of its public transport, the Casamance was in a state of permanent siege. But everyone was resigned to this, as they were used to concealing their anxiety about signals of war, trying to ignore the numerous military checkpoints along the road and the repeated attacks of the rebels.

The civil war had been rumbling on for almost twenty years. At first, the Djola rebels had fought to secede from Senegal, but after a time the rebellion had become little more than an excuse for banditry. The guerrillas stole cattle and crops of cashew nuts from the villagers near the border with Guinea-Bissau, forcing many of them to flee to the relative sanctuary of the towns. As we lurched along the battered road, through the glades and the marshes and the heat which sucked us eastwards towards the rising sun, I remembered a compound that I had visited in Dakar. There we had found an old fisherman sitting on a chair by the door, smoking a Marlboro and strumming on his guitar. The guitarist had begun to sing about the war in the Casamance, and one of the listening women, who had been swathed in gris-gris, had shuffled around the room in a mournful dance. The conflict had aroused such emotion in that small room that I had felt very sad, even though I had understood none of the words of the song.

Music is powerful in West Africa. The griots maintain oral history and sing the epics of their ancestors, thereby helping people to understand their lives. I turned my face to the window to watch the world and tried to imagine how it appeared to those who were travelling with me, which helped the time to pass, and also helped me to forget why I was travelling. Soon we would meet Asis, and I was apprehensive as to what we would find. I had come to look for Marabouts, but I was not sure if I wanted to find them. During my absence from West Africa I had managed to forget the intense passion with which people here believed in gris-gris, and it was impossible to know how ready I was to embrace this world again.

Eventually, after three hours, we reached Balimé. We clambered down from the bus next to a huge mound of oranges by the roadside. El Hadji talked to the old man watching over them, who picked out a dozen for us and refused any payment. Then we made for Asis's compound. I must have looked strange as I struggled along in my rags, shamed by El Hadji's neat attire. Not only was I dishevelled, but I was fairly dirty as well. However, the children did not seem to notice that the colour of my skin had darkened and, wherever I went in this part of Senegal, I was always pursued by the cry of *tubab*. I quickly discovered that this was inescapable and, although it was clearly absurd, the only appropriate response was a wave.

'*L'homme fameux*,' El Hadji called me.

We passed a man carrying an old rifle over his shoulder, prodding two cows that were yoked together and hauling an empty cart behind them which reared and skittered as if it had been drunk. The track gave way to stringy cornstalks hanging limply in the stillness. Then we turned into a compound, where women pounded millet in the heat. The sunlight glared off the sand. Beneath the shade of a mango tree, children played next to the goat that was tethered there.

We greeted everyone, and then El Hadji asked for Asis. We were directed towards a room in one of the buildings, and El Hadji ushered me under a curtain into a small enclave where the brilliance of the day seemed impossible. The thick walls had trapped a coolness that had long been dispelled from the village outside. Asis was squatting barefoot on a prayer mat when we entered, dressed in a bright green *boubou*. Behind him was a foam mattress with a mosquito net tied up above it, while stacked up against the wall nearest the entrance were several wooden tablets covered with Arabic script. Apart from two stools, and a tiny ledge hammered into the wall on which Asis had placed a bright red alarm clock, the room was without furnishings.

We introduced ourselves, and El Hadji and I settled onto the stools. Asis sat watching us minutely, while El Hadji began to explain our purpose in the Mandinga language. Asis nodded occasionally, and murmured responses as required. His skin was smooth, like stones in a riverbed. While El Hadji spoke, Asis looked at me every now and again, and fingered the yellowing pages of his Qu'ranic books.

When he had finished speaking, El Hadji turned to me.

'I have explained that you have come a long way,' he said, 'because you are interested in his powers.'

'It is also important to explain that I want to be able to convince people in Europe that these powers really do exist.'

El Hadji nodded and translated, and Asis bared his teeth in a smile – 'Yo,' he said, more than once, betokening his approval. Then he began to speak rapidly, and it was El Hadji who listened. There were two things with which he could help us, he said. The first was that, if ever we wanted to take some merchandise from one place to another, and we were worried that the police were going to create problems for us, we had only to place his gris-gris beneath the merchandise and no one would be able to stop us. There was also a gris-gris that would protect us from all gunfire – we could attach it to ourselves, and no one would be able to shoot us.

I explained to El Hadji that, since I did not want to become an international smuggler, the first charm was not for me. Invulnerability sounded more interesting, but I did not see how we could possibly test it. But El Hadji told me that it was easy, since all we had to do was tie the charm to a tree stump, and then fire at it. According to Asis, one of two things would happen. Either the gun would not fire and water would pour out of the barrel instead. Alternatively, the gun would fire, but the area where the bullet struck would be protected by frozen water.

'And what about invisibility?'

El Hadji turned to Asis, and put my question to him. Asis smiled, and composed his answer. In the momentary silence, I heard the mundane noises of life from the yard, conversations interspersed with the thud of pestle and mortar, the giggles of the children and the bleats of the goat. Everything seemed so ordinary in this place, so unexceptional, that it was difficult to believe that I was at that moment seriously engaged in a discussion of invisibility and invulnerability.

Eventually, Asis replied, and El Hadji translated for me.

'Yes,' he said, 'invisibility exists. But he does not know how to make it.'

We agreed that Asis should make the gris-gris against gunfire for us. We would wait two days for him to finish his work. A price was fixed, and we all shook hands and nodded deferentially to one another, before El Hadji and I ducked back out of his room into the heat of the compound, where nothing much had changed since we had last seen it. We walked through the village with the children still calling after me. The houses sat stolidly in their ground, fanning out southwards from the main road, drifting slowly towards the bush and then dwindling into that mysterious blur of sand, scrub and emptiness. To me the bush was monotonous and utterly unremarkable. But most of those I lived with saw a completely different land, one peopled by djinns, spirits and devils. It was as if we inhabited different worlds from one another, and there was a real sense in which this was true, for my technological world was largely alien to this place where magic and undiluted faith were so important.

Before leaving for Senegal, I had been worried that the preceding four years would have seen the West African belief in magic ebb away. After all, so much had changed in my own country during that time. It was virtually impossible to take stock of how much my world had been transformed by the constant development of new technologies, and of how these transformations had taken place almost without our having had the chance to consider their merit. But while my country had spun its revolutions, comparatively little of this had filtered through to the Senegalese bush where I now found myself. It seemed as if the earth had begun to split in two, and it was difficult to see how the two halves could ever be fused. North and south might as well have been on different planets.

In Balimé, time advanced very slowly. The heat was so heavy that it sapped my brain completely, and I began to look at this village through sleepy eyes. Everything became an effort. El Hadji and I walked falteringly towards the compound where we had arranged to meet Omar. As we went, we greeted those who sat outside their homes in deckchairs made from old rice sacks and bits of wood.

'How does Asis work?' I asked El Hadji as we neared the compound.

'He won't tell you that,' he said, laughing. 'That's his secret. But he certainly works with djinns; he calls them down and prays for them to do as he asks.'

We rounded a fence and climbed up to the veranda of the compound, where Omar was sitting with his back to the mud bricks of the house.

'I suppose you could call it the Muslim Internet,' El Hadji told me, smiling mischievously and sinking my prejudices.

Now he introduced me to Omar's maternal relatives, who all lived in this compound. Omar's cousin, Fatu, was married to Cheikh, a Tukulor man from the north of Senegal. Cheikh had worked in Mauritania for twenty years before coming to the Casamance and settling as a fisherman. In the mornings, he would go out to check on his catch, but the rest of his day was spent sitting on a mat inside his house, mending the rips in the nets caused by crab pincers during the previous night.

We went into the living space of the family's house, and spent the rest of the afternoon together. Cheikh sat across from us, toying with the huge white expanse of netting which billowed and gleamed like waves beneath a high sun. Scores of brown bats hung down from one of the cross-beams that supported the zinc roof, twitching all afternoon long. Fatu sat beside her husband, breastfeeding their newly born child. Once the boy had finished, she clutched him to her chest, oblivious to the breast which still hung out over her wrap.

Minutes often passed without anything being said. El Hadji toyed with the small blue kettle on the hot coals, and Omar and I shelled groundnuts absent-mindedly and watched him, mesmerised, as he poured the tea from one small glass to another and worked up a froth. Once the first glass of tea had been taken, Omar began hesitantly to ask Cheikh about the Marabouts in the area.

'There are some very powerful Marabouts here,' said Cheikh. 'But there used to be many more than there are today.'

'Why is that?'

'People only used to want gris-gris for good reasons. Invisibility was an important weapon against forced labour from the colonists, and invulnerability was invaluable if the colonists tried to shoot you. But today ...'

Cheikh shrugged, and his amiable features clouded over.

'People only want gris-gris for personal profit,' he said eventually. 'And Marabouts only make them for money.'

He chuckled to himself.

'What's so funny?' Omar asked.

'There used to be an old man who lived on the far side of the Casamance river,' Cheikh said. 'He was so powerful that if you wrapped his gris-gris around your waist, and happened to be in a pirogue which sank far out in the ocean, you would still be able to walk unharmed to the shore.'

'Walk on water?'

'Yes! His sons are still at work, and claim to be able to make the same gris-gris as their father did. But whereas the old man charged only 500 CFA, they charge 50,000. If the boat sinks, there's no doubt that the gris-gris will go down with it too.'

Wealth was such a short cut to happiness, Cheikh said now, the money they earn will be spent soon enough, and of what value is such wealth when its cost is wisdom? He shook his head, and returned his attention to the holes in his net.

'These things are true,' Omar said to me, after a while.

'The problem,' I said, 'is that where I come from people will not believe unless they have concrete proof.'

'I know something about this,' Cheikh said, overhearing me. 'When I was in Mauritania, I met a *tubab* who said that he would pay a great sum of money to anyone who could show him the gris-gris that made him invulnerable to gunfire. A Marabout responded, and the *tubab* asked to test it.'

'That's right,' I said. 'In Europe, we say that seeing is believing.'

'Well,' said Cheikh, 'I witnessed the occasion. Three men came up and fired rifles at the gris-gris, yet the guns could not discharge their bullets. But the *tubab* still wanted to be sure, so he fired his own rifle, and the bullet came out. He said that the gris-gris had not worked.'

No one had ever heard of him again. I am sure, Cheikh said, that he did not really believe that the gris-gris could work. Faith was so important where God and miracles were concerned, but in a faithless world little seemed to characterise experience other than the creeping deterioration of everything around us.

We spent two days here, waiting for Asis to finish his work. Stress and hurry were unknown in the compound, which subsisted according to the daily round of praying, washing, cooking and drinking tea. Fatu prepared enormous quantities of food, and was determined to see me put on weight. On one occasion, as we sat down to lunch, she chastised El Hadji for talking to me during the meal.

'Shut up!' she commanded. 'You're preventing him from eating.'

She and her husband both possessed large bellies and round, wholesome faces. They felt no self-consciousness about their bodies, but, unlike me, they had not been brought up in a world where the image of the body was often seen as a commodity, or a sexual fetish. The only fetishes around here were objects in the homes of the animist peoples, the Manjacos, Balantas and Bainungs, which connected people to the spirits of their ancestors, and joined together the worlds of the living and the dead.

On our third morning with Fatu and Cheikh, we received a message that Asis would like to see us. He had finished his work, and showed us the gris-gris, a piece of paper covered in Arabic script. He explained that now we needed to obtain a ram's horn, and press the paper inside the horn together with some gunpowder. Then melted wax should be poured into the opening of the horn, so that it was sealed, before the horn was wrapped in a piece of red cloth belonging to a mute. Finally the whole thing needed to be sewn up inside a piece of animal skin.

The instructions were so complicated that he had to repeat them several times before El Hadji was satisfied. We left carrying the piece of paper.

'Surely that can't all be in the Qu'ran, can it?'

'That's his secret.'

Back at the compound, Omar told us to leave the rest to him. He visited a friend to obtain rifle cartridges, and called in a favour from another man who he knew kept a supply of mutes' cloth solely for mystical uses.

'Won't he mind?' I asked.

'Of course not,' said Omar. 'He came to see me himself, about six months ago. He needed a green parrot for a gris-gris of his own, and the only one he knew of was one that I kept in Dioupar é as a pet.'

By lunch, Omar had also managed to procure a ram's horn and some gunpowder. The horn had been filled with the powder, and the paper that Asis had prepared had been placed inside it. Then the horn was treated with the wax and enveloped in the mute's cloth. We took the parcel to the shoemaker, who wrapped it in an animal skin. The gris-gris was ready to wear. Omar put it in his pocket, and we went to see his friend, Pape, who had a rifle.

Once the worst of the heat was over, El Hadji, Omar, Pape and I set out through the bush. The burning clay of the track was the colour of dried blood and it cut between shoulder-high elephant grass which gave an illusion of privacy in the emptiness. Birds called from the thorn trees and occasionally swooped low over the track, plummeting without warning from the painfully blue sky. But once we had left the village behind us, there was little to distract us from the heat haze which sat low above the silent earth.

We none of us said much. Pape fidgeted with the strap of his rifle, and El Hadji, Omar and I walked stoically through the loose sand. It was only now that the enormity of what I was doing struck me, and I realised again that I had no idea what I was getting involved in. Surely, I couldn't believe that the gun would not fire? I knew that at the beginning of the colonial period many African peoples had believed themselves to be invulnerable to gunfire. It was with this belief that the Kuba had risen up against the horrors of the Belgian press-gangs in the Congo during the rubber fever at the start of the 1900s. The Tuareg had rebelled against the French in Mali from the 1900s well into the 1920s, following the formal assurances of their leaders that the French rifles would only shoot water, thanks to the grace of Allah. Meanwhile, in East Africa, the Ungoni people of Tanganyika had believed themselves protected from German gunfire by their *maji*, or holy water, and had risen up against the Germans and their askaris. Yet all of them, Kuba, Tuareg and Ungoni, had been slaughtered. African history did not permit such miracles; even to consider them was to ignore the fact that the passage of time had presided only over the gradual disempowerment of Africans.

I watched my companions closely, but they seemed not to want to communicate now. Moving haltingly across the earth was effort enough. We walked on into the bush, the loaded rifle swinging against Pape's back and the sun beginning to weigh down upon the horizon. The rifle gleamed in the glaring afternoon light, and I realised that I had no control over the situation. In contrast to Pape, the only weapon I had here was faith in my friends. In Africa such a sensation is common enough, for both Africans and *tubabs*, but coming from a place where people have successfully created the illusion of self-determination, I found the burden of so much trust especially heavy.

No one spoke.

After half an hour, Pape led the way into a small clearing. Omar took the gris-gris out of his pocket and attached it to a tree stump. Pape put the rifle to his shoulder, and I noticed that El Hadji, Omar and I all wanted to stand as far away from the gun as possible. My earlier moment of scepticism now seemed petty and undignified.

Pape pulled the trigger and the rifle fired loudly. A haze of smoke quickly rose above us, and we rushed forward to examine the tree stump, which was scorched.

'It didn't work,' I said to El Hadji.

'Not this time,' he said. 'But that doesn't necessarily mean that it would not work if your life depended on it.'

Trying out a gris-gris was always a risky business. The djinns did not like to be tested, and sometimes they deliberately withheld their powers.

'I know of a man who had a gris-gris against gunfire,' added Omar. 'He had it demonstrated to him before his eyes, and then he called all his friends round to witness the miracle. When they fired the gun again, the gris-gris did not work.'

It was with arguments such as these that the Ungoni had persisted in their war against the Germans. Some of the men had no faith in the *maji*, but their chief, Chabruma, forced them to drink it. Nevertheless, doubts persisted, so Chabruma devised a test. The *maji* was administered to a dog, who was then shot at. The dog died. But as the dog was a mere animal, some elders held that the *maji* might still work for a human being. Chabruma suggested testing the water on Mgayi, a young man who happened to have seduced one of Chabruma's wives. Mgayi also died.

But, said the medicine man to the Ungoni, the *maji* will still work in a situation where your life is at risk. Such false trials do not test the efficacy of the charm. You must have faith, the Ungoni were told. The Ungoni continued to believe in the powers of the *maji*, they bathed in it before their battles against the Germans, and then marched into the blazing gunfire that knocked them down remorselessly, levelling that brave and blindly faithful people with not a hint of mercy.

We made our way back towards Balimé. I felt dismal at the failure of the gris-gris and, not for the first time, I wondered why I had ever believed that such things might work. Of course, I thought, if a *tubab* turned up with money, asking to see some examples of magic, he would be sure to find any number of people happy to oblige his whim. Everyone assumed that I possessed unlimited wealth simply because I was white. This meant that, just as tourists are targeted by the unscrupulous in Europe, Asia and the Americas, so complete strangers would approach me with absurd requests. Often, they asked me to pay for their airfare to Europe. Every beggar demanded alms with the glow of righteousness in their eyes. And of course, these requests were to some degree justified by history, since whiteness and wealth had been synonyms for centuries in this part of Africa. So the idea of poor *tubabs* or of *tubabs* with modest incomes did not just strike a false note: the very notion was obscene and contradicted all appearances, even though it happened to be true.

No one likes to feel that their good faith is being exploited, and at this point, as we walked through the gathering dusk, the darkness matched the thoughts circling in my mind. Yes, we would meet many Marabouts, and yes, they would write gris-gris for me. But none of the charms would work, and they would all demand money. The kinder side of me tried not to be so cynical – I was richer than everyone I met, after all, and my doubts did me no credit. But really I was struggling against four centuries of accumulated prejudice, and the battle was frequently beyond me. I knew that, ever since Europeans had begun to trade along the West African coast, they had taken exception to the constant demands for trifling items. Smeathman, an official of the Sierra Leone Company at the end of the eighteenth century, could not abide this tendency, for, he wrote, whatever abundance a man may get by assiduity will be shared by the lazy, and thus these people seldom calculate for more than the necessaries. The law of hospitality, he went on, doubtless unaware of the transparency of his Anglo-Saxon miserliness, is obstructive of industry.

It has always been difficult for Europeans to enter into the mindset of people who see it as a fundamental obligation of the wealthy to offer gifts to those poorer than themselves. This was the problem that I now faced. Today, just as in Smeathman's time, things are measured in terms of profit and loss, and this elastic notion of 'gifts' – instead of contracted payments – is difficult to accept. My personal quandary had existed for centuries, and it was that of the collision of my world and an African one. Perhaps anything that I learnt from this journey could only be measured in terms of how much I accommodated the place in which I was. But, as we walked back into Balimé, this sort of equilibrium seemed more distant than ever.

We strolled along the main street of the village, greeting the acquaintances of El Hadji and Omar as we went. This was quite a lengthy process, since Omar had been brought up in this village, and El Hadji had often played football here as a child.

'If you had seen me play!' he would say to me. 'I dominated the pitch.'

All the girls loved him for his skills. His first ever girlfriend still lived here, a pale Moorish woman who worked at the market, where she sold onions and stock cubes. As we passed the stalls, she ran out and proffered her hand to El Hadji. They talked quietly, looking deep into each other's eyes.

Omar and I soon tired of being ignored, so we walked on. As we were about to turn towards the compound, however, a young man called out and pulled Omar to one side. Omar and his friend talked rapidly and seemed greatly excited. When they had finished, a broad smile was on Omar's face.

'You see,' he said to me as we walked on, 'it is always important to think ahead. Six months ago, a friend shot a hyena, and I managed to steal its nose.'

'What for?'

'I wanted to be prepared. Everyone knows that, if you have a hyena's nose, you become very popular.'

Omar had once had a friend who had secreted a hyena's nose, but its effects had been so pronounced that the man had thrown it away. He had become afraid that otherwise he would never be left in peace. The friend who had just accosted him, Moustapha, also knew all about the power of the hyena's nose.

'He heard the rumour that I had it, you see,' Omar explained.

Moustapha was a close friend, and had offered to pay a large sum for some of the hyena's nose. What was more, Omar had explained to him that he needed a gris-gris for invisibility, and had discovered that Moustapha's brother, who lived in the nearby town of Bolana, was thought to possess this secret.

'If we go to Bolana,' Omar told me, all smiles, 'we may be in luck. I know Moustapha's brother. He lives in the house next to my uncle.'

So the next morning, we travelled fifteen kilometres down the road to Bolana, where we stayed with the uncle of Omar and El Hadji, who lived near the port. When we arrived, Omar went to look for Moustapha's brother, and found him working at his stall in the market. We would have to wait for the evening before talking to him, and so, after we had greeted everyone, we settled down on the cracked concrete veranda and began to make tea. Bolana was such a sleepy place that it did not seem to be in the midst of a rebellion. Twice a day, the dock became a frenzy of activity, as the pirogues unloaded their catches of prawns and stevedores packed them into the lorries that would take them to Ziguinchor. But the rest of the day was always characterised by inertia. People were afraid to leave the security of the large military camp based here, in case they came across the rebels. Instead of going into the bush, they spent their days in one another's compounds, making tea and eating oranges.

The only person who appeared not to be subdued was the eldest daughter of the uncle of El Hadji and Omar, Oumi Ndiaye. Oumi was a large, effervescent young woman, who quickly decided that she would take steps to improve my Wolof. In practice, this meant that she would gabble away at me for minutes on end, and then profess surprise when I was unable to respond with anything sensible at all.

'*Dedet,*' she would say, if I replied in French. '*Deguna Wolof. Wolof rek.* Only Wolof.'

Then, when I still failed to understand her, she would put on an act of anger.

'She says that you understand what she's saying,' Omar told me once, 'but you just don't want to talk to her.'

Oumi flounced around the compound in her many brightly printed dresses, along with her mother and Siré, the fiancée of her brother Maodo. Bolana was so hot that the women changed their clothes three or four times a day, each time donning a spotless new outfit. While the women did the laundry and prepared lunch and dinner, Maodo worked at his upholstery workshop near the market, and his father spent most of his time reading the Qu'ran or praying silently in his room.

After the evening prayer on our first day there, Omar, El Hadji and I sat in a small room, waiting for Moustapha's brother. It was dark before he arrived, and we silently watched the dancing shadows cast by the candlelight on the walls. When Mohammed eventually appeared, he stooped as he entered the room, and we performed the ritual greetings in Mandinga.

'Kortanante?'

'Tanante.'

'Sukononkolo?'

'Ibi Jay.'

'Yo...'

Mohammed was wearing filthy white trousers and a blue T-shirt. He sat on a stool, while I sat on the bed and El Hadji and Omar took up positions on the prayer mats. Omar began to speak, but Mohammed was diffident, and looked down into the blackness of the floor. He barely glanced at me, as if the presence of a white man in Bolana was nothing unusual.

Omar explained that Moustapha had let us in on his secret – that we knew that Mohammed might be able to help us with the matter of invisibility. Mohammed smiled, and played with his round felt hat while he thought about it.

'The secret exists,' he said eventually. 'But the gris-gris has no effect unless it is wrapped in the skin of a black cat, and is written in the black cat's blood.'

'The black cat,' Omar murmured. I, too, had heard of this before. When I had been in Guinea-Bissau in 1995, I had been told that the black cat was a prerequisite for invisibility. Now I remembered all the times in my childhood that I had read books where witches and black cats had worked together. But I had never realised that these stories described a real world.

'Ask him if he will make it for us,' I told Omar, 'and how much it will cost.'

47

They spoke some more, and then Omar told me that Mohammed would do it.

'But he cannot put a price on the gris-gris,' he said. 'He says that the knowledge of God is not for sale, and no one can name its price. You must just give what you can afford.'

'It's one thing that he'll do it,' said El Hadji slowly, after Mohammed had gone. 'But where are we going to find a black cat?'

'There has been one around the compound for a while now,' Omar said excitedly. 'For at least two weeks.'

The cat came and fed on fish heads at mealtimes. News of its presence had spread, and several people had come to the compound and offered 5000 CFA to the children if they caught it. But as soon as they began searching for the cat, it would vanish, never to be seen again until the fish heads were served up at the compound.

'These cats are very clever,' Omar said. 'They know how much we need them! There are many people who never wanted a black cat, and were used to seeing them all the time. As soon as they needed one, though, they never saw one again.'

We walked back to the yard, where dinner was ready. Oumi Ndiaye had prepared a dish of rice and fish, and we all squatted round the bowl, mixing our portions of rice with hot chilli. As we ate, I looked over to the wall that separated us from the latrines, and saw the green eyes of a cat surveying us.

I nudged El Hadji.

'It's the cat.'

'It's over there,' he said, 'but that's no use to us.'

We continued to eat. One by one, the others finished and got up, but when I tried to do the same Oumi Ndiaye grabbed my wrist.

'Toby, *lekal.*'

Reluctantly, I finished the rest of the rice. Then she scooped the backbones of the fish out of the bowl and dropped them onto the ground. At once, two large piebald cats came to eat. But the scrawny black cat kept her distance, eyeing us as warily as we eyed her.

We all stood up, and tried to appear indifferent. Oumi Ndiaye carried the dish into the house, and El Hadji went to perform his ablutions. Omar and I stood near the fish skeletons, and the black cat finally hopped down from the wall and joined the other two. Omar sauntered onto the veranda, and returned with a basket, which he then held above the black cat's head while it picked away at the bones.

He brought the basket down over the cat and trapped it. It tore at the wicker with its claws and howled in anguish. Then it ran from side to side of its prison. But Omar held firm, and weighed the basket down with two bricks so that the cat could not escape. The cat wailed again, but gradually fell still, as if it had already given up its useless struggle with death.

'We have to kill it as secretively as possible,' El Hadji told me.

'Those women are incurable gossips. If they see what we do, the whole of Bolana will hear of it,' Omar added, displaying the Wolof man's instinctive mistrust of the women who work away steadfastly and uncomplainingly in their homes. *Jigéén, soppal te bul wóólu*, says their proverb – love women, but don't trust them completely. Oral history has it that Samory Touré's* capture by the French only came about because of one of his wives, who told the Europeans the time at which he washed each day, when he would be denuded of the protection of his gris-gris. Otherwise, how else could the French have caught him?

It was a moonless night, and we sat in darkness which was dimly illuminated by the glow of the hot coals. Maodo, Omar and I watched El Hadji make the tea. Beyond the compound, the street was quiet, only occasionally disturbed by the barely visible shadows of people making social calls, their *boubous* rustling in the gentle breeze that blew in from the port. Everything was at rest apart from the wind, even the cat. It was almost impossible to conceive of that world of teeming spirits, interacting with the mundane and almost changeless scenes which constituted daily life in Bolana. But the reality of that invisible world for people here meant that things were never as simple as the banality which a person saw before them. The true extent of the world could not be revealed in a word or an image or a sound, and was perhaps nothing but a feeling, a sense that so much of what defined reality would never be seen.

* See Historical Notes, p. 274.

49

The cat began to wail again. Its howls were frenzied, and continued for several minutes. We looked at one another and, once we had drunk the next glass of tea, Omar rose resolutely from his stool. He disappeared, and returned quickly with Maodo's apprentice, Lamin. Lamin was experienced in such matters: this would be the third black cat that he had killed in the space of a year.

We all stood up, and moved away from the central part of the yard. El Hadji claimed that he had to go to the latrine, and disappeared with unseemly haste. Omar and Lamin displaced the bricks from the basket, and began to slide it across the concrete, to the accompaniment of scratches from the cat. I should have been disgusted, and sickened, but, as I watched the two of them raise the rim of the basket and jam it down on top of the neck of the cat, who stared up in absolute terror at the jagged blade of the knife which was used to slit its throat, my principal emotions were fear and guilt, fear of the unknown world which I was entering, guilt at the fate of the cat, this largely defenceless creature which we had forced into being a part of our plans, and now had so ruthlessly destroyed.

The guilt could easily have been avoided by not murdering the cat, but I had a dream of invisibility and the book I wanted to write, El Hadji had a dream of the gift I would give him when we had finished our journey, and the death of the cat was the price of our sugar-coated fantasies. The easiest and most sensible course of action, of course, was now to forget all about the murder, so that later I could disclaim all responsibility. I did not even have to tell anybody what had happened. If we none of us kept a record, the cruelty of this death would quickly vanish into the forgotten. To all intents and purposes, such an event would never have happened.

But the cat was dead. Lamin and Omar skinned it on the veranda, peeling the skin away from the body, the pink flesh of which began to glow eerily in the darkness. Beside us was a plate with the blood, which El Hadji laced with salt so that it would not coagulate. We went to see Mohammed, who looked on in surprise at our gruesome trophies. He would begin work in the morning, but to ensure that the rats did not get at the remains of the cat we had to put them in the room which I shared with Maodo.

Maodo was asleep when I entered with the skin and the plate of blood. I put them behind the bedstead, and clambered onto the mattress. My heart was still racing, and I only closed my eyes with difficulty. My mind teemed with questions, and I could not sleep. I wondered if the gris-gris would really work, what invisibility would be like, and whether such a thing was really worth the price of the cat's life. Blood was so easy to spill; you took a life and then it was gone. Thus had so many people vanished from here, and with fates that had been even more brutal than that of the cat. Their ghosts wandered through the glades and the rice-fields of the Casamance, this remote place which, together with Guinea-Bissau, had been known as a slaver's paradise by the Portuguese. I was but dimly aware of the reproaches of those silent and invisible figures of the past, and only gradually did they start to haunt me.

I could not sleep. When I was on the point of dozing off, I heard a shriek which I thought belonged to an animal. I was terrified that it was the ghost of the cat. Maodo slept fitfully. I lay still and tried to make out what I had heard. There was another shriek, and then a prolonged wail. In the morning, I discovered that a baby had died in the compound that lay across the street from our room. His mother had cried out, and was still sobbing at daylight, as mourners gathered from around Bolana and began to pray to Allah for the baby's soul, for redemption.

We waited two days in Bolana, while the gris-gris was prepared. On the first morning, we made the statutory visiting rounds. One of the compounds we visited belonged to a family who had fled Diouparé because of the rebel attacks. Already, the day was hot. The men were brewing tea, while one of the younger women was plaiting a girl's hair in a corner of the compound.

It had been a long time since El Hadji had met this family, and they had not known about the loss of his finger.

'El Hadji!' exclaimed one in distress. 'How did this happen?'

El Hadji explained his story, and everyone offered their sympathy.

'But,' said one, 'there is another person from Diouparé with a poisoned hand.'

'He must go to the hospital,' said El Hadji.

'They won't take him,' the man said.

'Come on.'

El Hadji stood up, and looked at Omar and me. 'I'm going to go and talk to them.'

We walked along, past the pickets that marked one compound from another. Children played in the sand, but they stopped as soon as they saw me. Some of them wanted to shake my hand; others were rooted to the spot. We passed a clutch of vultures picking at the carcass of a sheep, while mangy dogs loped around beside them looking for something to scavenge.

After five minutes, Omar turned into a compound, and we greeted the senior men and women. Then El Hadji asked about the ill man, and we were ushered into a dark room. As soon as we entered, I noticed a putrid stench in the air, which made me blanch. The man lay huddled against the wall, wrapped in a white sheet. He raised himself onto his elbow with difficulty, and offered us his good hand.

His grip was weak. Even this hold felt clammy.

El Hadji asked to see his bad hand, and the man raised his left arm. The appendage was wrapped in a filthy piece of cloth, and the infection was so far advanced that pus was leaking through the material.

'But there's nothing to worry about,' the man said, avoiding our gaze. 'We're going to the sorcerer, who is confident that he can heal me.'

El Hadji began to talk. He showed his own hand to the injured man. The hospital at Ziguinchor had been very efficient. There was an antibiotic there which could resolve this problem very quickly.

'I am better off with the sorcerer,' the man said, still looking evasive.

El Hadji's face clouded over. He murmured a farewell and went outside. The man's mother was standing near the door, watching us suspiciously.

'You have to take him to hospital,' El Hadji said.

'The hospital's no good,' she said. 'Someone's put a curse on him. The only person who can resolve that is the sorcerer.'

'They will cure him at the hospital.'

'All they will do is cut off his hand.'

She looked at us defiantly, and I noticed that her face was cut with vertical ritual scars near her eyes and on her cheeks. She placed her hands on her hips, and then turned away and began to sort through the washing which was piled up in a plastic tub.

'Come on,' said El Hadji. 'There's no point in us staying here.'

Exactly the same thing had happened when he had fallen ill, he told me as we walked back. Some of his brothers had said that it was a mystical illness, that the hospital would maim him but the sorcerer would cure him.

'There are people who do not believe in physical disease,' he said. 'Everything is spiritual as far as they are concerned.'

What El Hadji said reminded me of a Senegalese saying that Maodo had told me the night before: 'Bacteria can't kill Africans.'

'I suppose the sorcerers are cheaper, and that's why people go to them,' I said.

'Cheaper!' El Hadji laughed bitterly. 'They're even more expensive than the doctors! Sometimes they'll ask for a whole cow before they work for you.'

As there was a pharmacy in Bolana, I decided that I would do everything I could to prevent this person from dying of gangrene. The pharmacist stocked the antibiotic that El Hadji had used, so, in the afternoon, I bought a course for the man and we sent it to his compound.

'If it works,' I said to El Hadji, 'he'll realise that he ought to take your advice.'

'Perhaps,' said El Hadji.

The truth was that I had been chastened to see how easy it was for the slightest wound to fester and become rotten. We were reminded of the fragility of life every day. I had stubbed my toe before arriving in Bolana, and had not even drawn blood. I now had two poisoned swellings on my foot. El Hadji, too, had an infected cut below his knee. Our bodies were so weak that it took only the slightest injury for them to deteriorate.

So we waited for the gris-gris. Mohammed had to work in secrecy, and he took two days. Omar assured me that the wait would prove worthwhile.

'There is no question that Mohammed has powers,' he said to me.

'And don't forget,' said El Hadji, 'that he has not commercialised his wisdom.'

The problem with gris-gris, Cheikh had told me, was that the person you need to find will often be nearby without you realising it. Mohammed was next door to the Ndiaye compound, the black cat had appeared as if by a miracle, nothing happened without the will of Allah, and, *insh'allah*, the gris-gris would produce a miracle.

On the second evening following the affair with the cat, Mohammed came to visit us. He rooted around in a plastic bag and unearthed the gris-gris. There were three separate triangles of black fur, linked together by a copper chain. Mohammed placed the chain over his head and then under his left armpit, and began to speak to Omar. The charm, he said, was ready. You wore it in the fashion that he was demonstrating and, when faced by a moment of great danger, pulled the copper hard down towards the ground. This would enable you to pass by unharmed.

I watched Mohammed carefully. When he pulled on the copper, there was a part of me that expected him to vanish. But, of course, nothing happened. His solid, diffident figure still loomed across the room, more real than a thousand dreams of invisibility could ever have been. Yes, life was hard and matter disintegrated at the slightest provocation. But a person could not be made to vanish into thin air.

'What about invisibility?' I asked Omar.

'He says that, when the time appears, you will know when the charm has worked. Your enemies will act as if they have not seen you.'

'But I thought he was going to make the gris-gris for invisibility?'

'We had a slight misunderstanding,' El Hadji said now. 'What he said was that the gris-gris existed, and that you need the cat skin for it. But he knows how to make a different gris-gris with that skin.'

I felt let down. But, at the same time, it seemed ludicrous to blame Mohammed for not possessing the secret of invisibility when such a thing seemed unimaginable in the first place.

'So what are we going to do with this gris-gris?'

'What do you mean?' asked El Hadji.

'We don't need it.'

'I need it, though,' he murmured to me.

'What for?'

'It could save my life.'

I looked at him dubiously.

'Why don't you believe something when someone tells you that it is true?' El Hadji complained.

'Do you believe everything that you are told?'

He said nothing, but I saw that, in many ways, he did. In Africa, where history is preserved by oral tradition, stories have a truth value that they do not possess elsewhere. When a man said that he had a gris-gris against gunfire, he was believed, just as people believed in the histories that were passed down to them by their fathers.

El Hadji turned to Mohammed and explained the misunderstanding. Mohammed said that we should not worry. He understood that such things happened. When the time came and the gris-gris was useful to him, El Hadji would know, and could come and make a gift that betokened his gratitude.

I smiled at him, touched at his lack of avarice.

Meanwhile, El Hadji stowed the gris-gris carefully in his wallet.

'This means nothing,' he said to me, as we left. 'You must not lose your faith.'

But I found that the open-minded attitude that I had tried to bring to this journey was beginning to wane. After all, I had been in Senegal for almost a month with no success.

'Toby,' Omar said to me now. 'You will find what you are looking for. God is great! Why, even the old man here has many powers.'

'Who?'

'Our uncle here. Ho! If you stay long enough, you are bound to see him in action. As soon as someone in Bolana gets bitten by a snake, they come straight here.'

Omar said that it was well known that the old man had secret knowledge of the Qu'ran. 'About six months ago,' he explained, his voice lowering and becoming strangely subdued, 'I was returning to Bolana late at night from Diouparé. I took a short cut along a track, and trod on a snake. The snake wrapped itself around my leg, and bit me twice. Almost immediately, the world began to swim in front of my eyes, everything was indistinct, and my leg started to swell up. I went to the military camp, but they had no antivenenes, and I felt the poison advancing. I started to see things, spirits and dreams, and the world became very strange. The soldiers took me to my uncle, who set to work at once. He placed his foot beneath mine, and recited a verse from the Qu'ran five times, before making a spitting gesture into my mouth.'

Omar looked at my frozen features and smiled. Almost at once, he told me, he had felt the poison rushing down his leg and leaving his body. Twenty minutes later, he had felt so much better that he had walked down the road and bought some tea. When his friends saw him going past them, they swore that it had to be impossible.

Yet, even though I later had Omar's story confirmed by two people who had witnessed these events, I maintained my disbelief. The charm against gunfire had not worked, no one had become invisible before my eyes, and the idea of real magic lying beneath the surface of this suffering place was ridiculous. Surely this spirit world was as imaginary as life after death, a product only of humanity's capacity to believe stubbornly in a thing when all the evidence points against it. Witchcraft is an imaginary offence, the anthropologist Evans-Pritchard wrote of the Azande in the 1930s, because it is impossible.

Before dinner, we went to visit the man with the rotting hand, to see whether he was feeling any better. As soon as we arrived in the compound, he came out to see us, smiling broadly. The contrast with the scene we had found the day before could not have been more pronounced.

'Have you been taking the antibiotics?' El Hadji asked him.

'Oh yes,' he said. 'But there's something even better. Yesterday we went to see the sorcerer again and he prescribed a new herb. Look how much better I am.'

'But that's because of the antibiotics,' said El Hadji.

'Oh no,' said the man, 'it can't be.'

Nothing El Hadji could say would change the man's opinion. When we came back from Guinea-Conakry, he told us, he would be back in the groundnut fields. But El Hadji and I could only conclude that it was more likely that he would be dead.

We walked back towards the compound. The night was still. A pale glow filtered into the streets from the candles that had been lit at the roadside stalls. Bats brushed past us, and the streets were filled with people, some of whom stopped to greet us before moving on. During these short walks we met so many acquaintances of El Hadji and Omar that, almost invariably, I very soon forgot what they had looked like and what they had been called. Within a few days, the crossing of our paths left no discernible mark on the surface of my memory and, as far as my recollection of that time was concerned, I might as well not have met these people at all. Yet we had met, spoken and shaken hands.

The images that I carried with me of those days at Bolana were soon so fragile that they left me with nothing but the sense that something strange had happened, only to vanish into the ether. Mohammed, his gris-gris, the black cat, the refusal to believe in physical illness – all these things seemed like fantasies. The world was a place in which people relied on their eyes and on the images that these brought before them. This was how evidence was produced in laboratories, and it was how companies sold their products with a glimpse of flesh, a hint of breast or chest or thigh, with a fast car and a false smile which took nobody in for a moment. Since things were no longer deemed valuable or important unless they could be brought before our eyes, there was no point in worrying about the troublesome and invisible world of the spirits.

PART II

'The fear must be symbolic'

We entered Guinea-Conakry in a Peugeot estate car which transported ten paying passengers and three children on the inside, and several goats, jerrycans, sacks of rice, suitcases, rucksacks and the apprentice on the roof. For most of the journey I gritted my teeth, in part to prevent myself from swallowing mouthfuls of dust, but also because it was difficult to be enthusiastic when the car was composed primarily of rust, and my body was squeezed so forcefully by the three people with whom I shared the back seat that it seemed as if I had fallen into a compression chamber. The road was in an even worse state than the car, rutted by holes several metres deep, and our conveyance wallowed gracelessly in the drifting piles of sand which all but obliterated the route.

It was a close call, but the driver managed to inspire even less confidence than his vehicle and the road. Although the Peugeot had to be jump-started, and there was scarcely any metal left in the bodywork, he delighted in keeping his foot firmly to the steadily disintegrating floor. His greatest pleasure seemed to consist in swerving haphazardly to avoid the herds of cattle that also frequented the track. The road was so appalling, the car so worn out and overcrowded, that the passengers were reduced to silence. One old man, an emaciated Peul dressed in a fraying white *boubou* and clutching his rosary, spent the entire journey murmuring prayers, voicing the fears that we all of us felt in our own ways. In this place, where life was such an effort, even the smallest and most insignificant act was impossible without faith. So travelling long distances by car required serious concentration on the divine.

For several hours, our rustmobile pitched along the laterite roads towards Koundara. We progressed so haltingly that the clouds of dust thrown up by our car seeped in like leakage through the feeble metalwork. My glasses were soon covered with a film of red dirt, their lenses opaque, so I put them in my shirt pocket and squinted at Guinea-Conakry as it emerged through the haze. A long table mountain rose to the north. Its boulders twinkled with minerals and reflected the evening sunlight, which poured through the leaves of the intervening trees and covered them in gold. On all other sides of the road, empty land swept away into tumbling plains of thorn trees and hot earth, punctuated by a few rocky hillocks which reared up from the bush like waves from a dusty sea. Occasionally a village surfaced, usually surrounded by mango trees and bordered by a glade filled with grazing cattle.

But the villages were widely dispersed, and often we plunged on through the emptiness for twenty minutes or half an hour without spying a soul. These settlements were collections of thatched huts set around the sun-baked earth. They seemed quiet and timeless, and yet history had ensured that this was impossible. It had been through this region that the Peul people had poured in and out over the centuries, beginning their migrations from Senegal's Fouta Toro region under Koli Tenguela* in the sixteenth century. The Peul had intermingled peaceably at first with the Djalonke who lived in the mountains, but then, in the eighteenth century, the Djalonke had demanded that the Peul perform their prayers to Allah in private. The Peul had risen up victoriously in jihad and elected Karamoko Alfa† as the first Almamy of the theocratic Islamic state of the Fouta Djalon. In the nineteenth century, the Peul had passed this way once again and had waged jihad against the Mandingas of Kaabu. The Peul liked jihad, it was a holy act permitted by the Qu'ran, and it was also a convenient way of acquiring territory and slaves in a region peopled largely by animists. Since the time of Koli Tenguela, peace had been rare in these lands of the Badiar, yet even so to my eyes the bush seemed frozen in time. The land around us was so still that Guinea-Conakry's convulsive history was almost unthinkable.

* See Historical Notes, p. 272.
† See Historical Notes, p. 272.

At Koundara, we descended in the flyblown market. Peugeots in various states of disrepair were strewn around the transport park, and we were quickly surrounded by sheep, goats, dogs, mendacious black-marketeers and people offering rustmobiles for private hire. El Hadji tensed at this treatment, so I asked the cost of a taxi.

'Two thousand five hundred francs.'

'Two thousand five hundred francs!' El Hadji exclaimed. 'We are all Africans here!'

I reminded him that the *Franc Guinéen* was a weaker currency than the CFA. He relaxed only a little.

'Don't you say anything,' he ordered me. 'They raise the price for you.'

'I like discussing these things,' I said.

El Hadji shrugged. 'Well, do what you want.'

He had never been to Guinea-Conakry before. Ironically, since I had greater experience in dealing with people from different cultures, I felt that I was better equipped to cope than he was. I turned round to the cluster of touts, picked one out and asked him to drive us to a hotel. Still sulking, El Hadji clambered into the back seat, clutching his backpack.

'It's no way to treat a foreigner,' he muttered. 'The Peul – you can never trust the Peul.'

Our driver told us that the price was high because it was a long way to the hotel. Then he drove us 200 metres through Koundara's dust and pulled up outside the Hôtel Boiro.

'You can never trust the Peul,' El Hadji said again as we walked into the shadowy bulk of the Boiro, which had the misfortune to share its name with the most notorious death camp in Guinea-Conakry's history. What was more, the name was not the only quality that the two had in common, since the Boiro's rooms were rambling cells enveloped in darkness and the whole place was swathed in an air of decline. The cracks of the patio were thick with weeds and the walls of the al fresco bathroom crumbled onto the adjoining football pitch. Inside, long and gloomy corridors were sandwiched by sordid sleeping areas on the one side and worm-eaten shutters on the other.

We settled into our fleapit, and I tried to recall why I was here. We had come to Guinea-Conakry because the Marabouts of the Fouta Djalon were supposed to be among the strongest of West Africa, having inherited the secrets of the theocratic state. At first El Hadji had been reluctant but once Mohammed's charm had failed, he had agreed to the journey.

'We'll have to go to the land of Lansana Conté,*' he had said, referring to Guinea-Conakry's president.

'He's not popular, is he?'

El Hadji had shaken his head, sighing inwardly at the prospect of the long journey ahead of us. Now he scowled as he watched me brushing down my filthy white trousers and T-shirt, and wiping the dusty smears from my forehead. Then, for the first time since we had crossed the border, he smiled.

'Well,' he said, 'at least no one will think you're a white man any more. You've turned red. You must scrub hard to get that out.'

By now, El Hadji had decided to adopt me as his younger brother, so he felt entitled to make personal comments and issue orders.

'So will you,' I said, looking at the film of clay that had grown up around his eyebrows. The dust was so red that it threatened to eclipse the colour of his baseball cap.

After washing, we wandered to the market. The only food on sale was beef grilled by a gaunt Peul, who ladled bits of fat and bone into scratched plastic bowls and watched us eat in silence. Beyond his lantern, the streets were dark, and the air was filled with the bleating of the sheep that now occupied the transport park. We did not speak at all as we ate, for we were shattered and this was the first food we had touched all day. The night hummed with stillness and unspoken thoughts, and fear seemed to pervade the town. We shared three bowls of the meat, and then walked back to the Boiro in silence, past the stallholders who sat out in the dim glow of their lanterns, selling powdered milk, coffee, sugar, tea and torches, with which people made their way through the intense darkness that swallowed Koundara at night.

* See Historical Notes, p. 272.

Back at the hotel, we sat in the yard and brewed tea. We kept our voices down. Under Guinea-Conakry's first president, Sékou Touré,* foreigners had found it virtually impossible to visit the country, and suspicion of *tubabs* still lingered on. What was more, our hotel was the watering hole for many of Koundara's important people. That night, while we were talking outside, the bar filled with lubricious government functionaries ogling the town's whores. At the border, we had been greeted with a poster proclaiming the motto of Lansana Conté, who had been Sékou Touré's successor: *Démocratie, Sécurité, Développement* – three words that appeared to describe the antithesis to the regime presided over by President Conté. At the customs check, officials had demanded 'import duty' from one passenger, a student of Islam, claiming that his Qu'ranic books were being brought into Guinea-Conakry for commercial gain. Subsequently our only halts had been at the police checkpoints so that the requisite bribes could be paid before we were allowed to continue. Representatives of Koundara's forces of law and order now sat in the bar, drinking away the money that they had earned through extortion. Their venality was easily audible in the crude and bellowing laughter which periodically echoed around the courtyard, visible in their jowly faces and in the lewd sparkle of their eyes.

'El Hadji,' I murmured softly, as we sat outside in the darkness.

'Yes?'

'Corruption is a big problem in Africa, isn't it?'

'Oh no,' he said loudly, sucking on his pipe. 'It's no problem at all. If you want to bribe someone, you just go ahead and do it.'

Nevertheless, I got the impression that even he felt uneasy with the atmosphere in the town. Certainly, there was little to encourage us to remain in Koundara, and we decided to head for Labé, the heartland of the Fouta Djalon. The next morning, while we waited in the transport park for our rustmobile to leave, El Hadji met an old friend from Bula. The two were delighted to see each other, and exchanged news of Bula and Ziguinchor. Soon El Hadji's face clouded over because one of his friends had died. An inconsequential illness, El Hadji told me, one that

* See Historical Notes, p. 274.

a simple medicine would have cured, but Bula was so poor. After a time, he asked his friend in a low voice why this town seemed even poorer than Bula. Guinea-Conakry was supposed to be a big country in West Africa, yet in Koundara the streets were all of laterite, there were scarcely more than ten telephones and there were no shops worthy of the name.

'I don't understand it,' said El Hadji. 'Look at the table mountain. There must be diamonds up there.'

'Of course,' said his friend. 'But no one ever goes there.'

'Why not?'

The man, who regularly did business here, told us that devils lived on the mountain. Those who went there never returned. Why, even the pilots of Air Guinée made sure not to fly over those heights, since their planes would be brought down.

'But what people need to do,' El Hadji said, 'is to come to an arrangement with the devils. Enter into a dialogue, and let them know that it will be to their benefit too if the diamonds are exploited.'

His friend smiled and seemed to agree, but there was an evasiveness in his eyes that indicated that no amount of mutual benefit could justify a man entering into a compact with those devils. Eventually, when the car was full, we set off again through the bush, which was even emptier and wilder than the land north of Koundara had been. Dust flared behind us, the diabolical road swung through a forest of low trees, a group of baboons sat by the roadside, our knees and our bodies were all crushed together, and the only way that I could comfortably fit into the car was to lean right out of the window, gazing back at the mountain behind Koundara, which hung threateningly above the town like a thunder cloud.

The road pitched from crest to crest of the hills, which grew in size and gave increasingly extensive views of the plains and the haze that hung like a dirty fog above the emptiness. The outcrops of broken rock became more widespread, the potholes deepened, and the ridges of sand that were reclaiming the road grew softer and more pronounced. This new country was like a magnetic void, the further we went the emptier it became, but still it drew us inexorably into its vacuum. My thoughts dissolved into those blank plains so that I did not have to be reminded of the excruciating discomfort of travelling in this car but, more than an hour after leaving Koundara, I was heaved back into reality by one of the most extraordinary sights that I had ever seen. A python, at least six metres long, was shooting down the middle of the road. The road was so bad and our car was so old that the snake was travelling almost as fast as we were and, as we passed it, it reared up in fury and looked for a moment as if it would try to leap in through the window. There were yelps of fear and astonishment from the passengers, who stared at the snake as it wove from side to side and seemed ready to attack at any moment.

Less than a kilometre further on, we came to the first village we had seen since leaving Koundara, a small agglomeration of huts in the lee of a hillock. The proximity of the snake to the village brought to mind the reputation that people from Guinea-Conakry have as allies of serpents. The writer Camara Laye, a Malinké from *Haute Guinée*, has described the way in which, as a child in the 1930s, he once spied a black snake heading towards his father's workshop. Laye ran to warn his mother, whose practice was to beat such creatures to a pulp. But she warned him off. The snake must not be killed, she said, since it is your father's guiding spirit. It is to this snake that I owe everything, his father later added, it is he who gives me warning of all that is to happen. Then, explained Laye, I understood why, when my father came back from a walk and went into the blacksmith's workshop, he would describe in detail to his apprentices the appearance of every person who had come to the workship in his absence and the work that they had required him to do. The snake often curled up in a corner of the workshop, as if it had been a trusted friend, and from this point on Camara Laye was never surprised to see it being caressed by his father, especially when he was working with gold.

When confronted with stories like this, the analytical mind seeks a rational explanation. Perhaps snakes of this type are prone to being domesticated, and the blacksmith had a trick that made people believe that he had foretold things when this was not the case. Or perhaps such a thing would only work if you were born into this belief system. But this sort of easy cynicism does not tally with the mystical experiences of some Europeans in West Africa. An English colonial law officer, James Neal, spent over a decade in Ghana in the 1950s and 1960s, and soon found that his work brought him into close contact with magic. In his fascinating book, *Ju-Ju in My Life* – now sadly and predictably obscure – Neal tells how he arrived in Ghana with complete scepticism of West African mystics. His opinion only began to alter when he was contacted by a colonial engineer working on a new port project, where a tree was interfering with the works since it could not be uprooted. The team had tried bulldozing it and attaching metal cables to it in an attempt to haul it out, but it remained intransigent. Then the local workmen suggested calling a 'ju-ju man', who informed them that the tree was inhabited by an ancestral spirit. The man poured a libation, made an offering and began to talk to the tree. After a while, he told them that the spirit had agreed to move to a different tree. The engineer prepared to get the bulldozer. But the 'ju-ju man' told them that this was unnecessary, now that the spirit had moved on. And the tree was uprooted with the help of just four labourers hauling on a rope.

After this, and other strange occurrences, Neal became increasingly intertwined with this mysterious world. He involved himself with an Islamic mystic called Malam, who guarded him from the many criminals who tried to put curses on him. Malam produced a charm which protected Neal's bungalow from every evil. One day, Neal and his servant watched with mounting horror as a colourless snake of a species that Neal had never seen before came straight towards his bungalow from the surrounding shrubbery. Neal's servant was terrified, for he knew it to be a 'bad snake' sent by a bad 'ju-ju man'. Then, to their astonishment, the snake came to a dead stop when it reached the terrace, as if it had hit an invisible wall. Malam's work meant that the snake was unable to continue, and the servant beheaded it as it lay there struggling.

But the snake did not bleed.

On returning from Ghana to England, Neal mused on the many strange things that he had seen. Thinking back to the moment when he had finally left Ghana, Neal wondered at the prejudiced scepticism with which he had first arrived in the country. He had heard so many references to the 'Dark Continent', he wrote, thinking of his last view of Africa, many of them by people who used the words lightly and casually. But the words had a greater significance. There was something mystifying and frightening, he thought, about the quality of this particular 'darkness'. Back there on the quayside, and in the hinterland that lay behind it, was a force more powerful than many people cared to admit.

Reading stories like this before my departure had made me wonder about the cosseted rationalist world that I inhabited. And seeing the python steaming down the track reawakened these thoughts. Once we had passed the village, I mentioned to El Hadji that the speed and purposefulness with which the snake had been travelling, and its proximity to the settlement, had made me wonder if it was not responding to the call of one of those people who were famed for their relationships with snakes.

El Hadji looked at me as if I was mad.

'That thing was just going for a stroll,' he said, a smile twitching on his lips.

The Peugeot pressed on through the emptiness. For hour after hour the track clung to the rocky hillocks that pimpled the bush. The plains were dully coloured, greys and dark greens, and the only brightness was in the sky, a blue so piercing that it swallowed the drabness below. As we travelled, El Hadji struck up a conversation with the man next to him and, after an hour or so, he turned around in the front seat and asked me what I would think about going to stay in the man's village.

'There may be some Marabouts there,' he said softly.

Certainly, we would be able to make enquiries. We clambered out of the car at Komba, a large village near a river, where El Hadji introduced me to Ablai.

'His village is only a few kilometres away from the road,' said El Hadji. Ablai nodded in agreement, grinning as we shouldered our luggage. He was slight and compact, and had a perpetual smile, but he seemed subdued as we began to walk away from Komba.

'He did not want you to come at first,' El Hadji told me.

'Why not?'

'I think he is ashamed.'

We would never have known that the path existed had it not been for Ablai. From the main road, we picked our way between two posts at the side of a house, and struck out along a stony path which cut steeply down through a swathe of trees and disappeared into the river. Logs and branches had been tied together and turned into the most flimsy of pontoon bridges.

El Hadji laughed loudly when he saw it.

'Guinea-Conakry is going to be interesting,' he called out.

The heat was beginning to wane, and the river was shaded by the trees that clung to its banks. The water was clear, fast flowing and flickered in the sunlight which filtered through the thin canopy of leaves. I followed Ablai and El Hadji onto the bridge, keeping my balance by holding onto the creepers which had been lashed together at hand height. There was not a sound from Komba or the road to disturb the birdsong that hummed from the branches around us, and the monotone of the Peugeot's engine already seemed inconceivable. At the far side, the path passed through a village and negotiated a wooden kissing gate, before climbing through a lush cassava plantation to begin the ascent of the steep table mountain which loomed above the plains. We dodged between the thorn trees, scrambling over the boulders and broken stones, watching the river plain spread out beneath us like a relief map. We could see the distant mountains on each side of it, the plug which rose erect near the river, and we could follow the course of the stream from the curves of the thickest patch of forest. Each time that we stopped, El Hadji looked at the spreading panorama with increasingly wide eyes.

'I never would have thought that you could see so much from up here,' he said.

'This is only a little bump,' Ablai pointed out.

But El Hadji found the hill hard going. He wheezed and panted, and repeatedly called out for us to rest. Then he would turn and look away over the plains, as if what he was seeing was nothing less than a God-given miracle: those trees, that ethereal light, the hills soaring in a silver glow in the distance, and the sheer extent of the panorama which rolled on in an endless dream of transparency.

'You know,' he said to me, when we rested near the top of the escarpment, 'I never thought that I would see a mountain.'

Senegal is unremittingly flat, and so is Guinea-Bissau. It was almost impossible to imagine, but El Hadji had never even seen a hill before, let alone a small mountain like this, and the sudden opening of his mind to a perspective that he had never dreamt of created a world so fantastical that it was virtually unreal. We broke the back of the climb, and walked on along the top of the mountain, where the path was scattered with the black-and-white of porcupine spikes, shiny and smooth as marble. But although we had left the view behind us, El Hadji's eyes were still wide.

We walked on and saw the tell-tale mango trees that signalled the approach to Ablai's village. We climbed over two stiles, and then Ablai turned off the path and cut through the broken earth of a cassava plantation that had recently been harvested. His mother was sitting beneath a stunted mango tree. She was taller than her son, and had a gentle and creased face which was briefly transported by stares in our direction before she turned back to Ablai. He greeted her and introduced his guests but, considering that he had been away working in Bissau for two years, there was very little outward display of emotion. It was almost as if she had been expecting him, even though she had no means of communication with the outside world, and Ablai had not been able to send word that he was coming.

Ablai led us to a low hut, fronted with thatch that descended almost to the earth. He pushed open the door and we entered his home, which was bereft of all furniture except for a bed made of branches lashed together, and an old foam mattress. He swept out the dust with some twigs tied together with string, and told us that we could sleep there. Then he left El Hadji and me alone while he went to arrange dinner, and we sat on prayer mats outside the hut and awaited the advancing dusk. Soon we were surrounded by a group of young Peul children who stared at me and at my skin as if it had been magnetic. They pointed at me and jabbered away, but El Hadji quickly settled into his familiar

71

routine of issuing orders to those younger than himself – fetch us some water, brush down this prayer mat, don't just sit there watching. He seemed to bark the commands without any sense of being a stranger. But his eyes were still wide with fear of this new, mountainous world.

After the evening prayer, Ablai returned with a bowl of white rice. We added some evaporated milk and sugar, and made a meal of the rice pudding. After we had eaten, El Hadji and I listened to the musical chorus of the crickets. I turned my eyes towards the sky and watched the stars, which shone in the darkness. Beyond them, on the far ridges whose outlines could not be seen at night, bush fires burnt out of the blackness like devilish eyes. This was such a remote spot, so far from anything familiar, but it was no surprise that I had needed to come such a great distance to enter into a different world, where snakes and people understood one another, and devils glowed from the hills around me.

'You know,' said El Hadji, 'this whole day has been like a dream to me. I never thought that I would see mountains like these.'

Only God, he said, could explain such mysterious formations of rocks which rose in outlandish shapes, as if voided of all reason. I told him that, in Europe, people sought a scientific explanation for such things, but El Hadji laughed scornfully at the thought. He had been amazed by this experience, just as all the millions of slaves who set out from the flat coasts of West Africa for the Americas must have stared in disbelief at the strangeness of their new home across the sea. At the acme of the trade, many of them went to the silver mines of Potosí, which at the time was the second-largest settlement in the world. That Bolivian city is one of the highest on earth, at over 4000 metres above sea level, and is surrounded by the Andes, whose snowy peaks must have made those slaves imagine that this really was a new world, a place that had previously been unimaginable, where distinct rules applied and life was nothing but a dream which opened their eyes, wider and wider, to so much that was cruel.

*

Chelekoto was a large village of several neighbourhoods, spread out between mango trees and plantations of cassava. Although *tubabs* had rarely been seen here before, there were few displays of astonishment at my presence, and only once, on our first night, did a young boy run in terror when he saw me. But the Peul elders, tall and slim to a man, greeted me courteously as we exchanged the ritual greetings:

'*On Djarama.*'

'*On Djarama.*'

'*Tanalaton?*'

'*Djantum.*'

'*Marsude?*'

'*Seda seda.*'

These older men were so thin that it was easy to believe that slenderness was their genetic inheritance. But, as much as anything, their frame was determined by diet. All there was to eat here was rice mixed with a thin vegetable sauce, with oranges for afters – and this was the season of plenty. Children appeared to be several years younger than they were, simply because their growth was stunted. El Hadji told me that at the end of the wet season people could often go for days without food, during which time they would gather firewood which they would then sell for a few handfuls of rice. The Peul of the Fouta Djalon had yet to recover from the combination of forced labour and the cultivation of cash crops prescribed by the colonists, which had prevented farmers from keeping stores of grain as they had been used to doing before. By 1948, a study of malnutrition in francophone West Africa noted that, during the rainy season, the daily ration of an adult might fall to 208 calories, and that this was not during famines but simply at times of shortage. So great was the surprise of the personnel in France, wrote the author of the report, that they suspended their investigations, believing that this figure arose from an error on the part of those who compiled the facts. But there was no error.

El Hadji quickly tired of the meagre food. He was used to the Senegalese staples of rice and fish, but the constant supply of vegetables – cassava roots and cassava leaves, sweet potatoes and the leaves of the *bissap* nut – left his bowels working overtime to cope with the strain.

'Every day,' he would say, 'the same food. Never any fish. It's enough to drive you mad.'

He did not thank me when I reminded him of a Senegalese proverb which he had taught me: that when you go to a country where people dance on one leg, you must dance on one leg too.

I wanted to begin our investigations straightaway, but El Hadji told me that we had to tread carefully. Marabouts and magic never manifested themselves at a first glance. So instead, we spent our first two days exploring the bush. Ablai introduced us to his nephew, Moustapha, who led us along narrow paths that skirted the edge of the escarpment. El Hadji and I dressed in long trousers and trainers to protect ourselves from the snakes. We passed through thickets of brittle canes and thorn trees leading to clearings where cattle grazed among the tinder-dry grasses and swished their tails in a vain attempt to dispel the tsetse flies and their threat of sleeping sickness.

Moustapha was cheerful, with a toothy smile and an air of jovial self-possession. He had a heavy face and a strong jaw, but he was very slight, and I did not think that he could be older than ten.

I asked him if he went to school yet, and he replied that he did; in fact he had almost finished there.

'How old are you?'

'Fifteen.'

The school was in a hut much like all the others, and was run by the man who was Chelekoto's local government official. This man had quickly heard of my presence, and had been impatient to greet me. When Ablai took me to see him on the second day of my stay, he sized me up suspiciously.

'Yes,' he said, talking to me from a stool in the cool passage that encircled his hut, 'they told me about you. Why are you here?'

'We met Ablai in the bush taxi, and he invited us to see his village.'

'Why does it interest you?'

'Well, it's nice to walk in the mountains.'

'Don't you have mountains in your own country?'

I explained that our mountains were not like these ones. He asked to see my visa and, once he had checked my papers, he seemed to be satisfied, although he clearly still believed that little could pose a greater threat to Guinea-Conakry's national security than a foreigner walking in the hills. He had to be suspicious of strangers, he said now, especially with the rebellions in neighbouring countries. Guinea-Bissau was only just recovering from its civil war, the revolt in the Casamance was ongoing, Sierra Leone and Liberia had collapsed into anarchy throughout the 1990s, and there had just been a military coup in Côte d'Ivoire, so really it was only Guinea-Conakry, with its blatant corruption and tangible air of fear, that had managed to maintain any security at all. Security had been a watchword of Sékou Touré, who had spent most of his twenty-six years in power fighting the 'permanent plot' against Guinea-Conakry, denouncing at various times conservatives, intellectuals, merchants, cadres of state enterprises, the military, the Portuguese, the West Germans, the French, American veterans from Vietnam, and Presidents Senghor* and Houphouët-Boigny† of Senegal and Côte d'Ivoire. All were said at one time or another to be engaged in conspiracies to overthrow the PDG, the *Parti Démocratique de la Guinée*, whose chairman, President Touré, was re-elected to his fourth term of office in 1982 with a highly creditable 99.98 per cent of the vote.

The government representative watched us go uneasily. Ablai led us through a plantation of *bissap*, and took us to the hut where he lodged with his cousin Sherif. That afternoon, Ablai and Sherif led us through the bush to a waterfall. We heard the roar of the falls, and descended through increasingly lush vegetation, past banks of red and purple flowers, until we reached a spot where we could watch the veil of water cascading down from the plateau like white mist, towards the valley, the river and the road. The water fell for a clear thirty metres into the tangle of greenery that engulfed the valley floor. Yet again, El Hadji's eyes clouded over with the beauty of this world in which he saw only the fingerprints of the gods.

'I have only ever seen photographs of these waterfalls,' he said to me. 'For me, it is a miracle to be here and seeing this in reality.'

* See Historical Notes, p. 273.
† See Historical Notes, p. 272.

We sat for half an hour in thrall to the force of the water. Then a middle-aged man came up the path carrying an old rifle over his shoulder. He was tall and well built, with darker skin than most of the Peuls whom I had met.

'A white man near Chelekoto,' said Alasana. 'What can bring you here?'

'My friend Toby has come to see Guinea-Conakry for himself,' said El Hadji, taking the words out of my mouth. 'Then he can tell people in Europe how hard life is here in Africa.'

'That's good,' said Alasana, chewing on cassava as he listened. When El Hadji had finished, Alasana picked up Ablai's catapult and took aim at a monkey which was hooting from a tree higher up the escarpment. He fired and missed.

'Why didn't you use your gun?' I asked him.

'I've got no money to buy bullets,' he said.

He smiled broadly at his position.

'Come on,' he said, ignoring his bad luck, 'let's go back to my village.'

He led the way back up the path, pausing only to duck into the bush and defecate. Then we climbed over a stile and entered the village, where a group of women sat in the shade of the largest mango tree, next to a bull feeding on cornstalks. Alasana called out greetings as we went, and I too said my *On Djaramas*. He took us to his hut, outside which was a cloth covered with oranges and a few drying tamarind fruits. At the entrance to the hut, three men sat in the shade of the thatch. We exchanged greetings, and El Hadji spoke to one of them for a moment, an old man dressed in a white *boubou* brocaded with gold. I sat on a log, silently watching the haze and the dust and the roots of the cassava crop, utterly still beneath the breathless sky. Every so often the old man looked at me out of the corner of his eye, and then El Hadji turned and told me, in a low voice, that the man was a Marabout.

Alasana grinned at us now, and ushered us into his hut. We sat on the prayer mats that ornamented the dusty floor. My head felt heavy, and I stared with a glazed expression at the curious etchings that someone had made in the walls of the hut, depictions of figures and shapes and lines, all interwoven and possessing a meaning that was not easily apparent. Alasana then upended a basket of oranges. El Hadji peeled the fruit with a knife, before slitting the pith from the tops of them and handing them around. He gave two to me, and asked me what he should say.

'Ask him about invisibility, and the knife.'

'This *tubab* has come a long way, to seek this man's wisdom,' El Hadji explained to Ablai. 'In Europe, people do not believe in gris-gris, but this *tubab* would like to show them that African wisdom is a reality. He wants to discover the secrets of invisibility and invulnerability.'

Ablai translated El Hadji's Wolof to the Marabout, and I watched closely. The old man had a cyst on his nose, and a watery gaze which seemed to look through me when he glanced at me. After Ablai had spoken, the Marabout picked up Alasana's rifle, pointed it casually in our direction and started to laugh. Again, I felt uneasy about associating with guns in such a foreign place. However strongly I tried to dispel my fears, they grew with each mysterious encounter. The Marabout seemed placid enough, but where djinns, spells and gris-gris were concerned, it was impossible to be sure.

He put the rifle down and replied that we should go and visit him in his compound on the following day. Ablai led us back to Chelekoto, where we spent the afternoon resting. The meeting with the Marabout had made me uneasy about this world which was so alien. But El Hadji was confident.

'He would not have told us to visit him if he could not help,' he said.

'You think that he can even do invisibility?' I asked, struggling to believe this.

'Everything is possible.'

Yes, perhaps everything was possible, and I would not have been here had I not been open to this way of looking at the world. Yet, looking around this impoverished place, it was difficult to understand why this place was so poor if magical secrets really existed. Chelekoto was a village where women hoed the cassava plantations with their babies strapped to their backs by a length of cloth. Fresh water was a recent addition, hunger a mundane fact of life. Illness was endemic, medicines did not exist, the sun burnt, and much of the day was a bubbling cauldron when there was little to be done other than avoid a scalding. At all times, the earth teemed with ants, spiders, beetles and all manner of organic life which thrived on the steady disintegration of matter. If magic existed here, why was nothing done to change the material hardships that kept everyone down?

I put this question to El Hadji that afternoon, as we sat in Ablai's hut.

'You have to remember,' he said, 'that material and spiritual wealth are incompatible.'

'That is possible,' I admitted.

'Africans are very envious people,' he went on. 'Instead of using our powers to get ahead, all we do is harm others mystically. Someone sees his friend with something that he wants and, instead of working hard so that he can have such a thing for himself, he puts a curse on his friend out of spite.'

Ablai nodded in agreement. 'Look at Guinea-Bissau,' he said now. 'There are so many people with magical powers there, but all they do is throw curses onto one another. That is why the country is so poor, for really, magic is only one side of the matter. It is nothing without the intention with which it is put to work.'

'Is that why these secrets are so difficult to come by?' I asked.

'Of course,' said El Hadji. 'In the past, people did not use their gris-gris for bad ends. Now, Marabouts are afraid of the uses to which their powers will be put.'

'But it's curious,' said Ablai, thinking again of the Marabout we had just met. 'I never knew that that old man had this secret. He really kept it well.'

It just showed how jealously such things were guarded. Unless someone came looking for these secrets, they would lie untroubled for such a long time that eventually they would be buried beyond recall. The magic would be unseen and forgotten, and would inevitably fall into a world where only other spirits and animals could see it. Dogs, Ablai and El Hadji agreed, were particularly skilled at spying out spirits and, strangely, that night Chelekoto was filled with the fractious barks of a dog, whose howls echoed discordantly against the familiar refrain of the crickets. For an hour or more, the animal kept me awake. Its howls seemed eerie to me, and once more I could only wonder at the forces that my journey was disturbing.

In the morning, we breakfasted on stale bread whitening with mould. Then Ablai came to fetch us, and we set out across the bush to the Marabout's village of Busurah. We crossed a river by a pontoon bridge, and then climbed up a steep rise, past the voluptuous purple flowers opening up on the trees of a banana plantation, until we reached the village and the Marabout's house. The house was large and crowned with the prestige of a new zinc roof. The Marabout was on the veranda, sitting cross-legged on a prayer mat and staring through thick glasses at wooden tablets which he had inscribed with prayers from the Qu'ran. He placed the tablets to one side when he saw us, rose and donned his white leather sandals. Then he ushered us into his home, an airy place with wide corridors and several bare rooms sheltering beneath the shade of the zinc. He led us to the end of the corridor and showed us into his room, before leaving us alone for a while.

We removed our shoes and sat on the prayer mats. There was a bed, and a table on which stood a pile of yellowing Qu'ranic books. Under the table were two battered leather valises. When the Marabout returned, he sat on a pink blanket, fingering the tablets inscribed in Arabic, while we ate a mixture of cassava and *bissap* sauce which his daughter had prepared. Then he broached the topic under discussion, the small matter of invulnerability.

'I have a secret from the Qu'ran,' he told Ablai, 'an ancient prayer which has been interpreted by the Khalif of the Tijanniya in Senegal. No gun will be able to harm you. No knife will be able to break your skin. Even snakes will be unable to bite you.'

This seemed like an opportunity that was too good to pass up, and I explained to Ablai that I hoped that the Marabout could show me the reality of African wisdom.

'The contacts between our ancestors were full of misunderstandings,' I said, feeling strangely emotional. 'It would be wonderful to be able to base our relationship on something better.'

The Marabout seemed pleased by what I had said.

'If people in Europe do not believe in this,' he said, 'I am prepared to demonstrate the power of God to the whole world, if only they will come and visit me.'

The main problem, he went on, was that this gris-gris was an extremely complex one. We would have to be prepared to wait for up to a week before the Marabout could guarantee to have it ready.

'That's no problem,' I said to El Hadji. 'But what about the price?'

'Oh, you won't need to worry about that!' exclaimed the Marabout, when El Hadji had translated. 'We won't argue about that. You will simply pay what you can afford.'

So we waited with Ablai in Chelekoto. El Hadji and I slept together on one mattress in Ablai's hut, with the apparently inevitable consequence that El Hadji tended to push me onto the floor. During the day we explored the bush and the waterfalls with Ablai and Sherif. They led us through savannah where the cattle grazed habitually, and we passed clear brooks where bushes hung with green pods, desiccated by the onslaught of the dry season. Sherif knew of one place at the edge of the escarpment where the mountain literally fell away into the valley, and here we stared down as if we were floating, intangible, above the villages and the forest and the monkeys swinging through the trees. Up here, with this strange mixture of stillness, dust, gris-gris and the devils of the night fires, it really did seem as though I had fallen into a lost world.

After two days of walking in the shadow of the hills, however, El Hadji began to find the whole thing tedious.

'*Marcher, marcher, marcher dans la brousse.* Walk, walk, walk in the bush. Here's a mountain, there's a waterfall. The same mountains, the same waterfalls, the same faces. Every day.'

It seemed that even the heaven of a new earth became mundane after a time. We soon spent our days indolently in the grove of trees beside the village well. The copse was usually filled with shadows. Ablai always brought his radio, and we listened to the latest in *m'balax* from Dakar and *soukouss* from Kinshasa. Each afternoon we sat amid the crinkled leaves and drank the tea that Sherif prepared.

But the first time that he tasted it, El Hadji almost spat it out.

'It's too weak,' he said. 'Let me do the next one.'

But this was how the Peul drank their tea, and El Hadji had to be satisfied with the weak brew. He didn't like it.

'They don't know what they're doing,' he told me in English, one afternoon. 'They can't make tea, they don't even know how to pray properly. Their food's no good. They all stare at us.'

He reclined on the leaves, examining the sky. His limbs were heavy, and he stretched out as if he had been struck down by sleeping sickness.

'I can't wait to go,' he said. 'I wish the Marabout would hurry up.'

But the Marabout was occupied with too many things to worry himself about El Hadji's culture shock. In the meantime there was nothing to do but spend our days wallowing in Chelekoto's inertia, drinking tea, washing, listening to music in spite of the flat batteries, and dreaming of this magical world where the tedium of everyday things was turned upside down by gris-gris. Life appeared so thoroughly boring that, had it not been for the supernatural promises of the imagination, it might have been impossible. Only in the evenings, once the heaviness of the day had lifted, did things lighten up. We would be surrounded by groups of women and children who came to join us as we brewed tea outside Ablai's hut. But we shared no common language, and staring was the favoured form of communication. Ablai would chase the people away, and then we would recline and watch the silvery darkness of the night sky, wishing for the magic to begin.

On the eighth day after the Marabout had agreed to work for us, we woke once again in Ablai's hut, with the same view as ever, of chickens and their broods rooting around in the dust, listening to the thud of pestles in mortars and the sound of crowing cockerels which would continue throughout the day. El Hadji prayed, and then we sat listlessly inside the hut. We had both wanted to find these gris-gris, but the boredom and discomfort that went with it were hard to take.

'You know,' El Hadji had said to me the night before, when there was still no sign of the Marabout's gris-gris, 'when you said that you

81

wanted to come over and look for the gris-gris in Guinea-Conakry, I thought we would be doing it in a different way.'

He had imagined a four-wheel drive car and the best hotels in Guinea-Conakry. Rusting Peugeots and Ablai's hut did not quite come up to his expectations.

'*C'est difficile,*' he had said. 'Toby, *vraiment, c'est difficile.*'

The morning wore on. We watched the dust fall imperceptibly over the village, and the sun rise above the treetops. Then, without warning, things began to happen. Ablai appeared with a dish of food, which he said had been brought to him by the Marabout's daughter. She had told Ablai that her father would come that morning. I put the dish under the bed, and we sat, seething with impatience. After an hour, the Marabout arrived, accompanied by his brother, who was the Imam of Busurah. They sat at the other end of the hut facing El Hadji and me, while Ablai sat on the bed.

'*On Djarama,*' said the Marabout.

'*On Djarama. Tanalaton?*'

'*Alhamdoulilah,*' he responded. There was a pause, and then the Imam rustled around in a plastic bag and revealed about thirty sheets of paper. On each of them, the same Arabic sentence had been written painstakingly many times over. The Marabout explained, through Ablai, that the work had been finished, *alhamdoulilah*. For the charm to be successful, it would be necessary to take the papers with the prayers and place them in a wooden bowl filled with water, until all the ink had dissolved. Then, starting the following Sunday, we would take a piece of cloth and place it in the water, and we would wash ourselves with the cloth that morning, noon and night, repeating the process for seven days. By the next Sunday, our bodies would be protected.

'And don't forget,' the Marabout added, 'the charm protects you against everything – guns, knives, snakes, all impediments. Of course, when I do this work in Senegal, I charge one million CFA, but since you have come to see me, let us settle on a cheaper price, let us say 100,000 CFA.'

The Marabout allowed a small smile to break around his lips, and sat looking at us out of the corner of his eyes. El Hadji translated, talking softly, and avoiding my gaze as he mentioned the price. One million CFA was about £1000 – three times a typical annual wage in Senegal. Even 100,000 CFA was a fortune in this part of the world.

'It all sounds fine,' I said to El Hadji, 'but I think the price is too high.'

'We can't let him get away with charging that,' El Hadji agreed. 'In Senegal, those gris-gris don't cost more than 15,000 CFA.'

So he explained to the Marabout that we were delighted and honoured that he had finished the work; words could not express our fulsome admiration of his powers, which, it had to be said, did not come cheaply.

'Well,' said the Marabout, 'let's just say that, once you've tested it out and it works, you can give me 500,000 CFA. That's a compromise.'

It was at this moment, as I remembered the days we had spent in Chelekoto, and the Marabout's assurance that we would not argue about the price, that my blood first began to boil. I reminded El Hadji that it had been to prevent this sort of situation that we had asked the price in the first place. But the Marabout responded that, of course, he remembered that we had asked him this, but we must see that he had thought that we had asked him this question simply because we already knew the price.

'Tell him,' I said, marshalling all my willpower so that I did not storm out of the hut, 'that I apologise for the confusion, but I simply cannot afford that price.'

The Marabout then asked what price I could afford, and I offered 60,000 CFA, still well above the going rate.

'So,' he said, 'you'll give me 60,000 CFA now. What will you give me later?'

I was so furious that I began to stammer. Beneath the fury, I also began to feel afraid. Arguing with a man who worked with djinns was not a recipe for a trouble-free existence. This was exactly what I had feared before arriving in West Africa. I explained, quietly, that he had asked me how much I could afford, and that I believed in responding truthfully to such questions. I could afford 60,000 CFA. Then he said that, God knew it to be the truth, the work he had done was worth more than what I could afford. He rose from the prayer mat, and the Imam collected the papers. The two men shook our hands urgently, but El Hadji then asked them to wait.

'Say a prayer for us all,' he urged. The five of us clasped hands in the hut, and the Marabout murmured in Arabic. His grip was strong, and for all the world it appeared that he had forgotten our dispute. But then they left us, their white and purple *boubous* rustling away through the haze.

'You can never trust the Peul,' El Hadji murmured, beneath his breath.

Neither of us could believe that the old man preferred to have nothing at all rather than receive a price that was twice that charged by the Marabouts in Senegal. Even if the Marabout had explained his rationale to us, we still would not have understood. Some instincts were buried so deeply that no one could comprehend them even when they eventually emerged.

'I don't understand,' I said, again and again, as we sat there.

El Hadji listened to me sourly, pulling at his pipe.

'The thing is,' I said in the end, 'you can never know what another person is thinking.'

'Especially not in Chelekoto.'

El Hadji smiled for the first time in an hour.

'Still,' he said happily, 'at least we can leave now.'

I looked out at the village once again, at the huts, the mango trees, the cassava and the chickens. In the distance, a baby was crying. The air was yellow with dust, and the view of the plains was becoming obscured by the gathering winds. Poverty flourished here, you could see it in the leathery faces of the old Peul who passed the hut and feel it from the rumpus kicked up by the steers which locked horns in a small clearing nearby. There was a way of living that lay so deeply rooted in this place that not even those leaden days, absorbed in the bush, could reveal it.

*

Ablai felt uncomfortable. The Marabout was one of the elders of the community. Getting embroiled in an awkward situation between him and foreign visitors was no good at all.

'I wanted to ask you to raise the price,' he said to us later, 'but I knew that the amount you had offered was fair.'

'And he wouldn't lower his price,' said El Hadji.

No one could believe it. In the evening Ablai's friends gathered in the hut, as bewildered as we were by the turn of events.

'To be frank,' said Sherif, 'we were amazed when Ablai told us the situation.'

We sat in the candlelight, talking things over. Sherif spoke the most, with his lisping voice. As he explained the awkwardness of the predicament, his open mouth betrayed his splayed buck teeth and his jutting lower jaw. He wanted me to offer just 15,000 CFA more, and they would go back to talk to the Marabout. But I said that the whole thing was better left alone.

'Firstly,' I said, 'I can't afford 15,000 CFA more. And secondly, the Marabout was unhappy with 60,000, so I can't see that 75,000 is going to make much difference. We'd better just forget it.'

After all, added El Hadji, when the man said prayers for us, Toby gave him 5000 CFA as a gift for kola nuts. When Ablai's friends heard this, everyone agreed that it was better to leave the incomprehensible in the past, rather than to stir it up.

'You have done the right thing,' Sherif said, approvingly.

They soon left with Ablai. He would come in the morning, when we planned to leave Chelekoto and walk thirty kilometres over the mountains to Tianguel-Bori. One of Ablai's friends regularly undertook that journey, but Ablai was adamant that he should accompany us. As he put it, we were his foreigners.

El Hadji and I sat outside the hut after they had gone, watching the stars. The moon was high, and children were playing under a nearby mango tree, building a hideaway with broken branches. They shouted and laughed and giggled, running a little wild in the moonlight.

'Chelekoto,' El Hadji muttered. 'It would be a bad place to grow up.'

'Why?'

'When you went to the city to work, you would never get over the shock.'

Of course, Ablai had told us, people went. All the young men left for Conakry, Bissau, Dakar and Abidjan.

'Why would they want to stay here?' asked El Hadji, rhetorically. 'They starve in the rainy season, and are completely cut off from the rest of the world.'

'Do you think places like Chelekoto will still exist in thirty years' time?'

El Hadji didn't think so. People go to the cities, they get used to electricity, television and comforts, so why would they ever want to return? Even the Marabout at Busurah had spent years abroad, as evidenced by his zinc roof.

'Will the Marabouts ever disappear?'

'No!'

'Even with the modern world?'

El Hadji smiled.

'This one isn't a real Marabout,' he said, jerking his head towards Busurah. 'No Marabout would do what he has done to us. The real Marabouts still live out in the bush and shun the city.'

They were the ones that we had to find. El Hadji was sure that they would never die out, because Africa breathed through its faith, whereas, over the centuries, Europeans have developed a general attitude of doubt.

But in spite of El Hadji's unshakeable faith in the Marabouts, I was rapidly becoming disillusioned, and had begun to ask myself why I had ever been crazy enough to believe that his stories could possibly be true. Magic went against all reason. Almost by definition, it was impossible. At that moment it seemed to me that, in the West, we lived in a rational, materialistic world of the mind, and nature was governed by rational, materialistic forces, while in Africa people lived with djinns and spirits in their souls, and so they saw the bush as peopled by these very same djinns and spirits. But really, in spite of El Hadji's protestations to the contrary, the land was very monotonous.

In the morning, we waited for Ablai. We waited until half past eight, but he did not come. So then we cut through the bush to the hut where he lodged with Sherif, and knocked on the door. There were groans from within, and Ablai eventually emerged with bloodshot eyes and a swollen, sleepless face.

'I'm sorry,' he said.

'It's not right,' El Hadji murmured to me as we left. 'First he wouldn't let his friend take us. Now he goes out drinking and doesn't sleep, even though he knows how far we have to go.'

Ablai led us into the bush, along a narrow path that wound through the thorn trees, following the edge of the escarpment. The view tilted down towards the forests of the plain, but we kept to the higher parts. As we went, we negotiated small inclines, and El Hadji began the war against his enemies:

'Up, down. Up, down. Never a change,' he said. 'Mountains are my enemies.'

'I swear,' I said to him, 'by the time we leave Guinea-Conakry, I will have converted you into loving mountains.'

'It's impossible,' said El Hadji. 'You can't make someone love their enemy.'

We crossed one stream, a lush ribbon that sparkled like diamonds in the scrub. For ten metres on either side of it there was a smattering of grass and small purple flowers. But then the aridity returned, and the haze from the valley spread up over the hills. We forded another stream, and Ablai stooped to drink at a rock-pool, trying to dispel his hangover. On the far side stood a circle of small stones, surrounding a large boulder half concealed by leaves. Ablai told us that this was a sacred rock. If anyone picked it up and took it away, it would always return to this same spot in the hills.

Ten minutes further on, we reached the first village beyond Chelekoto. The entrance was marked by a kissing gate, beside which a bullock was grazing on discarded cassava roots. We walked on between the huts and greeted the village elders, who were beneath a mango tree even at this early hour. The only one of them to speak French greeted me kindly, and led us to a compound of three huts, where we sat on wicker matting which had been stretched out between sticks and tied to them with twine. We bought some small bananas, green and fresh, and ate them before continuing. As we walked on through the village, Ablai called out to El Hadji in Wolof.

'He says that these people are the slaves of his village,' El Hadji told me.

'What does he mean?'

Ablai said that their grandfathers had been the slaves of his grandfathers.

'But it's not right that he should say that,' El Hadji said to me. 'That is why slavery will be impossible to eradicate in Africa.'

When he said these words, I was surprised, because I had thought that slavery belonged to the past. It was easier to live with this notion than to consider the tens of thousands of people who worked for nothing in the groundnut plantations of their Marabouts in Senegal, let alone the huge numbers of people who were trapped, sold, beaten and never paid, forced to harvest cocoa in the plantations of the Côte d'Ivoire. And this was quite apart from the sorry history that had brought us to this state of affairs.

El Hadji shook his head. He preferred to forget such things, he had told me, because otherwise he would get angry. But still, after recent events, I sensed that he was simmering.

As we were leaving the village, Ablai asked a man for directions.

'I thought he knew the way,' I said to El Hadji.

'He's only been this way once,' he said, angry again. 'Fifteen years ago.'

It wasn't right, he said. His friend had known the way, but Ablai had not wanted him to profit from our presence, since we were 'his' foreigners.

'That's the problem with the Peul,' said El Hadji. 'They don't help each other.'

El Hadji often explained to me that his prejudice against the Peul was not racism. Racism was white against black. He did not hate all the Peul. Djinaba had Peul grandparents, and some of his best friends were Peul. There were Peul, and there were Peul. His general distrust was, he said, merely the upshot of long and painful experience, during which he had learnt that one could not trust the Peul. The Peul, who are the largest ethnic grouping in Guinea-Conakry, suffered years of persecution under Sékou Touré, when they were forced to emigrate by the hundreds of thousands. But, said El Hadji, this did not excuse their wiles; Touré simply realised that they could not be trusted and that the only way to ensure their obedience was to take a firm line.

Touré had been a Malinké, a people related to the Mandingas of Kaabu whom the Peul had massacred in the nineteenth century. And President Lansana Conté was a descendant of those Susu who were driven out of the mountains during the earlier jihad, down to the coast and into the grasp of the European slavers. Slavery itself had persisted in the Fouta Djalon until well into the 1950s, long after the abolition of Europe's Atlantic trade, for the Peul had found it difficult to give up the habit of centuries. First, they had enslaved the Djalonke to work for them in the hills, and then the glory of the empire of the Fouta Djalon had been wrought with the help of slaves. A British traveller at the end of the eighteenth century, James Watt, was chastened to hear the Almamy of the Fouta Djalon admit that the sole purpose of the Peul wars was the procurement of slaves, with which European goods could be bought. But the Almamy was merely confirming the truism that every empire is founded on slavery. The Peul empire was no different to the territorial empires of the Romans, the Incas, the Spanish, the Jolof, the Omanis, and the British, nor to the current economic empire of the Americans. Everyone else in the region of Guinea-Conakry knew of the Peul and their slavish foibles, and they feared their wars of religion and greed. The stories were passed from generation to generation. Even now, the fear and hatred seep into the earth. The further you dig, the deeper these feelings bury themselves, because some thoughts can never be destroyed – neither hate, nor the absurd idealisation of the empires of the past.

Ablai led us through a glade rich in orange, banana and palm trees. We forded a stream where a girl was drying her washing on flat stones. Trees lined the watercourse and the branches touched over her head, filtering the sunlight which burnt the waters with a blinding whiteness. We paused to rest for an instant, and then passed on into the bush. We walked in single file, in silence. The heat and the dust and the impenetrable thickets reclaimed us. The track dived left and right, brushing through the shrubs and over the broken stones. The land spread out in the haze, empty and bright, swallowing whole the mirages of villages.

I walked ahead of El Hadji and Ablai, who seemed to be suffering. After a time, El Hadji called out to me.

'Ablai says that his foot is hurting.'

I stopped. Ablai did not look at me, but his face was transported by a grimace.

'Perhaps he'd better turn back.'

El Hadji looked at me as if I was mad. However, he said nothing. I stuffed some notes into Ablai's pocket, and he left us quickly.

El Hadji and I walked on for a hundred metres, and then came to a junction.

'Now what are we going to do?' asked El Hadji.

We turned left. At first, we talked loudly and happily, pleased to be free of any reminder of Chelekoto, Busurah and the Marabout. But then the path began to descend, inexorably, back into the valley.

'This can't be right,' I said to El Hadji. 'Tianguel-Bori is over the hills.'

'Don't look at me,' said El Hadji. 'I'm not the one who told our guide to go home.'

The path carried merrily on down the hill, over large boulders and past the deserted shanties of cowherds. The plug near Komba loomed through the haze, and we seemed to be heading straight for it. Then the path disappeared into a clutch of boulders, and we spent twenty minutes hunting for it.

'Toby,' said El Hadji, 'is headstrong. He thinks he knows the way, he sends the guide home, and twenty minutes later we are lost.'

Eventually we found a path, which began heading unfailingly towards the plug. The trees were thick on all sides, and now the dust hung above us and infiltrated our thoughts and our mouths. We stumbled over the roots, long and thick like pythons, and tunnelled blindly on through the undergrowth.

'Toby is not only headstrong,' El Hadji said now. 'He is also stupid.'

After ten minutes more, we heard the sounds of a woodcutter through the trees. Miraculously, the man spoke Wolof. 'No,' he said to El Hadji, 'you're well off the way to Tianguel-Bori. All I can do is guide you back to Komba.'

He walked ahead of us, a blunt axe dangling from his shoulder. The path seemed to split every two or three minutes, and we dived through the low bush, twisting in this labyrinth which had easily punctured my arrogant conviction that it would be easy to explore.

'Really,' said El Hadji, 'what a stroke of madness. How would we ever have found our way through thirty kilometres of this on our own!'

It would have been impossible. Allah had protected us, said El Hadji, for if we had continued we would simply have become even more dangerously lost, and our problems would have been correspondingly severe. Those jaundiced hills were now safely out of sight again, on top of that arid plateau where we had tried and failed to glimpse invulnerability.

The woodcutter led us to a ford over the river, and we walked on to Komba, arriving there five hours after we had left Chelekoto. All we had done that morning was walk in an extravagant circle. Over a week had passed since we had left Komba, but nothing seemed to have changed: the cows still chewed on discarded orange pith in the dusty roadway and young girls sat listlessly beside their bowls of fruit, waiting for passing traffic. We sat in the shade of some cowhides, looking for transport to Labé.

Two hours passed, and nothing came in either direction. Drivers preferred to travel after dark, we were told, since the policemen were too tired to extract large bribes at night. Flies buzzed mercilessly around us as we waited. Eventually we went into an eatery and sat, stultified, in a dusty and gloomy room. Two benches had been laid against the wall, while in the corner stood an urn of drinking water, protected from the flies by an enamel plate. Outside, in the yard, a pot of chicken stew simmered on a wood fire. When the food was ready, the woman who ran the restaurant came in and served it out into faded plastic bowls.

Some time after we had finished our meal an old Peul came in, clutching his rosary, and began to eat as well. El Hadji had meanwhile brewed up some tea, and he offered a glass to the elder out of respect. But the old man declined it, for, he said, he had not had any tea since he had been a soldier in the army, and had reached the rank of lieutenant with the French, during the wars in Indochina.

'Indochina?' I asked, astonished.

'Yes,' he said, 'but that was a long time ago. I resigned my commission in 1955, when I came back from Vietnam.'

Vietnam had been interesting, he said, so green and fertile. But it was frankly impossible to imagine anyone from this backwoods place ever having been to Conakry, let alone Vietnam. Yet so much that is unimaginable is or has been true, and this man had clearly belonged to the *Tirailleurs Sénégalais*, the regiment drawn from all over francophone West Africa which supplied 175,000 men to the French during the First World War, and was subsequently deployed during the Second World War and the campaigns in Algeria and Vietnam. Many of the Africans died, particularly in the 1914–18 war, even more nameless than that whole generation of young Europeans whose loss we still grieve today. The devastation of that war was followed by the worldwide depression at the end of the 1920s, stretching on into the 1930s, which reinforced the sense of how difficult it was to make up for the loss of youth in war, how impossible for Africa to recover from the five centuries in which her young men had been her prime exports.

After the Vietnam veteran had left us, we waited for transport. Nothing moved in the insufferable heat. Then one of Komba's storekeepers, an old Peul with a large wart on his nose, climbed onto the back of his friend's moped, and they sputtered off into the distance. Two Senegalese truckers wrestled with the nuts on one of their vehicle's wheels. Children sat around us in rags, watching. But nothing happened.

'*C'est difficile*,' said El Hadji.

Shortly after this, he glanced down at my leg and noticed that a tick had embedded itself into my calf and was slowly sucking at my blood. He pulled it out. We sat, waiting. But nothing happened.

'*C'est difficile*,' said El Hadji, and he went off to pray. Shortly after he had returned, a Peugeot stopped for us and we prepared for the one hundred kilometres to Labé. El Hadji looked at his watch. It was just after five.

'We should be there by nine o'clock,' I said, taking into account the appalling state of the road. But we did not arrive until two in the morning.

Our Peugeot stuttered out of Komba and then hauled itself unwillingly over the hills. The road became even more intolerable than it had been before. Our car ploughed through potholes that were as deep as articulated lorries, baboons laughed at us from their perches in the woods, dust flooded the car, and we rocked from side to side, faster and faster, as if we were metronomes set to perform with brio.

After we had travelled for an hour and a half, we reached Tianguel-Bori just before dusk, in time for the prayers. The driver, whose nickname was Guérrier, told us that we would have to wait for a friend to catch us up. El Hadji prayed, and then we sat in a restaurant, eating rice and meat. I struck up a conversation with the proprietress, and related the day's events. She listened to me with mounting horror.

'You're mad,' she said in the end. 'Why have you come over here simply to suffer?'

'Surely life is all about suffering,' I said naively. 'In Europe and America people suffer mentally, while here the suffering is mostly physical.'

She looked at me blankly.

'Here,' she said simply and categorically, 'we suffer.'

Soon she came and collected my scarred plastic plate and took it away to rinse. Then we hung about for an hour in the car, waiting to go, but Guérrier and his apprentice, Bala, sat stubbornly on a concrete wall. Guérrier fingered his earring and chain-smoked, while Bala – a tall, muscular adolescent – picked the dust out of his hair.

'Will we be going soon?' I asked Bala.

'No,' he answered, truthfully.

I walked through the streets of Tianguel-Bori, which were filled with scavenging cattle, trucks and Peugeots in varying states of collapse. You had to be careful walking along the dust in the dark, for the cows were fearless, and their horns were long and sharp. The reek of petrol fumes lingered in the air, almost obliterating the scent of the wood fires. People picked their way through the darkness with their torches, whose batteries were, almost all of them, dying.

When I returned to the Peugeot, El Hadji was talking with one of the other passengers, an old Senegalese man who lived near Labé. He explained that they had left Diaobé, in Senegal, two days previously. The distance was only 380 kilometres between there and Labé, but they had broken down. Now they were being delayed again.

We sat in the dark and the gathering chill. The hills around Tianguel-Bori were sprinkled with firelight from the villages but the hills themselves had vanished into the blackness and, had it not been for the fires, you would not have known that they were there.

'I've had enough of this,' said El Hadji. 'Bala!'

He called out for the apprentice, who did not appear.

'Bala!'

El Hadji clambered out of the back seat, and went to talk to him.

'Come on,' he said. 'This is ridiculous. We've paid you to take us to Labé.'

Bala and Guérrier prevaricated for no apparent reason. Guérrier lit another cigarette, but eventually we shamed them into continuing. We lurched off through the night, with one of the headlights broken. The road continued over a section that was so rutted that it would not have disgraced a lava field, and then climbed up a hill that proved to be too much for our Peugeot, whose engine promptly died. We all had to get out and give it a push start. Then Guérrier stopped the car ten kilometres later, and he and Bala spent half an hour trying to mend their tape player. They toyed half-heartedly with the ancient machinery in the torchlight, ignoring our imprecations.

'Bala!' said El Hadji. 'You've got to sort out your car. It's in a terrible state.'

We continued. A little way further down the road, we stopped at a police checkpoint. The policeman took one look at me, and smiled.

'Have you got your International Vaccination Certificate?'

'Yes,' I said, rummaging around for it.

'But he,' the policeman said, nodding at El Hadji, 'he hasn't got one.'

'Yes he has,' I said, handing them both to him.

The Susu officer of the law frowned. Then he turned to the other passengers.

'*Papiers!*'

He read the scraps of paper and identity cards unhurriedly, and then asked for the old Senegalese man's International Vaccination Certificate.

'I don't need one,' he said. 'I'm a resident of Guinea-Conakry.'

'Who are you to tell me whether you need one or not!'

'But . . .'

'*Moi, je suis militaire,*' the Susu officer bellowed drunkenly into the night.

We all looked at him tiredly, and awaited the next act of the charade with resignation.

'Get out,' he said to the old man.

The old man hitched up his *boubou* and followed the policeman through the dark to his hut, where they began to argue.

'It's difficult to understand,' El Hadji said, listening to the protracted dispute. The old man refused to pay a bribe, and the Susu shouted, threatened and bullied, but eventually relented. We all continued on our way. Then Guérrier stopped the car ten minutes later in a small town, Popodara, and announced that he had run out of petrol.

We waited in the car. Bala sat on the roof. Half an hour passed, and Guérrier did not return.

'Where on earth has he got to?' I asked El Hadji.

We went to look for him, and found him in a bar, dead drunk. The bar was lit by a lantern, but it only revealed the shadows and the all-encompassing drunkenness.

'Guérrier!' said El Hadji. 'What about the petrol?'

Well, Guérrier explained expansively, of course we could see that it was dark, late, Labé was still a distance away and, to be honest, petrol in Popodara was expensive, so surely it was better to wait for the morning.

'But we've paid you to take us to Labé!'

Guérrier said nothing, and returned to his drink.

'Bala!'

We all of us began to plead with the apprentice.

'Bala! You've got to sort out the car *and* the driver. You've got to get us out of here.'

Bala stumbled off into the night, and went to talk to Guérrier. We all sat fuming in the car. It was well past midnight, and Popodara was filled with shadows and whispers. El Hadji talked to the old Senegalese man. This used to be a good country, the man said, but now everyone had entered into this business of materialism. El Hadji explained that we had come to search for Marabouts, and the old man smiled.

'Twenty years ago, this was the place to come,' he said. 'But not any more. No one cares about anything except money.'

I told him about the Marabout in Busurah.

'You see?' he said. 'No, that sort of thing's all hopeless. This craziness about money destroys that sort of wisdom.'

He shook his head sadly. Those things really belonged in the past, now that everyone was so greedy. There was no other place for them. But all those stories are true, he said, shaking his head. Hard to imagine, perhaps, but true. There really used to be some magical people, up here in the Fouta Djalon, before everyone became so interested in this world of money.

A cold wind began to shake through Popodara. The streets were filled with the solitary glow of lanterns, set up by the stalls which stayed open into the small hours. The earth was covered with rubbish and dust, each layer slowly enveloping the next until it disappeared and was replaced by more of the same. Time passed with unbearable slowness, and eventually Bala persuaded Guérrier to pay for a different driver to take us to Labé.

Then we lurched on through the darkness, swallowing dust and paying bribes almost without a murmur, and crawled into the city at the dead of night. When we arrived, I felt exhausted and bewildered. My fellow passengers were all asleep. Slowly they awoke, bleary-eyed and startled by their forced readmission to the world of Guinea-

Conakry. We all looked out at the sleeping city, which seemed utterly still and uninhabited at this hour, a ghost town.

We spent a day in Labé, recovering from the rigours of the journey from Chelekoto. Also staying in the deteriorating remains of the colonial Hôtel du Tourisme was Paul, a Lancastrian who was travelling in Africa. He had fallen ill in Mali. He had had constipation for ten days and run a high fever. The doctors had thought that it was sleeping sickness, then that it was malaria, but blood tests had been negative. Then they had admitted that there were so many illnesses in Africa, so many microbes and so many ways for matter to be destroyed, that they could not give a proper diagnosis.

At any event, now he was better.

'I tell you one thing, though,' he said. 'I make sure now that I always take my Lariam pill.'

In the morning, I almost forgot to take my weekly anti-malarial pill. But then Paul said something about Lariam again, and I remembered it. We said goodbye, and El Hadji and I made for the vehicles for Koubia. In Koundara, two people had independently told us that this small town in the bush, sixty kilometres from Labé, was the place we needed to make for. Koubia was famous for its wisdom.

'Koubia!' one Susu boy had said. 'If you go to see the Marabout there, he will know that you are coming. As you are approaching his hut, he will come to the door and watch you arriving. If he can help you, he will beckon. If he cannot do anything for you, he will hold up his hand, and you must stop.'

He had written something on a scrap of paper for us.

'When you get to Koubia, just say this word, and people will take you to him.'

The word he had written was 'wrakadiang'.

When we reached Labé's *Gare Voiture Koubia*, we waited in the shade of a hairdresser's, eating custard apples and spitting out the heart-shaped black seeds into the dust. The *Gare Voiture Koubia* seemed a slightly grand name for a residential street with one old Land Rover which had to wait two hours that morning for enough passengers to justify the journey.

After a time, El Hadji and I clambered inside the vehicle, where we began talking to an old Peul dressed in a scarlet *boubou* and resting a knobbly cane between his legs. He asked us if I was going to volunteer in Koubia, and El Hadji explained that I was not in the Peace Corps; that we were friends, I had come to see Africa, and people had all told us what a fine place Koubia was.

The old man looked at us as if we were mad.

Then El Hadji got out the piece of paper, and murmured 'wrakadiang' at the man, who started, and sat bolt upright.

'He's dead.'

El Hadji and I conferred, and decided to continue anyway, since the area was sure to be a good hunting ground for Marabouts.

The Land Rover began to fill. A middle-aged man dressed in a tailored pink linen suit greeted us warmly and explained that he worked at the *préfécture* in Koubia. It was a pleasure to welcome us: which town did I volunteer in? Again, El Hadji explained that I was not in the Peace Corps, but that everyone had told us what a fine town Koubia was, so we had decided to visit.

'What?' he asked. 'You're just a tourist?'

'Yes.'

The functionary looked at us carefully. Another man, with a round face and a thick moustache, grinned at us from his perch by the back door.

'Welcome to Koubia,' he said, extending his hand.

Then we set off. Near Labé, the hills were green, and the road was shady and cool. But soon we were out into the yellowing grass of the plains, sprinkled with termite mounds and small villages. There were twenty-three people jammed into that small space, yet we all managed to sit with some degree of self-respect. I sat next to a solid, well-fed lady dressed in multicoloured wraps of cloth. She was returning from Abidjan, where she lived, because her sister had died. Occasionally, her even features hardened, and you sensed the growing incursion of the past as we hobbled over the appalling road towards her home town.

'Of course,' she said after a time, 'everyone in Abidjan is pleased by the military coup.'

'Pleased?' I asked.

'Of course,' said El Hadji. 'That old lot were no good.'

'They did nothing to protect the people,' said the woman. 'But the new government go out into the streets to hunt down the thieves.'

Twenty thieves or more lost their lives every day, she said, and this was only right. The thieves made everyone's life a misery, people were afraid, the country could not develop – look at us, she said, and the appalling roads that we have.

'Of course,' said the functionary, 'in England you don't have roads like this.'

I admitted that we did not.

'Well,' said the moustached man, joining in, 'we were set back a great deal by the first government of the country under Sékou Touré.'

'You could not leave to go abroad,' said the functionary, shaking his head, 'and in Labé, where I grew up, there were only three private cars. But at least,' he went on, 'there is now a telephone in Koubia.'

Everyone nodded their heads approvingly.

'In Senegal,' said El Hadji, proudly, 'we have electricity in the villages. Often the roads are paved. There are more phone booths in a small village in Senegal than in the whole of Labé.'

Everyone marvelled at the thought.

'I was in Senegal once,' said the functionary. 'I escaped over the border under the noses of Sékou Touré's guards.'

'Why did you go?' I asked.

'I only wanted to visit my sister, who lived in Dakar.'

'That was during the revolution,' said the moustached man, shaking his head.

'Revolution!'

The functionary sneered.

'Sékou was just inventing plots as an excuse to kill those that he didn't like.'

'The problem with Sékou Touré,' said the woman who lived in Abidjan, 'was that he threw all the foreigners out.'

'He wanted our country to develop on its own, but no man can do anything without the help of others,' said the functionary. 'And now look at us! Everyone is struggling, dreaming of an escape to Europe. No one has any work, people migrate, families separate, all the foundations of life that we knew are being eroded. *Guinée!*'

The bush seemed deserted. The plains vanished into the heat, and the air felt as if a tropical storm was developing, thick and foreboding. The colours were stark, the road was empty, and everything seemed to mirror the increasingly bleak thoughts that encroached upon us.

'I tell you,' said the moustached man, 'we are sitting on a time bomb here.'

No one spoke any more about it. The faces were bleak, set firm, and the smiles that had greeted me when I had climbed into the back of the car had gone. It was so easy, when travelling through Africa, to believe that the smiles you saw betokened happiness. This was what I had thought when I had visited four years earlier, and since then I had often seen things that had helped to strengthen this idea. When not confronted with pictures of starving African children from famine relief camps, I had often come across images of children grinning at the camera and exuding happiness in spite of their material poverty. Of course, these photographs of extremes presented a part of the truth, but sometimes it was hard not to think that they fostered stereotypes, not archetypes. As snapshots, they were by nature superficial. In Labé, the moustached man had smiled and welcomed me to Koubia, retaining the dignity of human kindliness, when really he saw the failings of his country and felt them so deeply that they shamed him into inner distress.

As we neared Koubia, the Land Rover stopped to collect some parcels. Everyone climbed out to stretch their legs except for a mother and her three daughters, who sat in silence near the driver's seat. The woman's chest was bony, and her jawbones were set so rigidly in a downward curve that her mouth seemed to be fixed in a permanent grimace. She had not spoken since we had left Labé three hours before, or even given any indication that she had been aware of our conversation. Instead, her eyes had been fixed at some point in the far distance, as if she could see things that we could not even begin to imagine.

'What's the matter with her?' El Hadji asked the moustached man as we waited outside.

'She's a refugee from the war in Sierra Leone,' he said.

When we climbed back into the car, both he and the functionary tried to talk to her, but she blinked and nodded, saying nothing. Her eyes were filled with a watery distance that was impossible to bridge.

'She's traumatised,' the moustached man told me.

The woman's young daughters, too, seemed strangely cowed and quiet, so muted by their suffering that they did not have the energy to talk of how awful their lives had been. Each time that the car pitched and rolled, the one nearest to El Hadji grabbed hold of his knee in fear, and looked behind her with piercing, terrified eyes. This happened again near Koubia, and El Hadji reached out and felt her forehead.

'She's got a fever,' he said, turning to me. I felt her skin, which was burning hot. The girl's pulse convulsed the base of her neck, racing uncontrollably.

'Is it malaria?'

El Hadji shrugged. 'Whatever it is, it's important to keep her positive. Even if a person's at death's door, you must give them hope.'

'I don't agree,' I said. 'If a person's dying, they've got a right to know.'

El Hadji said nothing more on the subject. The woman who lived in Abidjan had been listening to our conversation, and now she felt the girl as well and gestured to the mother that her daughter was ill. But the woman simply nodded and shrugged. Of course the girl was ill. Who would not have been?

When we reached Koubia, the woman from Abidjan was one of the first to descend. She hitched up her skirts, gathered her bags from the roof and walked back through the gate into her family's compound. Then she put her bags down on the floor and embraced her sisters and her mother. Then she began to wail. She beat her chest, and wailed again. Her sister had died and, since she had been away, everyone here had descended a rotten stairwell of suffering.

Koubia was a dust-blown town sheltering in a bowl from the pale hills. The stunted trees that covered them spread out over the surrounding area, giving the town the unlikely air of a clearing in a forest. But there was nothing luscious about Koubia. The only vehicle to be seen was the Land Rover that deposited us in the market, beside the shops and the goats and the scores of people who sat in the shade of corrugated iron, watching the immanent emptiness.

'Where on earth can we sleep around here?'

El Hadji looked at me. I had no idea. A heavy-faced young man with a black woollen cap and many gaps in his coffee-coloured teeth came up to us, grinning. He introduced us to a friend who spoke some French and was sitting outside a general store. El Hadji told him that we wanted something to eat, so the man rose, told his son to accompany us, and led us to an eatery, where there was a table and a bench and two pots, one containing congealed rice and the other lumps of boiled cassava leaves.

We invited the man and his son to share our meal.

'Peace Corps?' he asked.

'No,' said El Hadji, who sounded less convincing each time. 'Everyone told us that Koubia was a good place, so we came to see for ourselves.'

On hearing this patent lie, the man looked at us strangely.

'We're looking for somewhere to stay,' said El Hadji.

The man said nothing. His boy wiped a finger around the plastic bowl, and looked at us with wide, hungry eyes.

'Well,' said El Hadji. 'We are looking for a man called Wrakadiang.'

The man shook his head.

'Wrakadiang,' El Hadji said again.

But the man said that no one of that name existed in Koubia, nor in any of the nearby villages. Then, once his son had finished licking his fingers, he told us that he would take us to see the Deputy Mayor. But he did not look at us, or even seem to want to speak to us, as we walked through the town.

'Well,' I said, deciding that it was better to tell the truth, since it might actually allay his suspicions, 'we have come here because we were told that there were many powerful Marabouts in Koubia.'

The man's face relaxed, and he slowed his pace as we passed Koubia's bare football pitch, heading towards the white domes of the mosque.

'You were told to ask for Wrakadiang?'

'Yes.'

'But *wrakadiang* is the word we use for bad sorcerers. There are no people who practise that here. *Wrakadiang* is only used by the Susu.'

We walked into a compound shielded by mango and kola trees. Beyond the huts, the incline fell away into the bush where the cattle grazed. Outside one of the buildings, millions of shells had accumulated over the years, and lay like hardened, flanged snowflakes on the earth. Leaning against the side of the house, a stocky young man with a boyish face was reading a Qu'ranic book. We were introduced, and Sédhiouba went to find his uncle, the Deputy Mayor. We waited outside, with the sweat trickling warmly down our faces. Koubia was roasting like a groundnut, in its withered, yellowing shell.

After five minutes, Sédhiouba returned with his uncle, Mamadou Diallo. The Deputy Mayor stood beneath the thatched porch, surveying us with suspicion. He had a somnolent air about him. When he first appeared, I thought that we had awoken him from his siesta. But it soon became clear that he did everything in the same languid, flat way. Words escaped his lips in a slothful monotone, and even when he told a joke he did so in such a ponderous way that it was as if he was trying to satirise his own attempt at humour. His left eye was afflicted by a parasite and was virtually shut, so that, on laughing, he appeared to wink conspiratorially. But then his eyelid would flutter, and turn resignedly to survey the rest of the world. Slowly, I realised that the sense of conspiracy was permanent.

'Well,' said Mamadou Diallo, when El Hadji had explained, 'this is not a hotel.'

'Of course not,' I said. 'But when you go to a new place, it is always important to seek the advice of those who know the situation there.'

Mamadou Diallo looked at me unblinkingly. Then El Hadji began to explain the true purpose of our visit, and the Deputy Mayor's suspicions lightened. There might be a place for us to stay, he admitted, and later on he would introduce us to his grandfather, a ninety-year-old man with much Islamic learning.

Soon he returned to his office in the Administrative Quarter. We sat with Sédhiouba, grinding our stools down into the shells while he made the tea. The heat from the wood-burner suffused the air around it, and enveloped my calves. Sédhiouba began to flicker through the haze. His even features became coarser. Then, when he had stopped pouring the tea with what seemed to be pronounced deliberation, that sweet, fiery liquid did not quell the burning in my throat.

At one point, we looked over towards the mosque and saw the Deputy Mayor's grandfather shuffling towards us. The old man had a smooth face and a ready smile, which he directed at us as he entered the house.

'The old man,' I heard Sédhiouba say, 'has much wisdom. He banishes devils from the possessed.'

There were, he said, many devils in the bush, and much sorcery. The devils grabbed hold of your mind and refused to let you go. Only spiritual warriors could compete with such wickedness. El Hadji asked Sédhiouba if he had seen the man work, and he said that indeed he had, this was the very reason that he had returned from Conakry. When he had been in Conakry, he said, studying law at the university, all his friends thought that he was unhinged. You have a gris-gris against this, another against that, what sort of lawyer can a man be when he puts his faith in such irrational things? But those people were from the city and had no experience of sorcery, Sédhiouba went on, with his soft, harmonious intonation. He had been protected, but still the sorcerers had got to him.

His limpid gaze seemed to be set far away, alighting on those immaterial devils that had come from the fires to torment him.

'I used to say to them,' Sédhiouba went on, 'you have no experience of sorcery. If you had seen what I have seen, you would not mock me.'

He returned to his tea. Dusk was falling, and the brilliance of the light was fading as the distant hills on the horizon were absorbed by a haze of grey.

'What's the old man done for you?' El Hadji asked, after a time.

'The devils have gone,' said Sédhiouba. 'We heard them crying in the sky above my head when he banished them.'

It was a terrible sound, he said. As if the world had suddenly been possessed by a cloak of madness which was able to materialise at any moment.

After we had drunk the tea, El Hadji went to the mosque to pray. The wails of the Imam reverberated through the evening, dissolving into a soft burble of voices chattering around the acrid smell of the wood fires. A feeble glow emanated from Koubia's houses and settled uncertainly in the twilight. In a room behind me, boys practised writing their Arabic on wooden tablets. They muttered prayers, and the air was redolent with supplication, hovering intangibly over the town.

When El Hadji returned from the mosque, he came with Mamadou Diallo and the exorcist.

'Come on,' said El Hadji. 'Let's go and talk to the old man.'

I rose awkwardly. My legs ached and, although it was a warm night, a film of cool sweat had gathered on my forehead. I wiped it off distastefully, and then followed them into the old man's bedroom, where I sat with El Hadji and Mamadou Diallo on prayer mats, while the exorcist took the bed, an iron contraption with a sagging foam mattress. On the wall there was a calendar and a square clock, which chimed out the hours with tuneless regularity, day and night.

We sat exchanging greetings in Peul, and then El Hadji murmured that I could begin. My throat was dry, and I felt flushed. But I tried to regain my equilibrium, and said that I came from a country where sacred magic was deemed impossible, and many people doubted the existence of God. The wisdom of African holy men was not even considered as a possibility. I said that I wanted to discover proof that such wisdom existed, evidence that even my most cynical compatriots would be hard pressed to ignore. Tradition had it that there was a gris-gris for invisibility, and I wondered if the old man knew where this could be found.

As Mamadou translated for him, the exorcist scanned us alertly with his chocolate eyes. Then he nodded, once he had understood the question, and began to reply. Koubia was the right place for us to have come, and there were three men in the district who had this secret.

'El Hadji Bouabacar Diallo is one,' he said 'the third Imam of our mosque. He was in Liberia about five years ago, and visited a local church. Then the guerrillas came and murdered everyone who was inside. He was the only man to escape, thanks to his gris-gris, *alhamdoulilah.*'

But El Hadji Bouabacar Diallo was away in Senegal, and would not be back for two months.

The exorcist smiled. His white *boubou* hung loosely to the ground, and brushed over the dust that had gathered on the prayer mats. There was another man in a village fifteen kilometres from here who had that secret. But he had fallen ill, and the government had sent him to Spain so that the infection could be treated. Many important people knew of that man's powers, they called on him frequently and were eager to see his health return.

'But this man,' he repeated, 'is also abroad.'

'And what about the third man?' I asked.

'He lives over the hills, towards the town of Mali,' said the exorcist. 'But he has lost his sight, so he does not write gris-gris any more.'

I listened, and my head pounded. My throat felt drier than it had done before. The cold sweat was now even more apparent to me, and my mind was clutched by a miasma of confusion. Yes, said a voice, far away, there are secrets in Koubia. But even if people come looking, secrets are not always easily unearthed.

We went out into the warm night air, but I shivered. We planned to walk forty kilometres the next day. The dust from the dry earth stuck in my throat, and I said that I would have to go to bed.

Gris-gris were most powerful in the earth, I remembered, climbing onto the old bed. Asis had said so in Balimé; he had said that they must be buried there. In that way magic was like the human body, he had told me, which is also buried in the dust. The difference is that magic thrives in the dust and, the deeper that a gris-gris is buried and concealed from sight, the wider its spells cast their nets. But our bodies die before they are buried and, once below the surface of the world, they soon consist of nothing.

My eyes rolled as I looked at the incongruous and fading posters on the wall. Two of them celebrated footballing triumphs for Germany and Nigeria, and another had salacious photographs of a group of women known as the Samba girls. I sweated, and clutched my cotton sheet. The posters grinned at me, and I felt as if they were mocking me as I lay there, unable to move and running a fever.

My febrile thoughts passed into dreams, during which I sweated more and more. My sheet sleeping bag was damp and warm, but it was not comforting, and I felt stripped of protection. The heat spread across my body. Even the posters were glowing, so that everything in my world seemed to burn in a welter of images. Finally it felt as if even my soul was ashen, white-hot.

My body struggled, twisting violently with my thoughts. Ideas swam in and out of focus like the images around me, and I felt that I was starting to disintegrate.

Then I remembered Musil's masterwork, *A Man without Qualities*. If people are constantly encouraged to understand their thoughts as chemical secretions, says Ulrich's friend Walter, and even their impulses to kindness as a sophisticated form of egoism, whatever they have left of them that constitute, their soul will be lost.

In the morning I turned to El Hadji, and croaked to him that I was ill.

'I've got a fever.'

He felt my head.

'Do you think it's malaria?'

'Oh no,' he said. 'It can't be malaria. You've been taking your pills.'

'I must have caught a flu from that young girl in the Land Rover,' I said, relapsing onto the dank sheet. El Hadji did not reply. He turned over, and then rose and went to speak to Mamadou Diallo.

'We can't leave today,' he said. 'He's ill.'

He gestured into the room, where I lay on the bed, tired, flushed and sweating, inert until the afternoon. I had no appetite, and wanted nothing except water. I slept and dozed and dreamt and was interrupted by the methodical sounds of the day: the pounding of millet, the laying down and taking up of prayer mats on the veranda, the rustle of a rosary and the anguished wails of a young toddler in the yard.

After the others had eaten lunch, I tottered outside and watched the toddler crying. He was large for his age, and I had seen him playing with his friends in the dust, throwing stones and shells at the unripe mangoes hanging down like green bees' nests in the yard. But he had a fungal infection in his ears, and they had become inflamed. The infection looked as if it might spread to the rest of his face, which was swelling slowly and ominously.

'My sister had that illness,' Sédhiouba said, as we watched the boy's mother boil some herbs before treating the infection.

'Is it serious?'

'She died from it,' he said matter-of-factly. The toddler screamed again, his cries filling the air with terror, an emotion which, at that moment, everyone seemed to share with him.

My fever was still pronounced. The afternoon heat was thick, and we sat beneath the kola tree drinking tea. I listened with only half an ear to Sédhiouba, as I worried about malaria. The initial symptoms may be confused, said my handbook on tropical diseases, especially if the sufferer has been taking malarial prophylactics. At first, you may think that you have only a cold, or a sore throat, but gradually the fever takes hold, and the parasite spreads. It is vital to seek medical help immediately. A course of drugs will be necessary to clear up the strain; the drugs will crush the parasite and your symptoms will subside.

Koubia abounded neither in drugs nor in medical help. My mind was fevered, and I kept on wanting to say to El Hadji that we needed to do something about my illness. But he pre-empted me, telling me that my ailment would not be anything serious and that we would soon be walking on in search of the Marabouts, insh'allah.

'Don't be a hypochondriac,' he said.

He sat talking with Sédhiouba, and their conversation wafted over me like a strange, mystical song.

'Those devils,' Sédhiouba told us as he shook the teapot so that the tea was properly brewed, 'they nearly did for me.'

'They are bad,' El Hadji agreed. 'That is what is dangerous about Africa, people are willing to use their powers for evil.'

That Marabout in Busurah, I thought, he must have been annoyed. And I had nearly forgotten to take my Lariam pill in Labé. Perhaps the djinns had been circling around me, the good and bad spirits fighting over me. That was the only time when I had nearly forgotten my pill – and if I had forgotten it, I might have died. Perhaps I would already have been dead, I thought. I knew that this was malaria. I convinced myself. The devils lined up on either side. They swam invisibly in the air, but I knew that they were there.

'In Conakry,' said Sédhiouba now, pouring out the first cup of tea, 'when I was taking my law degree, things were very difficult. I had no money, not even to take a bus to the campus, so I had to walk five kilometres each way to go to my classes. But I studied hard, and played football well for a good team. My team-mates never understood how I could do both, they became jealous. One day, when I came back from training, I put on a T-shirt. It had been missing for a few days, and I had not seen it. But as soon as I put it on, I got a severe headache and fits of shivering. I became ill, and began to have dreams that made it clear to me that my illness was the product of sorcery, for in my dreams I saw a white man holding five black dogs on a leash. The dogs were all barking wildly at me. The white man was laughing and,' Sédhiouba said, turning to me, 'as you know, white men in dreams are symbols of a sorcerer at work. Of course,' he said, 'I only understood this after I had seen the Marabout, and he had explained about the T-shirt, which must have been taken by my enemies and given to a sorcerer. That was when I knew that I had to come back to Koubia, and see the old man.'

Even though I was feverish, I was aware that these words hinted at some deep-seated mental problem. El Hadji later confided to me that he had taken Sédhiouba aside and told him that he had to get over his preoccupation with sorcery. It was doing him no good at all. But nevertheless, exorcist or healer of mental illness, his grandfather had performed him a great service, and Sédhiouba was not about to downplay his skills. 'Devils,' said Sédhiouba, 'have come for me in the past as well. About ten years ago I was walking along the street here, and suddenly I saw a dark shape in front of me. I couldn't make out whether it was coming or going. I walked on, trying to keep my cool. Then I saw that it was an old lady walking with a stick, with her hair hanging down in plaits right down to her thigh. I knew she was a devil, so I speeded up, and so did she. Then I slowed down, and so did she. Then I recited a secret verse from the Qu'ran which I knew, and she vanished. Whoever heard of an old woman with such plaits! That was a sure sign of the supernatural. It does not take much to see magic: the djinns hang in the air with the heat, and the fear and the illness.'

Sédhiouba prepared the tea. The sweat stood out on my brow, and El Hadji looked at me in alarm.

'You're ill,' he said.

'It's malaria.'

'It can't be malaria,' he said. 'But we'll go back to Labé tomorrow, just to be near the hospital.'

He smiled at me. I could not be that ill, he said. I was strong, I was protected. Do not worry about the Marabout – you must not kill yourself with fear. But once you have begun to fall into the precipice of terror, it is difficult to climb out of it. I remembered the argument in Ablai's hut. And then I remembered walking along a beach in Chile, seven years before, in a region famous for witchcraft. The beach had been empty except for myself and one old woman who was riding horseback with two black mongrels for company. She had followed me along the beach and then disappeared from sight. Later, I had been told that the area towards which she had been travelling was uninhabited, and hardly ever visited by locals. As soon as she had disappeared, I had been attacked by wave upon wave of birds, who had materialised as if from nowhere, in front of me and behind me and above my head. I had sprinted along the beach in terror, and the birds had crashed into my back and brushed against my head. Then I had stopped and looked behind me, and a thick curtain of birds had risen from between me and the waves, thousands upon thousands of them. They had seemed to be laughing. Then I had walked on, in shock, wondering who that woman could have been – a devil, surely, or a spirit. A figment of the imagination, laughing at me whenever I looked back.

By the morning, my fever had abated sufficiently to allow us to catch the Land Rover back to Labé. Of course, in order to get there again, we had to squeeze together with the other passengers like chickens in a battery farm, and endure the dust and the thirst and the threats from the authorities. Such a journey could not be recommended even for people in the best of health – in fact, I suspected the appalling travel conditions to be a factor in my illness – but I was in no position to quibble.

I comforted myself with the thought that at least things were better for me than they had been for the first Europeans in the Fouta Djalon. Perhaps the most long-suffering of these was the Frenchman Gaspard Mollien, an enormously likeable adventurer who set out from St Louis on the River Senegal in February 1818 with the assistance of Boukari, a guide who was a Marabout. Mollien's aim was to be the first European to reach the sources of the Senegal and Gambia rivers. Having travelled through the bush and neared the Fouta Djalon from the north, however, he had a severe argument with Boukari, who resolved to leave Mollien to continue his journey without him. On the fringes of a hostile country, in exacting terrain, his prospects did not look good. 'I then took my horse by the bridle,' wrote Mollien, 'and prepared alone to commence a journey which presented nothing but innumerable dangers. Before me lay deserts which it would take me three days to cross. Without a guide, not understanding Poula or Mandingo, I saw myself exposed to certain death. Nevertheless,' Mollien said with understated lunacy, 'I resolved to prosecute my enterprise.'

Fortunately for Mollien, Boukari relented, and they continued together. But their trials were only just commencing. Over the succeeding months they starved, often going for days at a time without eating. After they were attacked by soldier ants, Mollien and Boukari eventually reached Timbo, the capital of the Fouta Djalon, and found the sources of both rivers. However, the Frenchman then fell ill with what apears to have been malaria, and was several times on the point of death. Boubou, a Peul with whom he had travelled earlier, then offered to shelter him. But the Peul's motivations were exposed when, as Mollien was beginning an unlikely recovery, Boubou tried to kill him and his guide with a dish of poisoned chicken. When this ploy failed, Boubou sent assassins to Mollien's hut at night, but Mollien and Boukari escaped. They sought refuge with the village chief, but were permitted to eat only a few handfuls of rice a day. 'I prayed to heaven,' Mollien wrote, 'to deliver me from a miserable life, which was only a burden to me.' He lodged many bids for freedom, and finally managed to escape with the help of a good and honest guide. So ecstatic was he to be free that he spurred his ass too fast, with the result that, within a few hours, his mount plunged over a ledge and left him paralysed on the ground for two hours before he was able to move. Even after recovering from this accident, and having travelled on successfully towards the coast, months of fever and inactivity awaited Mollien in the Portuguese settlements of Geba and Bissau. The fevers of West Africa did not relinquish you lightly, once they had taken hold.

So, as soon as we arrived in Labé, I became flushed again.

I lay on my bed in the Hôtel du Tourisme, listening to the shouts from the bar, where the city's well-heeled functionaries had gathered to watch the final of the African Nations' Football Cup, live via satellite from Lagos. Judging by the constant hubbub that I could hear, the afternoon passed in a perpetual frenzy of excitement. However, I could only experience it vicariously, since I lay, pasty and lethargic, sweating into my sheet. My thoughts almost came to a halt, and I only returned to any semblance of activity when El Hadji burst into the room to tell me that the match had entered extra time. But I was too wasted to share his excitement.

'El Hadji,' I said, 'I'm sure it's malaria.'

'Nonsense,' he said. 'Stop worrying. You'll be fine. You are a coward.'

He went back to the bar, and I sank back onto the sheets. The noise from the generator rattled in my brain, and I heard, as if disembodied, the thump of beer bottles and the shouts of the men. I was clutched by an indiscriminate fear. There were so many things of which it was possible to be afraid. Illness, bad magic, the police, the Peugeots which we travelled in – it was difficult to know which was the most likely to kill me. The fear bunched in my chest. I could not dispel it. The hotel generator rattled more persistently, the TV droned on, and I imagined that I had been transported outside into Labé's streets, with the diesel fumes from the mopeds, the dust that spread inexorably throughout the day, the broken tarmac and the lean, gaunt figures of the Peul, walking with dignity along the shady avenues.

The city appeared to swim through the haze, and I looked on in astonishment. It was hard to believe how much this place now held me under its spell. The mystery had bewitched me, and now my body was sick, I had lost all sense of reason, and any assurance that I had once had in my own beliefs was rapidly vanishing into a morass of relativism.

I turned to the wall and stared at the peeling paint. As I watched the mosquitoes, I remembered 'Rule Britannia'. That song was now infamous but until recently it had been taught at British schools, and I recalled learning the lines by rote: *Rule Britannia/ Britannia rule the waves/ Britons never never never shall be slaves* – a charmless verse that was often sung to the slaves by the British slavers in the eighteenth century. That was a difficult, dangerous life. You went off to the swamp coasts and fevers descended. Reason was challenged and many people died. But for the British, faith in their own reason always persisted, and only those who succumbed to the irrational were lost. An empire and two world wars had been won, and the direction of history had been altered, thanks largely to the conquering power of logic. If I let reason go now, I thought as my mind steadily became lost, that will be the end.

Then I fell asleep. Some hours passed. After dinner, the cook came into the room to examine me. Tal was from Senegal, and their shared nationality had created an instant friendship between himself and El Hadji. He was a large middle-aged man, balding, with heavy, drooping jowls that gave his face an air of permanent distress, and long ears that curved down towards the lobes. He did everything related to his work with immense pride.

He perched on the edge of my bed and looked at me.

'I've got malaria,' I greeted him.

'No, it's not that,' he said. 'You know, white men are not as strong as blacks. History proves that. That was why our ancestors were taken to the Americas, because they could do work that no one else could manage.'

He puffed on a cigarette.

'El Hadji has been telling me all about you,' he said. 'He says you're headstrong. He tells you to purify the water, and you don't bother. He tells you not to eat the cassava leaves, and you insist that you must economise. He suggests that you rest, and you say that you have to continue.'

Tal paused, and frowned.

'Anyone would think, you know, that you had come to Africa to look only for death.'

I was in no position to argue. Tal would cook good food for us, he said, for lunch and dinner – *bons plats*. He would make us *filets au poivre, pintade, pommes dauphines* and *cassoulet*. We would eat as well as we would have done had we been staying in Paris. Tal had been a chef to wealthy people in Europe and Morocco. He knew what I needed.

'Good food,' he said. 'Rest, sleep and relaxation. That'll sort you out.'

That night he cooked us an enormous meal. Then we had a large lunch with plenty of French bread the following day. But then, in the evening, I sweated profusely, and slept flatulently throughout the night.

In the morning, I was freezing cold. El Hadji had opened the window wide.

'Why did you do that?'

'I thought you were going to kill me,' he said.

I laughed. Then I ran to the toilet. I spent most of the morning there, and my guts flowed away in a continuous stream. I was lucky to have the privacy of a cubicle, rather than the usual latrine, but unlucky that the toilet did not flush. The smell seeped into my nose and gradually made me feel nauseous. But Tal still insisted that I eat some chicken stew for lunch.

Then I ran to the toilet again, only this time I was sick.

'Wonderful,' said Tal, when I returned. 'When you've had malaria, it's finished as soon as you are sick.'

'Malaria?' I asked El Hadji when he had gone. 'I thought I didn't have malaria.'

'Well,' he said, 'of course you did. As soon as you had a fever, I knew what was wrong with you.'

'Why didn't you say anything?'

'We've had this discussion before!' he said. 'When someone's ill, they need to be encouraged. You were so worried. The fear was bright in your eyes. If I had agreed, and said that you were very ill, you probably would have killed yourself with the worry alone.'

'But I *have* been ill.'

His eyes measured me.

'Yes,' he said, 'you've been ill. When I saw you last night, I was frightened. You had gone yellow. You were wheezing. And all those farts!'

He paused, blanching at the memory.

'But now it's over.'

Nevertheless, we went to the hospital, so that I could have a blood test. The test showed that I still had the parasite in my system, so I bought a course of drugs from the pharmacy and pumped my body full of Fansidar. That night my pulse raced, and my body became hotter than it had ever felt before. The heat roasted me, and my mind was once again convulsed with fear. But the next day the heat subsided, and I realised that I was cured.

Even so, Tal and El Hadji counselled me that we had to rest up. We were planning to walk 150 kilometres through the bush, in an area that was said to be thick with Marabouts, and this was not the sort of mission to be undertaken by someone who was still weak with malaria. So we spent three days eating copious quantities of meat, padding around the hotel in our sandals and embarking on an exercise programme.

At the back of the hotel was an old tennis court, which stood on a low rise above the buildings. The tarmac was cracked and the paint was old and chipped, but the court itself was a good exercise ground. Each evening, we went there to train, stripping down to our shorts and then running around the tramlines, hopping across the court and leaping up in the air in star jumps. El Hadji looked on with satisfaction as my mien became normal again, and the jaundice left my skin.

'You've missed out on your vocation,' I said to him once. 'You should have become a personal trainer.'

During these workouts, we were also joined by children from the neighbourhood. They had never done exercises like this before, and El Hadji was soon racing them against each other, while I looked on, resting against the wire netting at the back of the court. On the third night, he set the children playing football against one another, and their enthusiasm knew no bounds.

'You could have been a football coach too,' I said to El Hadji.

He smiled, and carried on shouting out instructions. I was tired, and went back to the room for a shower. When El Hadji returned, twenty minutes later, his eyes were shining with the fun. But then he sneezed, twice.

'You've got a cold.'

'If I come down with a bad cold,' he said, pointing his finger at me, 'you'll pity me. It knocks me out.'

We went through to the bar. Tal had cooked up another sumptuous feast of *filet au poivre* with a delicious green salad and sautéed potatoes. Once Doré, the waiter, had served the food, Tal appeared from the kitchen and came to watch us eat. There was a deferential air about him as he asked if we were satisfied. Was the sauce spicy enough, and the steak well cooked? Was there anything that was lacking? Then he sat at a nearby table and took off his spotless white chef's hat, which he rested in his lap as he beheld the television.

It was a Saturday night, and the large room had gradually filled with local functionaries and four Moroccan engineers who worked on a construction project nearby. The noise of the disco downstairs thudded through the ceiling, even though the night had not properly got under way. But the noise was less of a distraction from the television than the numerous whores who paraded up and down the room. However, even they did not divert the eyes of most of the men from the screen. Doré had switched the channel to Canal +, France's international cable station, which was advertising forthcoming programmes, the football tomorrow, the world championship wrestling the following day, not to mention the pornography that would be showing tonight, tomorrow night and the night after. *La Bonne* was the film for later on. The maid was an attractive figure and she worked in an imposing house. The images showed that it had an immaculate lawn, behind which were flower gardens and a rockery. There was also a small pond covered with lilies and duckweed. In the grand interior of the house, there was a carpeted hall and a wide stairway that led up past flattering portraits to a first floor on which were many bedrooms, with en suite bathrooms and soft and receptive beds with embroidered counterpanes on which the maid could slowly divest herself of her smartly pressed clothing, and begin her work.

'You see,' El Hadji whispered, turning to me. 'If I go to Europe, I will have a house like that.'

He smiled. His eyes returned to the screen, and we watched, magnetised, as the trailer came to an end and a new film began. It was about an American gymnast who was so obsessed by becoming an international star that she starved herself and became anorexic. The programme took us inside her parents' home, with the clean units of the kitchen, the well-stocked fridge, and her bedroom with its computer and television. The men in the bar watched with fascination as she went out to eat with her friends, and secretly put the food she had ordered into the bin. The food seemed so appetising, and Tal shook his head in bewilderment at this deliberate waste. With increasing astonishment, the audience watched her become thinner and more obsessive, her body wasting away, her face leaner, until she withered and deteriorated into a fragile shell. Such behaviour was impossible to comprehend. They watched with all the stark fascination of a group of anthropologists seeing a film about an unknown people from the Amazon rain-forest.

'You see,' El Hadji said to me at one point, 'she is mad.'

'No,' I said, 'she's not mad. There is an illness in Europe and North

117

America where people can't bring themselves to eat. She has that illness.'

El Hadji shook his head.

'It's not easy over there,' he said.

He whispered to Doré, who was sitting beside him, and told him of this strange European illness. I leant over to Doré and confirmed the story. Doré was a lean, jovial man with an elegant gait. He smiled and shook his head in mystification. The events that were brought to Guinea-Conakry by this screen every night were so alien that they seemed as magical as anything that the Marabouts could do. As I sat in Labé, the second-largest city in Guinea-Conakry, where there were no more than ten advertising hoardings, it was impossible to conceive of the bombardment of images of thin girls which afflicts women in so many other countries, where, even though we all aspire to live up to the images that surround us, it is difficult not to feel anything but alienated from the supposed goods which they represent. The most appealing option was often to withdraw from this world, I thought, watching the credits dissolve upwards as the film came to an end and my mind went blank.

El Hadji and I sat contemplating the screen for some time. Once the film had ended, a football magazine programme began, and we watched tales from the nether regions of the French league. Eventually we rose and returned to our room. El Hadji sat heavily down on the bed and looked at me. Suddenly I saw that his gaze had weakened. Beads of sweat stood out on his forehead.

'I'm not well,' he said.

'Is it just a cold?'

'No. I've got a fever as well.'

I felt his forehead, which was flushed and burning.

'Do you think it's malaria?'

'I think so,' he nodded. Luckily, I had the drugs with me now, so I gave them to him and he took three Fansidar tablets. He shivered and crawled beneath the blanket. We looked at each other in silence.

'How is it that as soon as I improve, you've fallen ill?'

'Malaria is a dirty, cunning illness,' he said, quietly. 'I've known it for a long time. That's what it does. Once one person is better, it goes and attacks one of his friends. It's always the same.'

Neither of us said anything for a moment, and we listened to the generator rattle outside the window. El Hadji sighed.

'*C'est difficile*,' he said. '*Vraiment, c'est difficile.* If I had realised how difficult this was going to be . . .'

He left the sentence unfinished. Soon he drifted off to sleep, but I could not join him. The generator kept me awake, and so did the noise from the disco downstairs. My mind wandered, and I thought of the time we had spent in this hotel. We had been here long enough to become a part of the household. The well-covered Peul woman who owned the establishment greeted us every morning and allowed us to share her tea. Then, in the afternoons, we usually lazed on the terrace beyond the bar. El Hadji would constantly refill his pipe and make tea, and we would while away the time playing cards. El Hadji had tried to teach me a Senegalese game, *mariage*, but I had never entirely understood the rules. I enjoyed playing it anyway, even though I always lost – something that everyone else in the hotel found very funny.

The life of the people who worked there was always fairly constant. The brother of the owner, a promiscuous man with a lean body, would often saunter past, watching our games and cadging cigarettes from Tal. Max, the thin Wolof who worked as the DJ in the club downstairs, would emerge from his latest love fest at around two o'clock in the afternoon and blink rapidly at the brightness of the day. And Tal would mutter about his life, complaining that he was wasting his time there, working for someone else, when he had once had his own restaurant and hotel in Guinea-Bissau. It had been destroyed during the civil war, and now he had nothing. Every day he tried to negotiate a better deal with the owner of the hotel, pointing out that it was his sumptuous cooking that kept the restaurant so popular.

Yet although we had made friends, our inertia irritated me. We were supposed to be travelling and discovering things, but we were stuck in the same place. While there, we became used to the strange routine of life in the Hôtel du Tourisme. We learnt about all the petty squabbles between the people who lived there, and understood their relationships much better than we would have done if we had only stayed for two nights. But the traveller in me wanted to press on and ignore such mundane realities.

This travelling business was such a strange one, I thought, as I lay in bed, listening to El Hadji's heavy breathing, and his laboured movements beneath the blanket. The whole world wanted to travel now, everyone dreamt of donning a backpack. It was such a mesmerising activity, yet often it was also difficult and tedious. It was impossible to deny that, during my years of travelling, I had experienced a great many moments of awe and beauty and felt an unparalleled sense of freedom. It was also true that my journeys had opened my eyes to many things, and fundamentally altered the way that I saw the world. Yet I had also often been bored and unhappy.

With a creak and a whine, the generator gradually slowed and came to a stop. The stillness of the night resurfaced from beyond the shuttered window, and I heard the incessant arguments of the dogs that paraded through the streets after dark. My head was cool and I felt alert. There was a shout from the bar, and I heard the echoes of footsteps striding down the corridor. Then there was the sound of voices, a giggle and a door slammed shut.

I found it hard to get to sleep that night. I lay there, turning over my past journeys. They had introduced me to many people, most of whom I barely remembered. Sometimes I thought that all I had collected was a barrage of superficial and false images of people and places, a feeding ground for my imagination. For I was increasingly aware that when I remembered a place or an experience, I automatically stripped the memory of all its difficult feelings – the uneasiness, the homesickness, the fear and the tedium – so that they became projections of myself, emotions. Any claim that a story was the unadulterated truth suddenly seemed hopeless. But this was what I had believed when I had first begun to travel, and had taken my first photographs and written my first diaries. I had not sensed how much memories became confused and layered, and stories became distorted, until they were so remote from the original experiences that they could almost have been fictions.

Hopes were so often frustrated, I thought, in the silence that had gathered around the shadows of the hotel. People left Africa for Europe expecting material riches, and I had left Europe for Africa expecting spiritual riches, yet now I lay inert on my bed, my friend was ill and we had spent over a week doing nothing in Labé, festering with boredom.

El Hadji took three days to recover from his attack of malaria. He spent most of this time sprawled on his bed, his solid limbs stretched apart as if in supplication. He rarely moved from this position, except to eat and to pray. I would go out in the morning and buy bread, coffee, powdered milk and sugar, and then, once he had breakfasted, he would go back to sleep.

On the third day of his illness, I decided that I would go to the post office, where there was a connection to the Internet – the only place outside Conakry where public access to the Web was possible in this country. I walked through the streets, past the filthy chaos of the transport park, where half the cars lay disembowelled in the dirt, and made my way to the post office, where I asked if it was possible to use one of the machines.

The stocky Peul who ran the centre said that it was.

'How much does it cost?' I asked.

'It costs 3000 *Francs Guinéens* to send and receive messages.'

This was only a little over £1, so I settled down to write home to Europe. I spent forty minutes wrestling with the intricacies of a French keyboard, and eventually signalled to the man that I had finished. I gave him one of the dirty 5000-franc notes which are the highest denomination of currency available in Guinea-Conakry, and awaited my change.

'You have sent ten messages,' the Peul said.

'I don't know,' I said. 'I didn't count.'

'I did,' he said. 'That will be 30,000 francs.'

'You said that it was 3000 francs.'

'Three thousand francs,' he said, looking away, *'per message.* You have sent ten messages.'

I started to argue. I said that he ought to have explained properly.

There had been a misunderstanding and he could surely make an exception. But the man refused to budge.

'If you won't pay,' he said. 'I may have to call the police.'

I paid.

Then I walked back to the hotel in a fury, and told Tal what had happened.

'They're thieves,' he said, his jowls wobbling with rage. 'They're impossible!'

That was Guinea-Conakry for you, he said. Of course, the man would have been in league with the police. He swore, and then returned to the kitchen, where he was putting the finishing touches to his *coq au vin.* Something special, he said, for El Hadji to recuperate – another incongruous offering of his *haute cuisine.*

I woke El Hadji, and told him that lunch was ready.

'Where have you been?' he asked.

I explained.

'This country!' he spat. 'All it has brought us is trouble.'

We went through to the bar and ate the meal that Tal had prepared. El Hadji was feeling better, and he wanted to leave Labé the following day.

'If we stay here any longer,' he said, 'this place will kill us.'

We had planned to walk from Pita to Télimélé through the bush, but now we had a change of heart. What was the point, said El Hadji, when we did not know for certain that any of the Marabouts we needed were there? It was almost two months since we had left Dakar, and we had still had no luck.

'We must go to Guinea-Bissau,' he said. 'We need to go to the region around Gabú. That's where the best Marabouts live.'

As we had seen in Busurah, corruption was so endemic in Guinea-Conakry that even the Marabouts were affected. If we did find a Marabout who claimed to be able to have powers of invisibility or invulnerability, he would probably pull a million-franc trick again. We would take a Peugeot back to Koundara, and then cross over to Gabú.

We told Tal of our plans when he came in with our dessert, and he said that he would prepare the bill that evening, after he had served us a dish of couscous.

'A good meal for your final evening,' he said. 'Something to remember me by.'

We polished off the fruit salad that he had prepared. Then El Hadji burped loudly.

'*Alhamdoulilah*,' he said.

I looked at him strangely.

'Why did you say that?' I asked.

'What?'

'Why thank God when you burp?'

'You only burp when you have a full stomach,' he said. 'And it is thanks only to God that I am full.'

'What about Tal?' I asked. 'What about the people who harvested the wheat and killed the chicken?'

El Hadji shook his head sadly at what I had said.

'You still don't understand, do you?' he said. 'You still don't have the faith.'

'It's not a question of faith,' I said.

But El Hadji clearly did not agree. Everything was thanks only to God.

'He doesn't believe,' El Hadji said, pointing at me, when Tal returned.

I explained the source of our latest dispute.

'The fact is,' said Tal, grinning, 'of course each person has a different perspective on their faith. But God is above everything.'

Then he grimaced, and went to buy a packet of cigarettes.

'I still think we should thank Tal as well,' I said, watching him go and feeling belligerent.

El Hadji looked at me, and sighed.

'Nothing changes,' he murmured. 'Toby is headstrong, and he thinks he knows everything.'

But I smiled at this latest criticism.

'Still,' I said, 'at least we are now well enough to argue.'

El Hadji was right; it was time to move on.

When Tal returned, we spent the afternoon on the terrace together with him and Doré. Tal was feeling more contented now, since the hotel owner had offered to give him the downstairs bar to run on his own account, provided that he continued to cook for the restaurant.

The terrace had a privileged view of the city, and of the innumerable mopeds that passed bearing government officials. On the far side of the road was a bar and a general store, while across the roundabout was a clutch of small stalls sheltering under corrugated iron, all selling the same wares – milk, sugar, coffee, tea and washing powder. The trees behind the stalls were black with vultures. A little way along the road towards the centre of the city was a Total garage where, at dusk, old Peul men gathered to pray on the forecourt.

That afternoon, I noticed that there was a policeman on duty in the middle of the roundabout. 'He seems to be affected by the heat,' I said to Doré, 'because he's a little uneasy on his legs.'

Doré laughed.

'He's drunk,' he said.

'Drunk!'

El Hadji could not believe it.

'He's an officer of the law, how can he be drunk?'

'*Ici*,' said Doré, '*c'est la Guinée.*'

El Hadji shook his head.

'That man,' Doré went on, 'is famous.'

He had raped his own daughter and she had given birth to a child. The man had not even been imprisoned. Now he was back at work. He whistled at a heavy goods vehicle, and tottered down the hill to talk to the driver, his blue uniform flapping in the sunlight. Some money changed hands.

'How can he have the nerve to work as a policeman, after what he has done?' I asked Doré. But Doré did not reply.

'It's difficult to understand,' El Hadji murmured.

Max made the tea, and when it was almost time for the evening prayer, Tal said that he would go to the kitchen to work on our dinner.

'*Un bon plat,*' he said. 'You will see. Even if you were going to stay here for a whole year, I could cook you up a new dish every day.'

After dark, he reappeared with the couscous, which was delicious. When we had finished and wiped the plates clean with our bread, I asked Tal about the bill.

'Ah yes,' he said, 'I will go and see.'

He went to talk to the owner of the hotel, and they conferred. We were only waiting on the payment for the previous five days, since everything else had been settled previously. Our terms had been agreed. Tal returned with the bill, and he brought it over to us.

I looked at the figures with some surprise. Every meal that he had prepared for us before had been charged at 4500 francs, and this had included a small salad. Now I saw figures of 7000 francs for dishes that were marked down at 4500 francs on the menu. And the salads, having been included in the price beforehand, were now charged separately at 1500 francs.

'Tal,' I said, 'I'm a bit confused by the prices here. Our chicken was 4500 francs before, but you've put it down for 7000 here.'

'Ah well,' he said, 'there's chicken and there's chicken! The one I did for you before was just a mangy little dish. This week I prepared a proper meal.'

'But on the menu, it's marked down at 4500 francs.'

'Ah well,' he said, 'but that's just the ordinary fare which I give to everyone else. *Your* meal,' he said, raising his eyebrows, 'was a special dish.'

'I always thought,' I said, trying to keep my cool, 'that it was common practice to charge the price that is on the menu.'

Tal smiled. The owner appeared and asked if everything was in order. I pointed out the discrepancies, and she said that she did not see what the problem was.

'I don't see,' I said, 'why the salad was free before, but now costs 1500 francs.'

'They weren't very good before,' said Tal, 'but I've really been putting some good ingredients together in the last few days. To complete your recuperation.'

There was a phone call for Tal, and he excused himself. El Hadji leant over and whispered in my ear.

'Toby,' he said, 'stop arguing.'

'I want to argue.'

'It's a waste of energy. We're in Guinea-Conakry.'

He was right. The owner of the hotel was a prominent figure in Labé society. It was said that she was a friend of Lansana Conté's. However much I protested, she presented an immovable object. She made some trifling reductions and then said that, thankfully, she thought we all understood one another now.

I stood up.

'Yes,' I said. 'We all understand.'

I flounced off and sat watching the television. My blood was boiling once again, not because the prices were unreasonable, but because of the underhand way in which they had been raised. I sat tapping my Coke bottle on the table, watching an anodyne film.

The man at the table next to mine leant over.

'You're the man who goes to work out at the tennis court, aren't you?'

'Yes.'

'My son's been going there too!'

His son had been very happy there. The man smiled at the thought. In fact, he told me now, dropping his voice, his son had confided in him that I had offered to take him back with me when I returned to Germany. Of course, he said, simpering, his son had been afraid to broach the subject at home, for fear of upsetting his mother. But he could assure me, he finished off, that as far as he was concerned, there was no objection. I was welcome to take his son with me whenever I wanted. He was sure that I would find him a suitable occupation.

I looked at the man open-mouthed.

'Your son,' I said slowly, 'has not told you the truth.'

Then I got up and went to bed. But neither El Hadji nor I could sleep. We lay fulminating until the small hours about the turn of events. It seemed that Doré too had been furious. At one stage, he had called El Hadji over and they had gone outside. He had told him that I could not accept that bill. When other guests stayed for long periods, significant reductions were made – not significant increases.

126

'She's not been intelligent,' he had said to El Hadji. 'What does she think he's going to tell people in Europe?'

El Hadji grimaced at the thought.

'Toby,' he said, '*here. Guinea-Conakry...*' He laughed curtly. 'They don't think about the future. Only about today. *C'est difficile.*'

Eventually, we slept. In the morning, we departed with as much grace as we could muster. Tal drove us to the transport park, and we arrived at about half past eight in the morning. The sun was already hot, and the red earth was strewn with rubbish and Peugeots. We were the first passengers for Koundara. A rakish old Peul with bloodshot eyes gestured at an empty car in the middle of the dust.

'You can put your luggage in the boot,' he said.

We settled our things, and then went to sit in a concrete shelter which was surprisingly cool. Even at this early hour, the transport park was characterised by inertia. Several Peugeots sat limply awaiting more clients, so that they could depart for Diaobé, Mali or Gaoual. The passengers stood listlessly in the heat, leaning against the rusting bodywork of their chosen vehicles. Their luggage was strapped onto the roofs with twine. The cars were so overloaded, and the bags teetered so pronouncedly, that it seemed as if they might collapse at any moment.

El Hadji and I sat on the concrete wall, surveying the scene with resignation. We bought some roasted groundnuts and ate them half-heartedly. A three-legged dog hobbled past with great difficulty, and began to scavenge in the dust. El Hadji told me that it would have lost its leg in a car accident, but it did not seem to have learnt from its tragedy, for it was nearly run over again by a rusting Peugeot which now arrived.

The driver swore at the dog, and it limped away, whimpering.

The car pulled up in a cloud of dust that spread across the transport park and hung above the dishes of cold rice and boiled cassava leaves which sat in front of the concrete shelter. The food was attended to by several women, whose wraps glowed brightly in the morning light, red and green and yellow, their flowers and distended shapes intimations of a brightness that struggled on bravely amid the misery.

The women sat talking by their enamel dishes. One of them was washing up the plastic plates on which she served out her food, using water that was so dark and rancid that it would not have disgraced a sewage works. Having cleaned the plate, she left it to dry in the sun. The women continued to talk, but their conversation was interrupted by the yelps of three dogs which scampered in front of them, two of them trying to hump a bitch on heat. The bitch turned around and tried to bite them. Eventually the dogs settled in the shade of a Peugeot, and fornication began.

An hour passed, and the heat intensified. No other passengers appeared for Koundara.

'How long do you think we'll have to wait?' I asked El Hadji.

'We have been here long enough,' he said slowly, 'to know that any predictions are useless.'

We watched the heat gather, the haze intensify, the suffering deepen. A mother appeared with a boy who was no older than four. His eyes were lolling, and his body was a dead weight. A man carried him over to a blanket where they laid the child down. I looked at the boy's dilated pupils and at his forehead, which was incandescent with the sweat of fever. It seemed certain that he was on the verge of death.

'He looks as though he has malaria,' I said to El Hadji.

'Yes.'

'Why don't we offer them some of our pills?'

El Hadji leant over and called out to the mother. He made the suggestion, but the woman said that it was not necessary, she had her own remedy. Then she began boiling up a pungent herbal concoction on a wood fire, next to the bowls of food, which remained untouched. The man wiped the sweat from the boy's forehead, but it continued to flow uncontrollably.

'Why won't she take it?'

'Surely after what happened in Bolana you've realised that it's senseless to try to intervene.'

'But he's dying. They have to take him to the hospital.'

El Hadji shrugged.

'Tell them,' I said. 'Tell them they have to go.'

'What's the point?'

'Tell them.'

'You've missed out on your vocation,' he said. 'You should have been a doctor.'

'El Hadji! Tell them.'

He called out to the woman. 'You have to take him to the hospital!'

But the woman pretended not to hear. He turned back to me.

'Maybe he'll die, and maybe he won't. But if he survives, another child will take his place. You can't get in the way of death.'

He spat in the earth.

'*Ici, c'est l'Afrique.*'

The boy would die, I realised miserably, simply because his parents did not have the money to take him to hospital. Even if they had accepted my offer of drugs, he might have fallen ill again, and then there would have been no one to step in and save him. At that moment, with the unshakeable air of illness enveloping the transport park, the fact that people in Guinea-Conakry managed to live ordinary existences at all seemed miraculous. I did not need to see invisibility or invulnerability in order to experience something of the magic and desperation of life.

After twenty minutes, they carried the boy away. His eyes had almost closed, and his limbs hung limply down towards the ground. The man carried him lovingly, but he walked with resignation, as if no one could really question the ending of this brief flirtation with life.

I, too, felt hot. The sun, the memory of my fever, my anger at this experience: everything compounded the swelling temperature. Furthermore, I had not managed to dispel my fears completely. It was impossible to feel secure in this place, where everything seemed so tenuous, especially the hold of life over death. Since witchcraft is impossible, Margaret Field said of the Ga people of Ghana in the 1930s, the fear must by symbolic. But this fear was real, it was burning and constant. The magic was a release from this creeping terror which seemed to engulf the living.

We sat for two hours more in the transport park, watching the misery. Near midday, three more passengers appeared for Koundara: a Liberian man travelling with a Sierra Leonean couple. They had travelled up from Conakry, and were heading for Bissau, whence they hoped to make for the Cape Verde Islands. Lewis, the Liberian, had arranged to meet his fiancée there, an American, and then planned to emigrate to Maryland. Rosetta and Amos, the Sierra Leoneans, were looking for Rosetta's family, who had originally come from Cape Verde.

Amos grimaced as he remembered the problems they had had travelling this far.

'When we reached the police post at the entrance to Labé,' he said, 'they asked us a hundred questions!'

They had asked where the couple were travelling to. Then they had asked how they planned to travel from Bissau to Cape Verde. Then they had asked if they had anywhere to stay in Cape Verde. Then they had asked why they were travelling together. They were in a relationship, but did they have anything that proved that this was true?

Amos smiled at the memory.

'I asked him, what did he mean?' he said. 'He said, did we have a certificate that said that Rosetta was my girlfriend?'

He roared with laughter. A certificate of being someone's girlfriend! Who had ever heard of such a thing?

'This country,' he shook his head.

'*C'est difficile*,' said El Hadji. 'They are thieves.'

'This is hard, man, this country,' said Lewis, in English.

'It's the worst country in Africa,' said El Hadji.

'This road to Koundara,' I said, 'it must be one of the worst in the region.'

'One of the worst,' said El Hadji, 'in the world.'

'The police,' said Lewis, 'they're always after us. We don't get a moment to rest, not in this country.'

He shook his head. We sat in the car. The shredded leather of the seats was baking hot. Flies flitted in and out of the windows, and our conversation lapsed into silence. Lewis picked up an A4 envelope, and got out a picture of his fiancée. I saw that he had scrawled poetry on the back of the envelope: *You say/ Will we be able to meet?/ Will we be able to marry?/ I don't know, honey/ but I believe/ I believe/ that everything is possible.*

'Liberia.'

Lewis shook his head.

'Man, that was a good country! We got diamonds. We got gold. All we need is a bit of peace, man. That's all we need.'

'Your country was a symbol of hope,' I said, thinking of the freed slaves who had returned to Africa from the United States.

'That's right!'

Lewis's eyes glazed over.

'Now, I'm just hoping to meet my girlfriend,' he said. 'Get married, go over to America. That's right!'

He smiled, and lost himself in his daydreams. For centuries, the prospect of a journey to the Americas would have instilled nothing but terror in Africa. When the first freed slaves returned to Africa from the Deep South, everyone would have envied them. But now a journey to America was the stuff of dreams. Everyone longed to escape and enter into wage slavery.

El Hadji's eyes lolled, and he began to sleep. Then a policeman ambled over to our car, and looked in at the five of us.

'*Papiers!*'

I rustled about for our passports.

'Vaccination Certificates!'

He looked at them slowly, and then grunted.

'What about you?' he said, turning to Amos, Lewis and Rosetta.

'Wait a minute,' said Lewis, in halting French, rustling in his bag.

'Wait! Why should I be the one who waits for you!'

'I . . .'

'Get out!' snapped the policeman.

Resignedly, Lewis swung his legs out of the car and emerged into the heat.

'Go and wait for me in the office.'

'Tell me how much I have to pay,' said Lewis.

'Go and wait in the office!'

'Just tell me how much I have to pay.'

'Go on!' the policeman screamed.

'How much?'

The policeman paused for breath. He was panting with the thrill of his power trip, and his eyes were shining. He glanced down at Lewis's International Vaccination Certificate.

'This,' he said, gesturing at the orange booklet, 'is not valid.'

'Yes it is,' said Lewis. 'They're valid for ten years. I had it done two years ago.'

He showed the stamp to the policeman.

'This is not valid,' said the policeman slowly, savouring every moment, 'because it has not been stamped in Labé.' He smiled. 'The stamp costs 20,000 francs.'

Lewis stood immobile in the heat.

'If you will not pay, we will have to send you back to Conakry.'

El Hadji leant over and whispered in my ear.

'There's no law here,' he said, 'no democracy.'

'The sooner we get to Guinea-Bissau,' I said, 'the better.'

It was a strange sentiment, since I never would have believed that I would have seen Guinea-Bissau as some sort of promised land.

Once he had paid, Lewis climbed back into the car, and we all grumbled about the situation. The hours passed with agonising slowness, but no one came who wanted to go to Koundara. At one point, El Hadji got out and asked the touts where the driver had got to. It being a Friday, we were told, the man was at the mosque.

Shortly afterwards, he appeared. His breath stank of beer.

'There's nothing to worry about,' he said, 'some passengers will be arriving shortly.'

We waited. Repeatedly, we were told that these mythical passengers would arrive at any moment. But they never came. Then, at six o'clock, a car arrived needing three seats to be filled before it could make for Koundara. Since Lewis, Amos and Rosetta made three, they were told to get in the car, and we were left in the position that we had been in when we had arrived at eight-thirty in the morning.

'I'll tell you what we'll do,' said one of the Peul. 'We'll drive around the town and see if we can't find any passengers for Koundara.'

'That's all right,' said El Hadji. 'We'll wait for you. Only please, tell us the truth. If you don't think you'll find anyone, don't say that you'll be back shortly.'

The Peul looked at him evasively.

'We can't lie to you,' he said, lying.

El Hadji looked ready to explode. He stormed off to the shelter and sat on the wall. I followed him, and we gazed at the miserable scene, unchanged since the morning.

It didn't seem as though we were ever going to discover anything.

El Hadji turned to look at me and spoke, very deliberately, in English:

'Fuck . . . off . . . this . . . country.'

The heat was ever-present, the light was blinding, the air had stultified us and we had collapsed into a lethargy that was spreading across us like a cancer. It was impossible to imagine anything magical or mysterious in this desperate place. Life in Guinea-Conakry was such an effort, so redolent with fear and despair, that without the promise of magic and a spiritual universe completely alien to this misery, it would have been impossible. People had nothing, and what little they had was stolen by officers of the state, who were equally desperate. Whatever the roots of this wretchedness, I thought, they were rotten beyond belief. That explained why they were buried, like the magic, all but imperceptible to the naked eye. I was searching for an invisible world but, at that moment, the only thing that was unseen by the eyes of the outside world was the suffering of Guinea-Conakry, and of other disenfranchised countries and peoples like it.

PART III

'He stood on the dark little landing,
wondering what it might be that he had seen'

When we arrived in Gabú, we instantly felt happier. Although the streets strained with people, an air of indolence and tranquillity slowly dispelled the tension that had crushed us in Guinea-Conakry. As we gathered our possessions from the rusting van, I was already aware that people did not stare at me or point as they had in other countries. They were more used to *brancos*, since the Portuguese had begun to build riverine settlements in the area at the end of the sixteenth century and had maintained a strong presence until independence was won in 1974. Guinea-Bissau, with its long history of Portuguese creolisation, was different.

Amid the distending chaos of the transport park, I tried to remember the way to the boarding house in which I had lodged when I had stayed in Gabú four years before. I knew that the place was somewhere in the maze of dusty side streets behind the market. So I led El Hadji across the paved main road, and then our feet raised small clouds of sand as we walked along the warren of residential streets, many of which were lined with stalls. Their unwanted goods spilt over into the road and stuck to the dust. But no one paid much attention to them. The heat of the afternoon was beginning to magnify, and people were occupied with tea-making duties.

Delving into the town, we passed the elegant façades of the colonial buildings. The roofs were tiled, and the slates were a similar colour to the laterite roads of Guinea-Conakry – sharp red, offsetting the fading whitewashed walls. As we looked uncritically at their exteriors, El Hadji's face developed a wide grin. He had never been to Gabú before, but the gentle sounds of Portuguese Kriolu filled the streets. He was back in Guinea-Bissau.

'I like this country,' he said, thinking of the seven years that he had spent in Bula before the civil war had begun in 1998.

He looked around again, and then added, 'I'm never going to Guinea-Conakry again. After Labé, this is paradise.'

Gabú was a strange location for a utopia. Nevertheless, after what we had been through, it was hard to disagree with him.

El Hadji was sceptical about my ability to find the way, but I soon spied the faded blue paint of the hotel's concrete veranda. It was the only sharp colour in sight. I clearly remembered drinking beer here, and talking to the *meistizo* man who had run this ramshackle and unappealing place back then. The establishment had only deteriorated with age, but, according to El Hadji, it could hardly be worse than the Hôtel du Tourisme. Perhaps those people had been poisoning us all along, he suggested to me with wild improbability, hoping to swindle us out of our money. Someone must have put a curse on us, otherwise that run of bad luck was inexplicable.

The boarding house was now managed by a *Fula Preto*, as the Portuguese knew them: a 'black Peul', a descendant of the slaves who had served the original Peul conquerors from the north. He led us to the annexe which was fronted by the shaded blue veranda. Then he took us along a musty corridor, dark and untended like a buried memory, before opening a door and showing us the small, unembellished room in which we were to stay. I passed through the entrance and lay, exhausted, on the bed. Outside, I could hear the sound of washing being slapped against stones, together with the murmurs of the town. Vultures scraped their claws on the roof, and rustled their wings in a cumbersome struggle against the air. The noises seemed somehow threatening, a challenge to my tired senses. I wanted only to rest inside.

While El Hadji went to wash, I dozed among the fleas in a red pool of my own dust. I thought back to my first visit to Gabú, which I seemed to remember quite well. The light had been colourless, exposed like a bare advertising hoarding, and the streets had been saturated with goods and vendors. I had bought some metres of cloth and then gone to one of the tailors that were strung out along Gabú's side streets. The tailor had made two shirts for me in a little over an hour. Then a rakish

Mandinga had inveigled me into buying a silver necklace, which had gone green shortly afterwards. I had eaten rice and fish by the light of lanterns in the evening, and travelled on to the Casamance the next day.

I remembered all of that quite clearly. But what I could not remember, I realised, was anything of this hotel. Although I had retained a clear image of the unremarkable façade of the building, I had no recollection whatsoever of what lay within. I knew that I had stayed here, yet, looking at the five nondescript doors leading into rooms – all of them virtually identical – I could not recall in which one I had stayed. When El Hadji had finished washing, I replaced him in the shower room, and looked at it as if for the first time. I remembered nothing of the toilet bowl, now floating with venerable turds, nor of the large barrel of water and the broken tub with which guests were supposed to wash. Light filtered weakly through the windowless hole in the wall, and wrapped the space in an apparently permanent mantle of grey. I washed reluctantly amid the filth, and then returned to our room, wondering what the point of my first stay here had been when my recollection of it was now so fractured. As I lay on the dusty blankets, the heat advanced with every minute, and the activities outside seemed to come to a halt as the afternoon entered its hottest part.

We both felt exhausted. When the heat had ebbed a little, El Hadji went outside and found someone to make us tea. Then we lay together on the bed, sweating and cursing Guinea-Conakry, while Papi brought us the first and the second brews.

When he brought us the third cup El Hadji asked him to wait, so Papi stood against the wall. A film of sweat clung to his forehead, and he watched us intently. He was a muscular twenty-year-old, with even features and a perpetual air of cheerfulness.

'We've come from Guinea-Conakry,' El Hadji said slowly in Kriolu, as though expecting sympathy.

'Ah,' said Papi. 'Guinea-Conakry. How is it over there?'

'Oh, fine,' said El Hadji, observing the ritual through gritted teeth. 'Were you working there?'

'No,' said El Hadji, decisively. 'This *branco* is looking for Marabouts, but we had no luck in Guinea-Conakry. We know that Gabú is famous for its Marabouts.'

Papi acknowledged that this was true. People came from Senegal, The Gambia, Mali and even from as far away as Algeria, simply to consult the Marabouts of Gabú. There are Marabouts in the town, he said, but they are not as strong as the ones in the bush. Out there, men could perform miracles in front of your eyes.

'These are the people we are looking for,' I said.

Papi smiled. El Hadji asked him if he would be our guide in the bush, and he said that it would be a pleasure. So the following day, once we had recuperated, we walked out along the road from Gabú, in search of the Marabouts.

The morning was hot, and we swung through the rising haze with a fast, regular pace. The road was shaded by cashew trees, which had been planted in groves on either side. This was the start of the season, and the trees were beginning to fruit with the red and yellow cashew apples which grew down curiously from the bottoms of the nuts that hung, green and unmoving, from the branches. Sometimes, Papi would stop by the roadside and throw stones at the fruits until they plummeted among the leaves that covered the earth. The fruits were succulent, and their juice was sweeter than coconut milk, but to look at the sharp warnings of their colours you might have thought that here were apples that should not be tasted.

'How far are we going?' I asked Papi, after we had been walking for an hour and a half.

'Oh, it's still a long way,' he said.

We continued for another hour. Then the road swept down a hill and curved round to the largest village that we had passed since leaving Gabú. There were scores of mud houses covered in thatch, and several stalls selling piles of oranges and groundnuts.

We stopped to buy some fruit.

'Don't you think we ought to ask around?' I asked El Hadji. 'Don't forget what Cheikh told us – often the Marabout you want will be right under your nose, and you won't realise.'

El Hadji talked to a man under a mango tree. We were looking for one of Gabú's *ommi grandes*, the big men, the Marabouts.

'Where have you come from?' the man asked us.

'Gabú.'

'But you've gone past the biggest one of all!' he exclaimed.

In Kabakunda, a village an hour back towards Gabú, there was a Marabout who was famous for his power to wreak invisibility.

'Talla Seydi,' he said, reverentially.

He demonstrated the gris-gris for invisibility in front of your eyes, the man told us, and sometimes kept a special supply of black cat skins for mystical ends.

'Now people really are going to think that we're mad,' El Hadji said to me, as we walked back the way we had come. Walking through the heat was strange, and a white man walking through the heat was stranger still – but a white man walking back and forth in the heat with no apparent purpose was so absurd that it was positively dangerous.

The haze was thicker than it had been when we had come, and the distant mango trees around Kabakunda oscillated in the heat. We walked past a dense cashew grove, and then the bush returned, yellow and sprinkled with strange trees and rocks rearing like unfinished creations in the dust. By and by, the first huts of Kabakunda manifested themselves on the roadside, and Papi led us down an embankment to where three women sat slumped and still while their daughters sifted through grains of rice on a frayed piece of sacking.

We greeted them in Peul, but they did not respond. Then Papi said that we were looking for Talla Seydi, and the women stared at us dumbfounded, in silence.

So we walked further along, until we saw a woman pounding millet in a compound on the far side of the road. We called out the Peul greetings, and then Papi asked for Talla Seydi.

'What's he done?' she asked, believing us to represent the authorities.

So we walked further still, and then met a young boy who told us that the Marabout lived near a mosque.

Kabakunda's mosque was a squat mud building covered with a zinc roof. When we saw it, we left the road and walked beneath a mango tree, approaching the hut that was nearest to the place of worship. Beyond the mango tree, we passed a pile of calabashes lying empty on the earth. Then we ducked under the thatch and introduced ourselves to the men who were there.

'*Salaam malekum,*' said El Hadji.

'*Malekum salaam.*'

One of the men, a Peul with a thin moustache and broken glasses which barely concealed his maddened, rolling eyes, rose from a flimsy hard-backed chair and insisted that I sat in it. Then he scrutinised me as best he could.

'*Branco,*' he said.

'*Sí.*'

'*Como di corpo?*'

'*'Sta bon.*'

'*Como di trabalho?*'

'*'Sta bon, obrigado.*'

I looked at the other men. One of them, a *Fula Preto* with an angular face and eyes set wide apart, was fanning coals with a piece of cardboard to accelerate the boiling of the tea. Two others were writing out Arabic script on wooden tablets, while the oldest man of all was reclining in an exceptionally decrepit deckchair, surveying the silent road and the misshapen sacks of charcoal that sat unattended beside it.

We exchanged pleasantries, and then El Hadji explained that we were looking for Talla Seydi. The man who was making the tea responded quietly.

'It's him,' El Hadji told me, gesturing at the old man in the deckchair who looked on impassively at these events, as if they did not surprise him.

The tea-maker was Talla Seydi's son, Mohammed. Now he rose, put his feet in his white sandals and gathered his *boubou* about him. Talla Seydi had likewise risen. Mohammed picked up the deckchair and carried it before him with reverence into his father's bedroom. He was followed by the old man. After a minute, Mohammed returned, and we were granted an audience with the famous Marabout.

We brushed through the curtain that guarded the old man's boudoir, took off our sandals and sat cross-legged on the prayer mats. Talla Seydi was sitting on the deckchair next to his bed. He was wearing a red skullcap and a dark *boubou*. His nose was long and his face was bony. The bed was shrouded with the veil of a mosquito net but, other than this and a yellowing pile of books beneath his bed, the Marabout possessed nothing of material value.

We began to talk. I spoke to El Hadji in French, El Hadji spoke to Mohammed in Kriolu and Mohammed spoke to his father in Peul. We explained that we had heard that the old man possessed the secret of invisibility. At this, Talla Seydi smiled, and stroked his lips with his hands.

'Yes,' he said, 'I have this secret. But I very rarely make it. There are so many bad people in the world now. Things are not like they used to be. Now, people want this secret for all sorts of evil. There are thieves, murderers and rebels. Look at the number of rebellions! In the past, people used these powers to protect themselves, but now they use them to attack others.'

The white man did not look like a bad person, but it was hard to be sure.

The Marabout's reluctance seemed to be a good thing. Had he been a charlatan, he would have been rubbing his hands together with glee. And, after all, his objection was a reasonable one. Being moderate was difficult where invisibility was concerned, I thought, remembering H.G. Wells' invisible man, Griffin, who had tried to use his powers to oppress others. When Griffin realised that his invisibility was perma-nent, he struck out with rage at the people around him and, wrote Wells of his creation, soon he set to smiting and overthrowing for the mere satisfaction of hurting. Later, Griffin related to a former friend, Kemp, how he had at one time attacked the owner of the house in which he had been hiding. He made me wild, expostulated Griffin, hunting me about the house, fooling about with his revolver, locking and unlocking doors. He was, said Griffin, simply exasperating.

It did not seem to matter that this was the man's home, which he was simply trying to protect, nor that the brutality imposed was unnecessary. But Wells' writing often had social and political under-tones, and his book was published in 1897, at the height of the European assaults on African homes and the viciousness that went with them, when the Belgians and French were raping the Congo, the English were massacring armies in Benin and the Sudan, the Germans were performing acts of genocide in Namibia, and the Portuguese were indulging in acts of pacification in Mozambique, Angola and Guinea-Bissau, which culminated in the battle of Cacheu in 1914, at which 235,000 cartridges were fired by the Portuguese at the 10,000 Manjacos who faced them. The Congo Reform Society fulminated, some liberal elements of society expressed outrage, but the atrocities in most parts of Africa excited little interest. The capitalist expansion continued and progress advanced with shameless nakedness, with the streets of the European cities proliferating with cars, the rubber tyres of which were in large part responsible for the decline of the population in French Equatorial Africa from 10,000,000 according to the 1913 estimate of the Parisian Bureau of Longitudes, to 2,860,868 according to the estimate of the 1921 census. The zeroes had been wiped away and they had fallen into the earth. The land had been pacified and tamed, and anyway, what were all these souls but invisible people?

It was hard, Talla Seydi intimated, looking at me, always to be sure that a person's motivations were genuine.

'Of course,' I said to El Hadji, 'I understand his worries. But you have to tell him that I swear that I only want the gris-gris for good ends.'

When I had first heard of this charm, I had thought of all the amazing things that I would be able to do with it. I had imagined walking into a bank and filling my pockets, or travelling wherever I wanted to go to in the world, whenever I wanted. It had seemed as if this gris-gris would make life trouble-free. But now that looking for it had brought me malaria, endless problems in Guinea-Conakry and fears of the unknown and unseen spirits, I had become aware that invisibility came with its own strings attached.

El Hadji explained that my reasons for wanting the gris-gris were honourable.

'As you know,' he said, 'no one can be certain in the world any more. There are too many people who want to harm us.'

Talla Seydi smiled in agreement.

'The only problem,' he said, reassured, 'is that we need the skin of a black cat.'

'How are we going to find another one of them?' I asked El Hadji.

'We'll have to go back to my family in Ziguinchor,' he said. 'Omar's friend there has kept it.'

'Which friend?'

'The one who made me the gris-gris with the cat skin.'

He explained to the Marabout.

'I will also need a piece of cloth from a burial shroud that has recently been used,' Talla Seydi said.

'We can find that easily enough,' El Hadji told me.

The most important thing about these materials, the Marabout went on, was that they should be seen neither by a woman nor by a boy who had yet to be circumcised – so it was lucky that I was Jewish.

'What about the price?'

Talla Seydi then said that he was a man of God, and the knowledge of God was not for sale. 'You will simply see how much you can afford,' he said.

'That's what the man said in Chelekoto,' I murmured to El Hadji, and he tried to press the point with the Marabout, who reiterated his refusal to name a price.

'Don't worry,' El Hadji said to me. 'I trust this man.'

We were in agreement. We explained that we would have to return to Ziguinchor to find the cat skin, but that we would be back within a week. I gave Papi a consideration for his troubles, and we prepared for the journey. It was annoying to have to return to Ziguinchor, but we had never imagined that we might need the cat skin again. From Kabakunda, El Hadji told me, we needed to make our way through the village of Diabikunda, and then carry on along the bush track that led over the border to Kolda in Senegal. So we caught a minibus to the turn-off for Diabikunda, and walked away into the dust.

The depths of the sky's blue was peerless that afternoon. The brilliant

145

light made everything appear to sparkle. The track was long and straight, and lined by a row of tall trees to the east. To the west, the dust was engulfed by a thicket of thorn bushes. A herd of cattle drifted across the track in an apparently unbroken line as they moved from east to west. Other than their graceless progress and our own marching feet, the bush was clutched by a gathering palsy, and seemed utterly devoid of life and spirits.

In the very far distance, piercing through the mirages of the afternoon, I could see the mango trees of Diabikunda.

'I have been here once before,' El Hadji told me, as we walked.

'When was that?'

'It was about five years ago. I came with a friend.' He paused, and his eyes shone in the bright sunlight. 'There used to be a big Marabout here. But he died about two years ago.'

He started humming to himself, *Diabi-kunda, terra sá-bia* – Diabikunda, a wise land – the lyrics of a song by one of Guinea-Bissau's most popular bands.

'Did you meet the Marabout?' I asked him.

'Yes,' he said. 'He was a very wise man. But he was old when I met him.'

The Marabout had divined that he was not long for this world, and his son had been hard at work learning his secrets. However, the old man had told his son that he could not transmit his knowledge to him until he had read the Qu'ran a certain number of times, and so, when El Hadji had visited, the son had been in the process of reading the holy book thirty times a day.

'That's impossible!' I said.

El Hadji stiffened. 'Can you read Arabic?'

'No.'

'Have you ever read the Qu'ran?'

'No.'

'So how do you know it's impossible?'

'It seems unlikely,' I said.

His expression thickened with annoyance.

'But,' I went on, trying to mollify him, 'everything is possible.'

Dawn at Chelekoto, Guinea-Conakry

Looking south from Gorée, near Dakar

The Ouésséguélé river plain, Fouta
Djalon mountains, Guinea-Conakry

Bushels of rice drying in a hut,
Chelekoto, Guinea-Conakry

The scars of gunfire from the civil war, Bissau

Old Portuguese cannons on the River Cacheu, Cacheu, Guinea-Bissau

Sharing food from the communal bowl, Bissau

El Hadji and child, the
Casamance, Senegal

Oumi Ndiaye

Newborn babies, the Casamance, Senegal

The griot plays the kora, Balimé, Senegal

Ablai's mother, Chelekoto, Guinea-Conakry

Owe, the author's 'daughter'
and El Hadji's 'wife' –
Kabakunda, Guinea-Bissau

Children, Jeta
Island, Guinea-
Bissau

Community prayers at the end of Ramadan

El Hadji pours the tea

Pounding millet, the
Casamance, Senegal

Talla Seydi's hut, Kabakunda,
Guinea-Bissau

February's Carnival, Bissau

A Marabout buries a
charm, the Casamance,
Senegal

Sacred stone in the Fouta Djalon, Guinea-Conakry

The strips of black cat skin, used for the gris-gris for invisibility

Bushfires at dawn, Diaobé, Senegal

Maraboutic tablets with secret verses from the Qu'ran, Guinea-Bissau

A gris-gris hangs at the threshold of a restaurant to entice the clientele, Guinea-Conakry

Fetish house for the worship of ancestral spirits, Jeta Island,
Guinea-Bissau

The cockerel is
prepared for
burial

The cockerel is buried by
Bouabacar, the Marabout

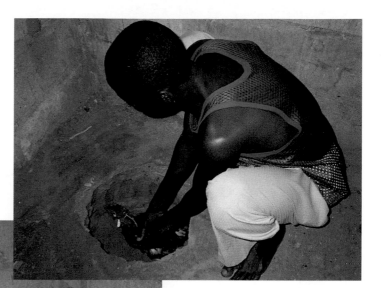

A week later, Bouabacar
digs up the cockerel

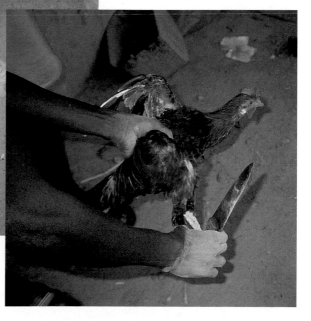

The cockerel emerges
unscathed.

The author is attacked with a knife by a
Marabout

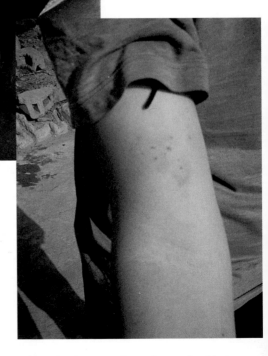

The author's arm 24 hours later - the skin is
bruised and marked, but it has not been punctured.

We came to the first compounds of Diabikunda. Used as I now was to the bush villages of this part of the world, I knew what to expect: thatched dwellings of mud huts, some basic stores and a fraudulent sense of nothing ever changing. Many of these attributes still clung to Diabikunda, like old clothes. Women balanced tubs of water on their heads, old men sat in shady spots and children raised clouds of dust in their early evening football games. Nevertheless, as we walked along the road, I noticed that Diabikunda was different from other bush villages. The houses were large, square and covered with zinc roofs. They led away from the road in straight lines and the blare of electronic noise filled the air above them: radios and televisions. Some of the sets were battery operated, but the more spacious compounds were adorned with satellite dishes and solar panels, glinting as they reflected the cloudless skies. It was in the driveways of these households that the cars were parked, old Mercedes and Renaults and Audis.

'El Hadji,' I said, as we walked through the village, 'why is this place so rich?'

'The Marabout,' he said softly. 'He was so powerful. People used to come from all over Africa to consult him.'

The old man had been a generous soul, he said. He had received riches in abundance, but he had kept none of them for himself. He had had no use for such offerings. Instead, he had used the money to send all of his sons over to North America to work. And of course, El Hadji said, each of them went with many gris-gris, so that they were sure to be successful when they arrived. Now look at the wealth that they acquired through magic, he said, looking approvingly at the village which, as he pointed out, was more developed than many of the *bairros* of the country's capital, Bissau. This was proof that magic worked, because it made men wealthy.

'Where did he get his wisdom from?' I asked.

'He did not go to Maraboutic school,' El Hadji told me. 'When he was a young man, he received a sign from God and went to spend many years in the bush on his own.'

According to El Hadji, while in the bush, the Marabout had divined his wisdom and powers from God and the natural world around him, in the same way that sages have often been supposed to.

We walked on through Diabikunda and reached the edge of the village. Then we laid our things down beneath a kola tree. El Hadji retrieved his prayer rug from his rucksack, dusted down an area of sand in the shade and faced to the east. It was time for his five o'clock prayer, the sounds of which soon echoed across the brilliant afternoon light along with the distant noises from the mosque. It was another faithful African scene, something that cried out to be trusted. But ironic cynicism seemed to be ingrained so deeply in my being that the smallest act of trust had the same effect as malaria – it brought me out in cold sweats. Every day, while El Hadji prayed at dawn, at two o'clock, at five o'clock, at seven-thirty and once before retiring to sleep, I sat awkwardly beside him, 'meditating', watching the space and doing nothing, listening to his faith grate like a scratched record in my brain.

I looked across at El Hadji, who had just finished his prayers. He rose from his rug, dusted it down, folded it and replaced it carefully at the top of his rucksack, ready for further use.

'Shall we go on?' I asked.

'We must,' he said. 'It is a long way to Kolda.'

We walked along the dusty road for a few minutes. But then El Hadji suddenly came to a stop.

'My friend, Toby,' he said, smiling. 'Who would have thought it when we met in Bula? That four years later we would meet and see so much together.'

'And go to Guinea-Conakry!'

He laughed.

'Never again,' he said, extending his arm and taking me by the hand in friendship. 'At least, not to Guinea-Conakry.'

We carried on walking side by side in this way for some time. Then our hands became sweaty and we walked alone. The trees encroached on each side, mingling with the low bush and the animal tracks which meandered away. There were still two hours left before twilight, and the sun remained surprisingly strong. Dust filled the air, cloaking it in opacity. The world beyond our road took such an effort to see, it was not surprising that we ignored it.

After a time, I became aware of something in the bush.

Then someone cried out in the silence.

'Look!'

El Hadji pointed under one of the trees, and I saw that a group of children were huddled there, wrapped in white robes. Behind them, an older man sat on a log, clutching a twisted cane.

'They're preparing for circumcision,' he whispered.

The children had seemed to draw even closer to one another when they had seen me. I could have been a djinn or an ancestral spirit come to prepare their initiation, but, when they realised that I was a mere person, their faces crumpled with relief and the tension dispersed into laughter. They crushed in on each other so that I could take their photograph, and bear witness to the bravery of these innocent and still virginal young boys, clothed in white and guarded from the unseen spirits by the old man and his gnarled piece of wood, which he continued to hold out erect before him as I pressed the shutter and the bulb flashed.

We walked on for two hours, until night had almost fallen. Then a blinding flash lit up the road too, and we turned to see a pair of headlights setting upon us like witches flying out of the gloom. An articulated lorry was carrying a tractor over the border to Senegal. We climbed up onto the back and sat amid the dust, in the cold and the dark, bouncing blindly onwards. The bush was thick and sparsely inhabited, and we travelled for almost an hour before we saw the first settlement, where a blazing fire had been lit a little way from the road.

The bright light revealed us starkly as we sat on the truck. The flames leapt and started in El Hadji's eyes.

'People,' I said.

'Yes,' he said, smiling in what appeared to be relief.

He said that they had lit their fire to guard themselves from the devils of the surrounding bush. They were protecting themselves with the flames and their religious fervour, reading and writing verses from the Qu'ran.

Around the fire I saw a group of the villagers, singing in their brilliant illumination of the night.

It took us three days to complete the journey to the Casamance. We made for Ziguinchor, where we retrieved the cat skin, procured the piece of burial shroud through one of Omar's friends who always kept a supply handy, and eventually found transport back towards Gabú. The distance between the cities was only 300 kilometres, and all the roads were paved. Nevertheless the journey, which was punctuated by border checks, internal customs checks, ferry crossings and two roadside fights between touts for rival bush taxis, took us an entire day. We only reached Kabakunda once the night had been lit up by the guileless luminosity of fire. Our bush taxi deposited us next to the sacks of charcoal, which appeared to have remained immobile ever since we had left the village, and we pawed our way into the darkness around Talla Seydi's hut.

His wife was busy stirring rice over a layer of hot coals. She straightened perceptibly in the darkness as she sensed our shadows stray towards her.

'*On Djarama,*' El Hadji called out.

'*On Djarama.*'

He asked for the old man, but Talla Seydi had gone to Gabú. He had not expected us back so quickly.

'I thought this might happen,' El Hadji muttered to me.

The Marabout's nephew, Sitafa, was squatting behind the low thatch of his uncle's hut. We could scarcely make him out amid the shadows. Talla Seydi's wife said something to him in Peul, and then he led us across the road to his own compound, where we could eat. We deposited our bags on the prayer mats that had been set beneath a large mango tree, lay down beside them, and then stared up at Orion and the Plough, glittering in the sequinned sky. The new moon had yet to appear, but the darkness was relieved by the sounds of conversations flowing softly in the compound. The cooking fire crackled on the veranda, and eased our fears of the silence that enveloped us as we lay there listening to the night.

Eventually, one of Sitafa's brothers, a crippled boy who supported his weight with an improvised crutch, swung towards us with a dish cradled beneath his right arm, which he placed silently on the ground. We ate the heavy rice and the bony fish that it contained. Then Sitafa led us to a small hut. Its external symmetry was appealing, with its roundness and the very low thatch that crept almost down to the earth, but, inside, the mud walls were cracked and the air was heavy with dust and abandonment. A disintegrating mattress had been placed on the floor, covered with a sheet of uncertain vintage.

It was hardly comfortable but, at that moment, washed out with fatigue, the only thing that mattered was rest.

In the morning, Sitafa walked to Gabú to fetch his uncle. El Hadji and I found it difficult to sleep beyond seven-thirty, since the heat permeated through the flimsy walls of the hut. So we sat up, bleary-eyed, and began to itch.

The hut was infested with insects which had managed to bite us to pieces during the night.

'What on earth is living in here?' El Hadji asked, scratching and staring up at the walls and the dusty thatch.

'It must be a sort of flea,' I said. Dirty huts could have devastating effects in these areas, I remembered, and were responsible for lethal outbreaks of Lassa fever and leishmaniasis.

I looked unhappily at the filthy walls and the thatch.

'C'est difficile.'

'What shall we do about it?'

'Well,' said El Hadji, 'I'm not staying in here any longer than I have to.'

So we went outside, and sat beneath a cashew tree waiting for Talla Seydi.

The tree lay between the road and the old man's hut. It was large and already fruiting. While we sat on prayer mats, cashew apples dropped between us. The other noise was that of the cars that occasionally tore past the village on their way to Gabú or Bissau. Their mechanical terror echoed brashly through the stillness long after they had disappeared over the horizon.

At first we were alone. Talla Seydi's wife brought us gruel for breakfast, and then El Hadji asked for the wood-burner and began to prepare tea. As the morning progressed and people saw the tea being brewed, we were joined by Mohammed, Domingos – the man with rolling eyes who had offered me his chair on our first visit to the hut – an off-duty soldier and, eventually, Sitafa.

'He's on his way back,' he said when he joined us, referring to his uncle. 'If there were more cars,' he went on, 'he would be here sooner, but . . .'

He shrugged, and we looked at the emptiness of the burning road.

'The war really hurt us,' he said now. 'So many people fled from Bissau to Gabú that you could not see the tarmac for all the people that were there.'

'Just like Bula,' said El Hadji.

'Were you here during the war?'

'Yes,' said El Hadji. 'I stayed at first. I did well.'

'What happened?' asked Sitafa.

'I left in the end.'

El Hadji's eyes clouded over.

'Here,' said Sitafa, 'there was nothing. There were no medicines, no supplies. All the whites left – only a Portuguese bishop helped us out a little.'

'What happened to the refugees?' I asked.

'They died.'

'Where?'

'In Gabú.'

The war had only been concluded nine months before, but I had seen no sign of this tragedy in the streets of Gabú, which had seemed full of bustle. Bloodstains did not last for long; their traces were soon invisible, even if their legacies remained. Memories faded, written evidence could be falsified, oral accounts often conflicted, so that all that was really left was a sense of the unspoken tragedy of Gabú, which had once been a great kingdom, the second most important branch of the Mali empire. With the invasions of the Peul from the Fouta Djalon in the nineteenth century, some Mandingas had fled to the Casamance, others had hurtled down to the coast, and others had stayed behind, forced to convert to Islam and left with only a vague sense of what was now an inaccessible greatness.

Thoughts like this troubled El Hadji. He would often tell me that his ancestors had lived to great ages, that life had been better and easier then. This was something that he genuinely believed, knowing how hard life now was in Africa and conveniently forgetting the histories of wars and brutality. But his eulogies of the past were curious, since those times had in many ways been far more horrific than the world was today.

'Yes,' said Sitafa, mulling it all over, 'many people died in Gabú.'

No one knew how many, or where they had all been from, or whether people missed them. Such things were unrecorded, those emotions were lost, but hate and resentment lingered on.

We looked out into the haze, waiting for Talla Seydi. A few cars passed but, as the morning wore on, the steady flow dwindled into a trickle. The air hung motionless over the village. No cars passed, and the Marabout did not come.

Even now, Sitafa told me, watching El Hadji brew the tea, things were bad. His wife had a fever, and she had been to the hospital three times. But no one could say what was wrong with her and, in any event, there were no medicines. So now they took her to the local healer. Perhaps he would cure her, perhaps he would not. It was difficult to say, impossible to be sure.

'You,' Sitafa said, looking at me, 'we need more people like you. More whites. We can't do anything any more. Our country is ruined.'

He sipped the tea that El Hadji had passed to him, but he found it too bitter. He spat it into the earth, and looked at me.

'You,' said another voice.

I started at the echo to Sitafa and, turning around, saw a pregnant woman approaching us. Sitafa told me that her name was Owe.

Owe was slight and had a round face with a small, delicate nose. She had arranged a strange collection of shells and defunct batteries into a necklace which hung disjointedly about her chest. Her hair was tied up in a black headscarf, and her eyes flitted from face to face.

'You,' she said, pointing at me, 'when did you arrive?'

'Last night.'

She screamed, 'Why have you been away for so long?'

I looked away, embarrassed. The others said nothing. Then Owe gabbled rapidly in Peul.

'She says that you are her father,' El Hadji told me.

She screamed, nodding angrily. Then she began to jabber in a mixture of Peul and Kriolu. She said that I was her father, and so I had to take care of her. She knew that she had to obey me, but she was even willing to make this sacrifice if I wished.

Then she abandoned her ravings, sat down on the prayer mat and took my hand, stroking it gently in hers.

'I am scared of whites,' she said, softly. 'We have not seen them since independence, so what are you doing here?'

'I have come to see Talla Seydi.'

She shrugged. 'You don't care about your daughter!'

She turned her back to me, and lay down against El Hadji.

'My husband,' she murmured, to El Hadji's shock.

'Husband?' he asked. 'How many children do we have?'

'You should know,' she said, 'since you were the one who fathered them.'

Sitafa murmured that this would be Owe's fourth child, but that no one knew who her lovers had been.

'That's terrible,' I said. 'She's clearly not in her right mind. That sounds like rape to me.'

Sitafa shrugged. He fiddled with the knobs on the radio, and we listened to the international Portuguese radio station, RTP Africa.

'*RTP Africa, 2 de Março de 2000. São nove horas — Cabo Verde, dez horas — Portugal, Guiné-Bissau e São Tomé, onze horas — Angola e meio-dia em Moçambique.*'

The programmes were transmitted from Lisbon for some of the most abandoned corners of Africa. The curiously musical sounds of Portuguese filled the blankness of the day, which wound on towards the next event of note – lunch. El Hadji brewed the last round of the tea and passed the cups to us, as we waited for the Marabout. But no cars came. The air filled with torpor, the day was still and the road was noiseless; even the village shrank into silence. Then, once I had drunk the third cup of tea and was feeling more slothful than ever, I turned around and saw Talla Seydi standing behind us on the veranda, as if he had appeared from nowhere.

He was bending over and washing his hands with water from a colourful plastic kettle. When he had finished, he dried his hands on a rag and then looked over towards us. He was wearing an embroidered white *boubou*, fronted by a maroon rosary and a multicoloured shawl embellished with long red tassels.

Now he stooped and put on his white leather slippers, before turning to look towards us again.

'El Hadji,' I said, jogging the leg of my friend.

He raised himself slothfully and saw the Marabout on the veranda. 'Come on.'

Mohammed rose and beckoned that we should follow him into his father's boudoir. We removed our sandals in the antechamber and went into Talla Seydi's room. This time the old man was sitting on his bed, surveying us with a soft smile as we sat down on the prayer mats and began the ritual greetings.

El Hadji explained that we had made the journey back to Ziguinchor with success; we had retrieved the cat skin and found the piece of burial shroud, *alhamdoulilah*. Then he nudged me and I rooted around in my money belt, where we had been concealing the accoutrements of our gris-gris from the eyes of women and of children who had yet to be circumcised, according to the Marabout's orders.

I retrieved the cat skin, which had been torn into four tufted scraps of fur, and Talla Seydi's eyes widened as he looked into the blackness, fingering it softly.

Then he nodded, and whispered something to Mohammed.

'This is it,' he said, 'this is it.'

He picked up the materials, put them back in the plastic wrapper in which they had been concealed and tucked them under his mattress.

Then he told us that he would do the work for us. The writing had to be done at night, and he would work for three nights until the gris-gris was ready. Then we would get a shoemaker to sew the charm and the burial shroud into the cat skin.

We shook hands and returned to our positions under the cashew tree. The day continued in just the same way as it had begun, as if this mystical interlude had never taken place. Tea was brewed and drunk, donkeys brayed in the desolation, chickens scavenged for grain beneath the tree and raised dust with their feet, young men played a game with unshelled cashew nuts, placing them in small piles on the ground and trying to gather as many as possible with one hand while throwing a nut into the air and waiting to catch it with the other, El Hadji procured a long stick and prodded the cashew tree with it to dislodge the riper fruit, prayers wailed like lamentations from the mosque, and we all waited for time to pass.

Nothing much had changed, except that now I was on my way to becoming invisible.

After a lunch of stodgy rice and *bissap* sauce, we retired to our hut. We lay on the mattress, but we had not been there for long before again we began to itch.

'I don't know what lives in here, but I don't like it,' said El Hadji. 'It's eating us alive.'

'Do you think they knew that these things were in this hut?'

'Of course!' he said bitterly. 'Why do you think that no one lives here?'

He stretched his limbs out heavily in a star shape.

'My whole body hurts,' he said, plaintively.

He yawned.

'*Marcher, marcher, marcher dans la brousse.* There's nothing – the same faces, the same people, the same food . . .'

He sat up, and looked at me resentfully.

'*C'est difficile.* If I had known what you were going to make me do . . .'

He left the sentence unfinished.

'Back in Europe,' he said, 'everyone thinks that Toby is having a good time. Lucky Toby! Off to Africa, the beaches, the forests, the women...'

He stood up, stooping beneath the lintel and moving outside to survey the village.

'Bring them here,' he said. 'They'd ask to get on the first plane back.'

The heat thickened. The inertia was crippling. El Hadji was soon back inside, and we stared blankly up at the thatch and the beetles and spiders that crawled happily across it.

'El Hadji,' I said after a time, raising something that was still troubling me.

'Yes.'

'This morning, when Talla Seydi arrived.'

'Yes.'

'How did he get here?'

El Hadji sat up and looked at me, his eyes shining.

'You know,' he said, 'I wondered about that myself.'

We had been sitting between his hut and the road. No car had stopped for at least half an hour beforehand. And then the Marabout had appeared behind us on the veranda.

'Perhaps he walked?' I asked.

'No!' said El Hadji. 'Walk? That's only for lunatics like you!'

Talla Seydi was about eighty, and Gabú was a brisk hour-and-a-half's walk away. There was no chance that this was something that he would have entertained. And even if he had walked, he should not have been able to go past us unseen.

'He was trying to impress us,' said El Hadji.

I fell into silence, staring up at the circles of the thatch and the cracks in the walls of the hut. A group of children sprinted past, shouting and giggling. These sounds of happiness hung in the air, together with all the unseen fears and powers that lingered on in this forgotten corner of the world.

'He must have transported himself psychically,' El Hadji concluded.

Like his grandfather, I thought, my mind working turgidly. The similarity was unsettling. I closed my eyes and tried to doze. I scratched through my dreams. When I woke, I found that I had scratched so forcefully, I had begun to bleed.

That afternoon, we went for a walk through the bush. Initially, though, El Hadji had not wanted to stir from his prone position in our hut.

'What's the point?' he asked. 'What do you think you're going to see?'

'I'm interested.'

'Interested!' He spat the word out. 'What could they possibly have that is of interest here?' He looked at me in angered bewilderment. 'It's all the same. Bush. Scrub. Villages.'

'Well,' I said, 'I'm going. I don't want to die of boredom in here.'

'No,' said El Hadji. 'You'd rather be bitten by a cobra outside.'

But he came anyway.

We walked away from Kabakunda along a path that was flanked with cashews whose leaves lay thickly upon the ground. Lizards dived off the path into their brown carpet. Many of the cashew apples had not yet ripened, and the trees were unrewarding to our poaching eyes. The groves then gave way to a plantation of cassava. The cassava leaves had already been harvested, and the tubers lay strewn about like corpulent earthworms. A man was hoeing in the field. He called out when he saw us, and beckoned. We walked over to him and he deposited eight thick tubers in our arms. As we passed through the nearby village, we bit off the crunchy white flesh in great hunks, spitting out the bitter brown skin.

On the far side of the village, several paths headed in different directions, and then disappeared into a lush glade which was green with rice paddies. A woman was drying her washing on the flat stones next to the well. In the far corner of the glade, a family had fenced off a section of land and had cultivated it with tomatoes, onions and banana plants, which three young boys were irrigating with large green watering cans. Eventually we found our way to another village nearby, where a football match was disturbing the late afternoon dust. The efforts of the players raised a haze that intermingled with the twilight and the Saharan sand in the wind, and rendered the air increasingly opaque.

The pitch was quite the worst that I had ever seen, with a large palm tree in the middle of it, sharp rocks sprouting at various points and a mound that was several metres tall. The players were all barefoot except for two. Of these, one had only one shoe and the other had two shoes that hailed from different pairs. The ball took wicked deflections off the rocks, and frequently bounded out of control into the palm groves that bordered the pitch. The players would often seize up with pain because they had trodden on some sharp piece of stone or a splinter. It was hard enough for them to kick the ball at all, let alone pass or shoot.

'Well,' said El Hadji, after we had been watching for a time, 'are you happy?'

'Happy?'

'You've seen the bush now.'

'Part of it.'

'There's nothing more to see.'

Soon he turned away and led us back towards Kabakunda, still seething at the discomfort of this escapade.

'*Marcher, marcher, marcher dans la brousse,*' he muttered. 'Terrible food. Terrible insects. Bitten to death.'

He swiped at the brittle grass with his hands as we went.

'He wants to kill me,' he said, looking back at me with a wry grin.

We laughed. Then I suggested that we ought to give something to the wife of Talla Seydi to contribute to our stay.

El Hadji nodded in agreement.

'Let's give her 5000 CFA,' I said.

'No. We'll give her 2000 CFA, but we'll give 3000 CFA to Sitafa's mother,' he said.

'Why?' I asked, uncertain of this tactless scheme.

'I think that she cooks better.'

El Hadji insisted stubbornly on this plan. The result was that, in the evening, we were provided with two identical meals of stodgy rice and bone-ridden fish. El Hadji made a token attempt to finish the first one, but when it came to the second bowl of rice, he had only one spoonful before standing up and moving away.

'What are you doing?' I said.

'I'm full.'

'You've got to help me,' I said. 'You can't expect me to finish all this on my own.'

'I can't eat any more.'

'She'll be offended.'

'How many stomachs do you think I've got?'

'I thought you had several,' I said. 'Like cows.'

He grunted at the joke, and moved off into the hut. Shortly afterwards, I heard him scratching.

'Toby,' he called out.

'Yes.'

'My whole body hurts.'

I went in to look at my friend, and found him lying in state like a corpse, motionless on the mattress. His eyes twitched along with the candle flames on the walls. They opened slowly as he sensed me watching him.

'We've got to pray,' he said. 'Pray that the Marabout gets this done with as quickly as possible. Otherwise, they'll kill us.'

He rose ponderously onto one elbow, and fumbled for his tobacco and his pipe.

'Otherwise, they'll kill us,' he repeated.

'He's working tonight,' I said. 'I've seen the light in his hut.'

The weak glow was just perceptible through the crack in Talla Seydi's bedroom door, which faced out onto a wasteland of broken roots and low termite mounds. That dun-coloured hut was an unpromising home for magic, but if wealth and mysticism were incompatible, as El Hadji had once told me I could not have found a better spot.

In the morning we lay in our hut, scratching. Then we pushed open the wooden door and saw two bowls of gruel waiting for us. We were also brought two bowls of rice and fish for lunch, and the same again for dinner. The following morning we woke and scratched again. Again, we saw two bowls of gruel awaiting us when we pushed open the door.

El Hadji picked up one of the plastic ladles accompanying the meal, and scooped out some of the grains. Then he let them plop heavily back into the dish.

'*C'est difficile.*'

'If I had 1000 CFA for every time you had said that, I would be a rich man.'

'Toby, *vraiment ... c'est difficile.*'

We looked disconsolately at the dish before us.

'We'd better eat,' I said.

'We've got serious problems,' El Hadji said. 'I've been constipated for three days. This food is going to do for us.'

'You know,' I said, 'you've made a serious error. You should never have given money to Talla Seydi's wife and to Sitafa's mother.'

'No,' he agreed.

We ate in silence. As we squatted on our misshapen stools, Domingos came strolling up the path. He was wearing a bright green shirt and fraying cloth trousers.

'I'll join you,' he said, 'if I may.'

El Hadji happily passed him his ladle, and Domingos ate assiduously.

'It's impossible,' El Hadji said in English, so that Domingos could not understand. 'This place is never going to develop. Who cares about Guinea-Bissau?'

'It's wrong,' I said.

'Travelling is a good thing,' El Hadji mused. 'It makes you realise that you should never complain when you are at home.'

The land was parched, especially now, in the dry season. Stores of grain rarely kept families free from hunger through the whole year, and the sparse plantations of fruit and vegetables were insufficient to quell the growing shortages all around. But Guinea-Bissau had not always been like this. The imposition of the groundnut and palm oil economy under the Portuguese administration had radically reshaped the country's agricultural constitution, so that it could benefit from free trade and global markets. Areas that had traditionally been given over to grazing and orchards were taken up by the plantations, and traditional techniques were forgotten. The contrast between the hunger that besets Guinea-Bissau now and the plentiful times of the past is shown up in the report of a very distant blood relation of mine, Joshua Montefiore, who wrote an account of the British attempt to found a colony under Philip Beaver on Bolama Island in the 1790s. 'In Bissau,' wrote Montefiore, 'the orchards were in great perfection, and contained orange, lime, lemon, fig, guava, banana, cocoa nut, and plantain trees, and also pine apples, water melons, cucumbers and cassava plants. Near the coast,' he continued, 'the country is most delightful, the sea abounds with the most delicious fish of every kind, and the land with buffaloes, deer, antelopes, wild hogs, and Guinea fowls, doves, pigeons, and several sorts of small birds. In it are also many elephants, monkeys and parrots, and the elephants often come down to the beach to bathe in the sea.' This was only 200 years ago, which is not so very long in the scheme of things, but certainly long enough for a country to be ruined.

In the interval since Joshua Montefiore moved on from Bissau, 'progress' has been visited upon Africa by the industrial and economic revolutions, which have presided over such events as the demise of the slave trade and the colonial project of inducting African countries 'into the modern world'. The Enlightenment has also presided over a decrease in wealth, resources and food supplies in Guinea-Bissau and in neighbouring countries. The land around Bissau is now bereft of the wildlife of the 1790s, hunting has become difficult and people go hungry, so that, in much of Guinea-Bissau, it is a sign of wealth when a family is able to eat twice in a day.

Like much of what had gone before, complaining about our food in that opaque and dusty place seemed contemptible.

But this did not stop us from feeling heavy and irritable. After Domingos had scoffed the rest of the gruel, we went over to the cashew tree and sat listlessly for much of the rest of the day, as we had done on all the other days that we had spent in Kabakunda. Conversation came and went, like the cars and the bowls of food and the seasons, never very fecund, but always managing to interest us for long enough to prevent us from crumbling into nothingness.

Thoughts turned inevitably to the war.

'It was terrible in Bula,' said El Hadji.

'Well,' said the soldier, 'you're near Bissau there.'

'The streets were filled with people. No one had anything to eat.'

'What did you do there?' asked Sitafa.

'I was in good nick, then,' said El Hadji. 'I used to import food over the border from Ziguinchor through a contact at customs. I smuggled goats in from Tanaff. I had an eatery, and everyone in Bula went there.'

He shrugged, and the words petered out. He seemed not to want to continue.

'Why did you leave?'

But El Hadji did not answer.

'My friend was near Bula,' Domingos said. 'At Canchungo.'

'What happened to him?' I asked.

'He was shot in the leg. They had no medicines. He died.'

It had been the rainy season when the war had begun, El Hadji said now. The whole country had been clutched by such a deadening heaviness that people almost ceased to care. Wounds festered. There had been no food, no protein. Nothing healed up. Everything deteriorated and the numbers of vultures proliferated. At Bula there were more vultures than people, and there were a lot of people, tens of thousands of people. But there was nothing for them to eat.

Many of them died, he said. Some of the richer men went up to the girls and offered them a loaf of stale bread if they would sleep with them. And the girls were so desperate that they complied.

But still they had died. Their bodies had littered the streets, swarming with flies, rotting, putrid. The dogs had fought with the vultures for the spoils. Some people had not even had the energy to bury the bones, but these were soon covered by the dust periodically blown in from the Sahara.

And back in Europe, I remembered, I had read two newspaper articles about the conflict, when it had just begun. The headlines and the stories had tried to tell me as much as possible, but sometimes I had sensed that what they had really done was alienate me from the events in this distant country. And then the currency of the situation had ebbed, information had become increasingly difficult to obtain, attention was distracted, images of other nightmares in other benighted regions surfaced, and the people had continued to die in Bula, invisible in the information age. Sitting in Kabakunda, too, it was possible to imagine that the war had not even occurred. So little seemed to happen here and, throughout the centuries, African villages had always given this misleading image of being timeless, changeless and constant. Yet great events came, perhaps with more frequency than they did elsewhere. They attacked like a guerrilla army: spasmodically, unpredictably, with great and uncontainable force.

'Did you see much of the war here in Kabakunda?' I asked.

'Only the people going on to Gabú,' said Mohammed, who rose now and sauntered over towards his father's house.

'And the planes,' said Sitafa, as we watched Mohammed go. 'Sometimes they roared overhead. But they never seemed to come down to the earth.'

Mohammed picked up one of the hens which was scavenging in the dust by the hut, and carried her over towards us, holding her by the legs. A young boy handed him a serrated knife and he slit the chicken's throat. I expected the ground to be covered with blood, as had happened with similar slaughters which I had witnessed in South America. But the chicken was so thin that there was hardly any blood left in its veins. A trickle was all that came, dripping slowly to the ground. The emaciated bird did not even appear to struggle.

'Here,' said Mohammed, giving the chicken to the boy. 'Take it to the women.'

The boy scampered away past rolls of wickerwork that had been stacked up near the veranda. Talla Seydi was sitting in his deckchair, unobtrusive as ever, and he watched the little boy go. The old man was so calm that he rarely made himself noticed. He preferred to sit quietly, like his village, keeping his secrets hidden from the destructive eyes of others, so that if you passed casually by you would never know that this impoverished place concealed the mystery of invisibility.

Like all the other days, we spent the rest of the morning silently. Owe came to join us, and I nudged El Hadji, who had been dozing.

'Your wife's here,' I said.

'Leave me alone,' he said. 'I haven't got the energy even to think about satisfying her.'

He dozed some more. At lunch, Talla Seydi's wife brought us a dish of rice and chicken stew. Owe leapt forward and siphoned off a goodly portion of the food onto a plastic plate which she kept hidden in her wrap.

'That's for me,' she said crossly.

'Aren't you going to share it round?' asked El Hadji.

'You've forgotten,' she snapped. 'I'm the white man's daughter, so I'm white myself. And white people don't share the food on their plates.'

Then, shovelling greedily with her spoon, she devoured the meal before her.

While El Hadji and I waited at Kabakunda, the actual purpose of our visit went unspoken. Although we made plans in case the gris-gris did not work, the issue of invisibility, and the gris-gris itself, remained unmentioned. This was a critical moment: we had had no luck thus far and, if this attempt failed, I knew that I would lose all that was left of my faith in the powers of the Marabouts. But what remains unspoken is rarely unthought and, at various times in that cheerless place, foreboding returned to envelop me. Stretched out beneath the cashew tree, squatting around the wood-burner, or staring up at the thatched roof of my hut, I found myself clutched by anxiety.

I had never thought myself a coward before, but I had many fears. They now seem completely ludicrous, but at the time they were absorbing. Sometimes I worried that the heaviness in my legs and my body was more than an effect of the poor nutrition of Kabakunda – secretly, I had the paranoid concern that we were being poisoned for some nefarious ritual. Whenever I considered the possibility that the gris-gris might actually work, I also worried that the djinns would dislike my motivations for searching the charm out – which, even now, I had not completely understood – and would work against me. But my greatest fear was that, if the gris-gris worked, I would not be able to make myself visible again, and would stumble around as if I had been a clod of air. Like Griffin in Wells' *The Invisible Man*, I would find that no one noticed me any more. My actions, my appearance and my body would be nullified, and I would walk blindly and unseen through the world. In this solitary universe, I saw two possibilities: either I would feel so dispirited that I would quickly cease to do anything at all, or I could imagine that, like Griffin, I would feel the sheer frustration boiling up, anger would come to a head, and my fury would be uncontrollable.

There was something about the nature of this search that seemed to bring me to the borders of sanity. In ordinary circumstances, these notions would all have seemed absurd, but I could not banish them. They returned constantly, especially at night, in the candlelight, as I lay on the mattress waiting for El Hadji to finish his evening prayers. On the third night at Kabakunda – the last night during which Talla Seydi was working on the gris-gris – I remembered that, in my world, visibility and existence were symbiotic. That was, after all, the insinuation of the empirical project, and of the growing importance of images in advertising and the media. What was not observable did not exist. God was dead, spirits were mental disorders, witches had been mentally disturbed martyrs and the invisible world was imaginary.

If I made myself invisible, I realised with a start, to all intents and purposes I would cease to exist.

But I did not have long to dwell over this disquieting notion. El Hadji now finished his genuflection and prostration, rolled up his prayer mat and lay down on the mattress beside me.

'Tomorrow,' he said, 'we will see.'

'What do you think will happen?'

'We must have faith,' he said. 'It will work.'

We lay side by side, deep in thought as to what this gris-gris would mean to us. I could only trust that everything would turn out for the best, and that visibility and existence were not completely interdependent. But it was difficult to be reassured. The hut seemed cold that night. I remembered that I had been ill. I scratched. I dozed, but I could not rest. My mind sought solace in some of the philosophy lessons that I had taken in the past, and I remembered being taught that it was precisely the unseen world of 'forms' that had been the summit of knowledge for Plato who, in the *Republic*, wrote that the visible realm should be likened to a prison dwelling, where our concept of truth is limited to the few shadows that we see before our eyes, and that we are otherwise cave-dwellers as far as knowledge is concerned.

So in a sense, my visible world was that of Plato's hoi polloi – but the Marabouts were the philosopher kings.

For a long time I could not sleep. I listened to the dogs barking in Kabakunda, and sensed the profound darkness of that night. This awareness of an unseen world came again to me in my dreams, and I tossed and turned, bitten by the millions of unseen insects that dwelt alongside me. I scratched. I opened my eyes and gazed blindly at the immanent darkness of the inside of that hut. When I did manage to sleep, I dreamt of my home country, where such fears had been buried. And, as my attention turned from invisible thoughts to the cavernous concerns of the visible world, I realised with dismay that some of Plato's essential qualities – goodness and beauty in particular – had ceased to be intelligible, and that I was no longer clear about what was true.

I dreamt a great deal that night. But the images from my home, of wealth and beauty and a superficial contentment, were so disconnected and difficult to interpret that they did not comfort me, and I woke feeling disturbed.

Then Sitafa brought us another bowl of gruel, and helped us to finish it.

'So,' he said, 'how long are you going to spend in Kabakunda?'

'Today will be our last day, *insh'allah*,' said El Hadji.

'Is my uncle finishing today?' asked Sitafa.

'Last night,' I said.

'He's a wise man,' said Sitafa. 'He spent fourteen years studying in the bush with a big Marabout. There was one time that I was having trouble with my schoolwork. I went to see Talla Seydi, and he told me that one of my classmates was working against me. Then he grabbed hold of my right leg and said that this leg was troubling me. And it was

167

true, every time that I stood up my right leg felt dead, as if all the life had been draining away from it.'

'He is very wise,' I said.

'We are all worried about what will happen when he dies,' said Sitafa. 'Then there will be no one to work for us in Kabakunda, and we will be at the mercy of the Marabouts of nearby villages.'

'Hasn't he passed the knowledge on to one of his sons?'

'Oh he's tried,' said Sitafa. 'But none of us have been able to understand.'

'But surely he only works with the Qu'ran?'

'Yes,' said Sitafa. 'Although,' he went on, leaning forward, 'sometimes he also calls upon the *irā*.'

At this, El Hadji stiffened and he stood up, leaving Sitafa and me to talk alone. His Islamic sensibilities had been piqued, since *irā* is the term used by Guinea-Bissauans to describe the spirits of their mystical life. At first, the Portuguese dismissed this as simple fetishism, but gradually, as the understanding of some of their number deepened, they came to realise that this word was – in the words of Teixeira da Mota, the greatest Portuguese historian of Guinea-Bissau – completely inadequate. The word is a symbol of our profound ignorance about these religions, Teixeira da Mota went on, since the Guinea-Bissauans discovered that its use was a handy way of freeing themselves from the curiosity of the white man. Thus, he said, anything that is incomprehensible to the European's mindset is said by them automatically to be linked to the workings of the *irā*. Witch-doctors, fetishists, medicine-men, shamans, ju-ju men, spiritual healers, call them what you will: English, along with other European languages, has many terms for the mystical workers of Africa, but not one of them does justice to the complexity of African theology. Among many of the peoples of Guinea-Bissau, this manifests itself with a belief in a universal God who has ceased to attend to human affairs after the act of creation, and a world in which everything has a portion of the universe's energy and contains a dynamic spirit, known as the *irā*, which can be invoked by those with the necessary knowledge.

'Does he use the *irā* often?'

'Only when he has a special problem,' Sitafa said, mysteriously. But he did not seem to want to discuss this any further.

Soon Mohammed appeared to collect the empty bowl of gruel, and told us that his father was ready to see us. So we followed him over to Talla Seydi's hut. The day was already sweltering, and a thin veil of dust was hanging over Kabakunda.

We took off our sandals, murmured our greetings and sat down on the prayer mats, facing the old man. He was holding a long piece of paper, which he had folded many times over into a thin strip. Once we had greeted each other, he reached under his mattress and retrieved the piece of burial shroud, which he then wrapped around the paper until it was completely enveloped.

As he did this, he spoke to Mohammed, and told us about the charm.

'This secret of invisibility,' he said, 'must not be misused. You must not rob people or commit sins. You can only invoke it when you want to perform some piece of work, and you do not want to be interfered with.'

His father had given him this secret. He had used the charm during the wars of Alfa Yaya*, the last ruler of the Fouta Djalon before the incorporation of the theocracy into France's West African empire. Those had been dangerous times, the enemy came from the north and attacked repeatedly, but his father would vanish as soon as they came.

Talla Seydi smiled at the thought. That had been when the charm had been used for good ends, when people had walked unseen past the eyes of their foes.

'My father,' said Mohammed in Kriolu, 'is the only person in Guinea-Bissau who still has this power. There used to be another man near Bafatá who possessed it as well, but he died. And his son has not taken up the secrets.'

Talla Seydi nodded at his son's words, even though he did not understand them. I looked at his delicate skin, still smooth in spite of his age, and remembered the sober way in which he did everything. His wisdom and his unhurried actions and his poverty all seemed to

* See Historical Notes, p. 271.

constitute a unity. In a world of frenetic activity, where time mattered more than people, he would have been lost.

Now he leant over to his son and said something else.

'The shoemaker will come this evening,' Mohammed translated. 'He will wrap the prayer in the cat skin, and then the gris-gris will be ready.'

We spent the rest of the day waiting. The heat swelled, dust filled the air, the branches of the cashew trees hung torpid and listless in the thick stillness, and there was little other than sleep to distract us from the slow passage of time. We ate rice and sauce, drank tea, slept and waited, mute, like prisoners awaiting sentence. Eventually, towards dusk, a solid man, dressed in a black-and-white woollen hat and thin black trousers, arrived on a bicycle from Gabú. He approached our group beneath the cashew tree and explained that he was the shoemaker.

'Who is the gris-gris for?' he asked, and Mohammed indicated the *branco* sitting on the prayer mat. The shoemaker's eyes widened with surprise, but he said nothing as he looked at me.

Then Mohammed led us inside Talla Seydi's hut, and the Marabout showed the shoemaker the prayer and the four pieces of black cat skin. The shoemaker laid the pieces of fur lengthwise on the floor and eyed them cautiously, as if the blackness itself contained a great secret. Then he tried to match them to the length of the paper. He took hold of the longer pieces of fur and tried to wrap them around the prayer, but they scarcely fitted. Mohammed picked up another of the scraps of fur and did the same. But it was clear that it was going to be a difficult task.

After some ineffectual attempts, the pieces of skin were left on the mat, and the shoemaker, Mohammed and Talla Seydi began to confer.

'Will he be able to do it?' I asked El Hadji.

'He'll cope,' he said.

Talla Seydi eventually explained that the shoemaker had to sew the prayer inside the cloth, and that I was not allowed to see him perform the task. Nor was I allowed to talk to him while he worked. He had to begin as soon as the prayer at sunset had been finished.

We went outside. By this time the light was fading fast, and the village was enveloped in greyness. The sparkle of fires shone from many

170

of the huts, illuminating the heavy leaves of the cashew trees. On the verandas, old men could be seen performing their ablutions in preparation for the evening prayers. We went and sat outside our hut, and the shoemaker and El Hadji talked desultorily about the events. Every now and again the shoemaker looked at me with fascination until, finally, he leant over to whisper something to El Hadji.

'He says that he doesn't know what sort of gris-gris you have obtained,' El Hadji translated. 'But when he touched the prayer and the skin, he felt the power of the spell.'

'The power of the dead,' as El Hadji later put it – or of the invisible world.

Then the Muezzin began to call out over the gloom, and they left me alone as they vanished in the direction of the mosque.

Once they had gone, the prayers of the men began to echo over the community. My thoughts turned to how much this gris-gris would change me. If it worked, of course, my perspective on the world would have to be transformed. So I realised that, in fact, I was longing for it to fail. If the charm did not work, I would not have to confront anything except for my gullibility. It would be far easier for me if this invisible world did not exist, so that I would not have to allow my values and prejudices to be challenged. Then I would be able to return home happily with the thought that life was simply a question of information: we were processors of information, and the unceasing glut of information empowered us, rather than rendering us impassive, like the keyboards that sounded out with the stabbing motions of our fingers.

After the prayers had finished, El Hadji wandered back from the mosque, together with Mohammed and the shoemaker. They greeted me, and then El Hadji lit a candle and ushered the shoemaker inside the hut. He did not stay with him for long, and was soon outside with us again. I sat on a stool hewn from a hollow tree trunk, while El Hadji and Mohammed sat on a small prayer mat. The evening was still, the roars from the vehicles on the road had ceased, what wind there had been had dropped, and only the golden flames of firelight intervened amid the blackness.

Then Mohammed began to speak.

171

'This gris-gris is exceptionally powerful,' he said. 'It must not be misused.'

I nodded my agreement.

'It is very easily spoilt,' he went on.

'Spoilt?'

'There are many ways in which the powers can be destroyed.'

And he began to explain the prohibitions. I could not wear it during sexual intercourse. After sex, I had to wash myself thoroughly before touching the charm, and the water with which I cleaned myself could not be soapy. If I took the gris-gris with me when I went to the toilet, it would be spoilt. If I took it with me when I went to a funeral, then its powers would be vitiated. Even if I just didn't look after it very well, it might simply disappear. It had a habit of doing that. But the most dangerous thing of all was to open up the gris-gris once it had been sewn together, and look inside.

'If you do that,' Mohammed said, 'you will go mad, and you will only be cured if you come back to this village.'

Looking around Kabakunda, and remembering the days I had already spent here, I vowed that this was something I would never be stupid enough to do.

Then, once he had listed the taboos, Mohammed told me how to work with the gris-gris. When you want to make use of it, he said, you must lean forward, close your eyes tight shut, clench your teeth as hard as you can, stretch your arms out behind your back, and then pull the charm as far up the right arm as it will go.

He smiled, and his white teeth glinted in the light of the crescent moon.

'No one will be able to see you! You will pass unharmed!'

With that, he sat back, satisfied that he had explained as much as he could.

Then we waited while the shoemaker worked. We could see the flickering light from beneath the door of the hut, but he stitched in silence. At one point, he called out to El Hadji, who went into the hut to try the gris-gris for size. El Hadji was not inside for long, and then again we sat, waiting.

Eventually the shoemaker emerged and said that he had finished the work. I ducked under the lintel, and he showed me a black bracelet lined with cat fur. The gris-gris fitted neatly around my wrist. Mohammed and El Hadji looked on in approval as I tried it for size, and then I suggested to Mohammed that I test it there and then.

But he disagreed.

'Wait!' he commanded. 'Let's go and see my father.'

Talla Seydi was waiting for us in his hut. The candle had guttered, and wax was dripping onto the floor, while the flames shimmied chaotically around the walls like the shadows of some unseen and drunken world. While we settled ourselves on the prayer mats, the old man reached under his mattress where he kept a secret supply of candles. He lit a new one, which he placed near the door.

Then we sat in silence for a moment. From his front porch, we could hear the murmur of young boys reading from the Qu'ran, their voices echoing militarily over the night, with the repetitions of their chants and the disharmonies of their notes. Talla Seydi's eyes observed me minutely as I took out the gris-gris and placed it on the floor.

He picked it up in his right hand and touched it approvingly. Then he replaced it, saying that he had done his work and he hoped that we were satisfied with it. By now I knew the form of these meetings, and I explained through El Hadji that I felt it was an honour that Talla Seydi had consented to work for me, and that I hoped he trusted me not to betray this act of his. I took out three 10,000-CFA notes and one 5000-CFA note, and placed them before him. It was not a fortune, I said, but it was a token of my gratitude, and the money was not a payment as such, but a consideration so that the Marabout could buy kola nuts.

Everyone seemed happy, since the knowledge of God was not for sale.

Talla Seydi picked up each of the notes. His eyes were wide as he held them before the candlelight, marvelling unashamedly at the wealth. It was quite clear that he had never seen so much money before. He stroked each note gently, while he listened to me explaining that we had faith in the work he had done, and hoped that its success would convince some people to take his powers more seriously than they did at present.

Talla Seydi nodded in approval. Then he spoke again about the gris-gris. He had never used it himself, he went on, but he had been told that it allowed you to see the stars even by daylight. We would have to test it out on public transport, he said, to see whether or not it worked.

'But I thought we were allowed to test it now,' I observed to El Hadji in French.

'We'll have to trust in it,' he said. 'I have faith in the old man.'

I nodded, and repeated once again how honoured I felt to have been with him. Then Talla Seydi fished around under his mattress and retrieved his final treasure, an ancient book which he himself had transcribed. The pages were yellowing, the colour of milky tea, and were thick and warped. Some of them were filled with rows of strange, apparently unintelligible symbols. Others were covered in neat lines of Arabic script.

'My father will say a prayer for all of us now,' said Mohammed.

We joined hands in the wavering candlelight.

'Each one must pray for the good and for the benefit of everyone in this room,' he said.

The old man began to murmur. His hands gripped ours with a gentle strength and, as the words slipped easily from his mouth, he scarcely seemed to need to look at the script before him. His prayers echoed the chants of his students, which filtered through to us from the dusty veranda as we bowed our heads towards the floor.

We left Kabakunda the next morning. Initially, I wanted to test the gris-gris on the bush taxi from Gabú to Bissau, but El Hadji talked me out of it.

'That's a sin,' he said. 'That's how they earn their living.'

In somewhere as poor as Guinea-Bissau, dodging fares was unthinkable – particularly on the most expensive journey in the country. But the truth was that I was easy to persuade. I was scared of this black bracelet which I now carried with me. And I had yet to summon the courage to confront my fears.

So we decided to wait until we went on a short hop, and paid for the privilege of squeezing together for the three hours that it took us to reach Bissau. As we went, the scrub of the east dried into shrivelled scoops of dust, like bushels of rice, but its desiccated expanses could not compete with the moist air nearer the coast. Glades took over, stretching away into palm groves which swayed on the horizon, while the fat apples of the cashew trees hung immobile by the roadside.

The verges thickened into a tangled body of greenery beneath a dull sky. When the air became almost insufferably humid, we knew that we were approaching Bissau.

We spent three days there. El Hadji wanted to catch up with all the old friends that he had not seen since the civil war, and I was quite happy to reacquaint myself with this dowdy and strangely memorable city. Four years before, at a moment that now seemed like a sliver of a different existence, I had returned with Evan from the Bijagós islands, and we had arrived in Bissau. Here we had met two refugees from Sierra Leone, Henry and Saliou. They had both fled from their country when the wars there had deteriorated, and had fallen in with each other on the road. When I had known them back then, they had lived in one of the slums of Bissau, in a decrepit old room with two disintegrating chairs and a mattress infested with bedbugs. Of course, they had insisted on our sleeping on the mattress.

I remembered that in the mornings, once Evan and I had scratched ourselves all over and breakfasted on gruel, we would go to nearby compounds, visiting other members of the Sierra Leonean community in exile and meeting many of the Liberian refugees who were also there. Henry and Saliou had always tried to refuse to let us pay for anything. If we went to eat at the Caracol market, they paid. If we went out to drink Bazooka beer from empty mayonnaise jars in the evening, they also tried to pay. It was only with reluctance that they had allowed us to buy them a drink.

After a time, Henry had started to talk about the mysticism of West Africa. During his flight from Sierra Leone, he told us, he had been helped by a leaf that grew in the bush. When he had chewed on this leaf, he had been protected from rain during storms, so that it had been impossible for him to get wet.

Then he had mentioned the black cat.

'This country is strong in that!' he had said. 'Very strong.'

He had found a Marabout who could make the charm, he told us, near Bafatá. Now all that he was looking for was the black cat. When he found that, he would stroll into the main bank in Bissau, raid the vaults and leave for Europe.

'That's all I'm waiting for!'

El Hadji had begun my flirtation with invisibility, but there was no question that this had been accentuated by Henry's stories. Now, even though I knew that I did not really believe that it could work, I was waiting for the courage to test my gris-gris. But Henry, I remembered, had been completely convinced by the legend. He had been so certain that he would soon find the cat that I had given him my address in Britain.

'I will go to Banjul and get on a flight to London,' he had told me. 'No one will see.'

But he had never appeared, and I had secretly been relieved. The black cat was powerful, after all, and I still found it difficult to confront it. This was why I was hapy to be leaving my bracelet untouched in my money belt when El Hadji and I arrived in Bissau that afternoon.

We were disgorged amid the chaos of Bandim market, where El Hadji telephoned one of his friends, who invited us to stay. We caught a taxi, which took us away from the crush and towards the ugly white water tower that heralds the city centre. Then we made our way towards a small roundabout, passed a night club and, with some surprise, I realised that we were heading for the very same street in which I had lodged with Henry and Saliou four years before.

I grabbed El Hadji's sleeve. 'Where are we going?'

'My friend lives here,' he said.

'But I've been here before.'

We climbed out of the battered blue and white car scarcely twenty metres from the spot at which I had last seen Henry waving to Evan and me, as our taxi had sped towards the transport park and the cars for Gabú. El Hadji shouldered his rucksack, and then led me past the compound in which we had stayed with the Sierra Leoneans. The whole thing was so surreal that I half expected to see them there, but a simple glance confirmed that the mechanics' workshop that they had run had closed down.

My friends had gone.

They must have fled when the war had begun, trying to move on to the next safe haven that would take them. Their only options would have been Senegal or Guinea-Conakry, but Senegal had closed its borders. And Sitafa had told me what had happened at Gabú to those heading for Guinea-Conakry.

We walked on a little further up the road, which was characterised by the same lines of basic general stores and the same disrepair that I had seen four years before. Reggae boomed out from a set of speakers, and a dated poster clung to the door of a barber's with faded resignation. When I had been here before, I had only been twenty-one years old, and I had believed that the smiling faces of the compounds hinted at a happiness that Europeans could only dream of. But now I sensed that the air was heavy with inertia and suffering.

It was impossible to know, of course, what had really happened, and how much – if anything – had changed, except for the fact that I had grown up.

We turned off the road and picked our way through the compounds nearby. We walked past flea-ridden dogs and piles of rubbish and women pounding millet on the cracked verandas of their homes. Hordes of flies buzzed like motors in spite of the heat. If my friends had failed to escape, I realised, brushing through the thick clouds of insects, they had probably died. No one knew how many had suffered that fate during the war, and foreign refugees were more likely than most to be buried in unmarked graves.

I remembered again the vast numbers of refugees from the struggles in Liberia and Sierra Leone whom I had met in Bissau. Many thousands of them had found their way here believing that this small country was safe. But now they had mostly gone. And no one seemed to know what had happened to them.

El Hadji led me to the house of his friend Joao, where we stayed. Joao lived with his wife Vitoria and their little daughter in a two-room flat. Joao was a tall Peul, with a solid, even face and a ready smile. He was fleshier than most of the Peul, but he had been working in Madeira, he told me, and I wondered again how much of the habitual thinness of the Peul was caused by genetics and how much was caused by diet.

Since Joao lived and worked in Madeira, the family's standard of living was better than most. The living room had a glass-topped table and tall wicker stands holding plates and glasses. We sat in comfy chairs as El Hadji and Joao caught up with one another and we discussed Bissau.

El Hadji and Joao talked of Europe, and of the effects of the war.

'Are you still in Bula?' Joao asked El Hadji.

'No, I'm back in Ziguinchor. I had to leave.'

They exchanged further news, and then Joao turned to me.

'Have you come for the carnival?' he asked me.

'Carnival?'

'It starts tonight!'

Guinea-Bissau, as a Lusophone country, celebrates Shrove Tuesday with abandon.

'You won't believe it,' El Hadji told me. 'You'll burst out laughing when you see what they wear.'

I asked Joao if he would come with us to see the parade, but he declined. Nevertheless, that evening El Hadji and I walked towards the water tower to join in the party. The streets were thick with people and lined with stalls selling palm wine, rum and beer. Guinea-Bissauans are renowned drinkers, and many of them were already staggering about, their eyes reduced to wild, glazed saucers. But the most extraordinary thing about the parade was the number of cross-dressers. Many of the men had adorned themselves with tight-fitting crinkled dresses and headscarfs, and some had even put on frilly knickers outside their shorts. Some had had their hair plaited, while others wore lipstick.

Many of the women, too, had dressed in tight men's clothes, and they minced around commandingly, mingling with the men and the children, whose heads were covered in ghoulish papier-mâché masks. Most bizarre of all was the cart being wheeled through the streets with a doll strapped to it, bearing the legend 'Virus da SIDA' (AIDS virus).

It seemed as if half of Guinea-Bissau was out to enjoy the carnival and, in spite of the dire warnings of Joao – who had talked of violent assaults in these difficult times – everyone seemed determined to enjoy themselves, this being the first carnival since the end of the war. The drink flowed freely, nods and winks were exchanged, and El Hadji constantly met former girlfriends.

One of them, Tô, joined us for a stroll along the main street. The evening air was heavy with the scent of bougainvillaea. She and El Hadji constantly eyed one another up, while I tried to resist the effects of the heat and the party.

'Let's go and have a drink,' I suggested.

We sat down at a bar, where I ordered a beer for myself and a Coke for El Hadji. This would be the first alcohol I had touched since meeting him.

'I'll have a beer, too,' said Tô.

'No,' said El Hadji, flaring up crossly.

'Why not?' I asked.

'It's forbidden by the Qu'ran,' he said.

'So is adultery,' I said in French, 'and the Qu'ran doesn't stop you dreaming of that.'

El Hadji laughed.

'You're very bad,' he said. 'I'm committing one sin, and now you want me to commit another one.'

'When you're in a country where everyone dances on one leg,' I reminded him, 'you have to dance on one leg too.'

This time he grinned. Then he turned back to Tô and continued his conversation. The Guinea-Bissauans, he told me, without a hint of prejudice, thought of nothing but drink and sex. I could take care of the one, and he could take care of the other.

Eventually, I went home before he did. Joao was waiting up for us, and Vitoria had prepared the front room, moving the table and chairs into the corner and placing a mattress on the tiled floor. I sat on the veranda with Joao, listening to the distant echoes of fireworks from the town and watching people huddled around their stores in the feeble glow of candlelight. A soft breeze hustled dust-devils along the road. Then it lapsed and the devils disappeared suddenly into the earth.

'How long do you think El Hadji will be?' Joao asked me.

'It could be a long time,' I said.

He soon left me to sleep. I lay on the mattress, staring up at the darkened roof and listening to the murmuring of Bissau by night. El Hadji arrived well past midnight. He washed himself, prayed in the corner of the room and then stretched out expansively beside me.

'You mustn't write that I slept with Tô,' he said, without preamble.

'What happened?'

'I thought of you telling Djinaba, and came home.'

I laughed at his reluctant fidelity. Then we were silent, and the space was suddenly filled with the sobs of a woman from a neighbouring room. They continued for a long while. Later, two babies wailed. The evening had so recently been one of celebration, but now despair had returned to hang in the air.

'The war was terrible, wasn't it?' I murmured to El Hadji.

'It was the worst thing I have seen,' he said. 'Toby, if you had been there, you would have cried.'

He sighed deeply, and I felt him stretch out on the mattress and begin to sleep. That night, as I lay beneath the zinc roof and tried to follow my friend's example, my head filled with memories of the comments that are habitually to be heard whenever we hear of our governments' efforts to prop up benighted countries such as Guinea-Bissau. The death toll had been high during the war there but, it was to be understood, it could well have been higher had it not been for the munificence of international organisations and governments, which spent months procrastinating over a humanitarian donation of less than US$10 million when, less than a year later, they would embark on a war in Yugoslavia that cost billions. The United Nations did, at least, recognise that the response of the international community to the crisis had been slow, and a member of the staff in Bissau wrote that refugees fled for the countryside, finding shelter with rural inhabitants, family members, friends and even strangers. Traditional hospitality dictated that no refugee was turned away, she wrote, and all was shared. El Hadji told me that he himself had lodged thirty people in his three rooms in Bula and had fed them all, even giving them tobacco. People with nothing but a roof over their heads had taken in up to fifty strangers each, and had run up debts so that no one would starve.

Eventually I slept, but the air was always heavy and uncomfortable, and I sweated in the night. At about six-thirty, the first rustles of the cockerels and the men going to work disturbed the morning, and I awoke. El Hadji soon followed suit, and he turned to me as soon as he was alert.

I thought he was going to say something about the war, but instead he reiterated what he had said the night before.

'You mustn't write that I slept with Tô,' he said.

Joao laughed when El Hadji told his story. Even Vitoria thought it was funny. Then I went outside, through the early morning fug of people and dust, and bought bread and butter for breakfast.

We sat around the glass table, eating our baguettes. Eventually, and inevitably, the conversation turned to the economic situation.

'This place,' said Joao. 'It's sinking.'

'What do you mean?'

'Before, everyone had something. But now people have to sell their bodies just to live.'

He had been away in Madeira during the fighting, and had only just returned.

'I've never seen Bissau so poor,' he said sadly.

Friends hurried to see him, he said, hearing that he was back from Europe, and begging for whatever small change he could afford. He never turned any of them away. One of them had come to see Joao on our first night, just before El Hadji and I had gone to the carnival. He had been a slight, diffident man, dressed in a ragged black T-shirt and ripped white jeans.

I had asked him what the war had been like.

'One of my friends died when a shell exploded next to where he was sitting,' he had said. 'The gunfire was everywhere. So we all left, and walked to Bafatá. But when we got there, it was even worse. The streets were crawling with people, many of them were dying, and there was no food. So I came back to Bissau and scavenged as best I could. I ate whatever I could find. Even rats,' he had said, blinking. 'But the city was deserted, there was hardly anyone else here.'

Everyone seemed to have vanished.

'Did you hear about the war when you were in Madeira?' I asked Joao that morning, as the crumbs of our baguette flaked to the floor.

'Of course,' he said. 'But what could we do?'

I stayed in Bissau, going from compound to compound and greeting old friends. One of these was Aliou. Aliou was from The Gambia and had been in Guinea-Bissau for six years. When I had left him, his batik business had been on the up, but now he was living in a musty room pockmarked with bullet holes from the war. The walls were so eroded by the gunfire that it looked as if mice had decided that concrete tasted better than wood. During the war, he explained, soldiers from the junta used to walk past every day with their sub-machine guns, drunk with alcohol and power. They would point their guns at random and fire, and Aliou would think, 'Only God, my fate is only in the hands of God.'

'There was one boy who was drunk and playing with his gun just outside in the road' – Aliou gestured at the dusty street, apparently like any other run-down street in a West African city – 'and he shot himself in the chest.'

Aliou shook his head.

'I walked past shortly afterwards,' he said, 'and his blood was dripping away into the sand. He was already dead. And I thought, "Only God".'

Other people in Bissau told me stories of hunger, of huddling in bomb shelters as the bullets and bombs whistled overhead, and of the dead lying untended in the streets. The war had smouldered on for a year, and then there had been the transition to democracy. But elections do not bring wealth and, shortly after the installation of the new president, Guinea-Bissau was recognised as the sixth-poorest country in the world by the United Nations' World Development Report. No one had any money and the city was in a desperate state. Everyone in Bissau plotted escape to Europe and, in Europe, the authorities plotted to prevent their dreams from being realised.

Inevitably, on my last day in the city, I felt depressed. The hope that had accompanied the end of the war seemed already to have evaporated, for there was no money and, as El Hadji and I quickly realised, people were desperate. They simply could not survive on the pittances that they were earning.

'Bissau is different,' I said.

'It has become a new place,' said El Hadji. 'And I don't like it.'

The war had left a profound impact on the city. As we had driven in along the only four-lane highway on our first morning, I had gazed with fascination at the relics of the conflict. On the right-hand side of the road, two tanks rusted among the broken glass and the brown stubble masquerading as grass. On the left were the shells of the buildings that had been blown to pieces by these same tanks during the war, with their roofs caved in and rubble strewn all around the earth. Tiles lay shattered, the redder brown mixing with the light colour of the dust, and blowing all over the streets in a poisoned cloud of forgetfulness. Windows were fragmented, walls had crumbled, ruins stood where once there had been buildings, and everywhere there were reminders of the fighting that had devastated this country and those who lived in it.

When the conflict had broken out, I remembered, I had listened to news of it with mounting horror. I had struggled to imagine the noise of the shells and the suffering engulfing this place that I knew, but I found it impossible. In my home country, I had tried to publicise the situation, and a well-known left-wing magazine had expressed an interest. But then the news had slipped out of sight, and that interest had waned as attention to the war was replaced by more immediate concerns. Everything was changing so quickly. Meanwhile, technology continued to empower us and was the crux to success. Less than a year after the ceasefire finally came in Guinea-Bissau, the discovery of the constitution of the human genome was hailed, paving the way to the eradication of many inherited diseases, so that people would live to an age that was previously unimaginable. Yet all these things were so alien to Bissau and the rest of West Africa, where wars came and went and there was not the money to pay for doctors or electricity, let alone DNA tests and computers. Unless subsidies were forthcoming, it was difficult to see how Africa could not suffer as a result of these changes.

At one point, I discussed the nature of genetically modified foods with El Hadji.

'The essence of our bodies and of the foods that we eat can now be pinpointed,' I explained, 'and then these can be altered so as to improve their strength.'

El Hadji listened with disbelief.

'Those people over in Europe are mad,' he said, shaking his head.

During my journey, it became abundantly clear that the vast economic and social differences between Africa and the rest of the world were only increasing with the advent of these new technologies. With things as they were, it seemed that the gap could only continue to widen. It felt as if some people intended a rift to develop in the human species.

We left Bissau for Bula.

At the transport park in Bissau, El Hadji and I huddled inside the unadorned cattle truck that would transport us and fifty other passengers to the ferry at Joao Landim. Watching the shameless way in which they were prodded and ordered around, I felt that little had changed since slaving times, when the ancestors of these people had been considered as animate objects and, like cattle, had been valued according to their weight.

Of course, Guinea-Bissau had been the slaver's paradise.

El Hadji and I were squeezed near the back end of the truck, where we had an excellent view of the hawkers selling Maxam toothpaste from China and fake Calvin Klein underpants, as well as of the clutches of oranges and bananas that were thrust in our faces and of the expected confusion outside. The transport park was a muddle of flies, litter, dust, battered tin trays, boys selling water in cellophane bags and impatience. There were some bush taxis there as well.

El Hadji sat nearest to the back of the truck, and so he bore the brunt of the hawkers. One man repeatedly thrust a tape of Alpha Blondy – an Ivoirian reggae star – under his nose.

'That's funny,' I said to him on the fourth occasion that the hawker assailed him. 'You don't look like someone who doesn't want to buy an Alpha Blondy tape.'

We waited for twenty minutes. Every time that it seemed that no one else could possibly fit into this boxed space, someone new was squeezed inside, together with their chickens, goats, pigs or jerrycans of palm wine. By the end, when I looked down at my limbs, I was amazed that they could fit into such a tiny space.

We left, and our conveyance hobbled towards Joao Landim. We stopped several times to jam still more people inside. The sun beat down on the metal of the truck, which was hot to the touch, and the only way I could sit without getting a crick in my neck was to stare down at the holes in the floor.

It felt as if we were back in Guinea-Conakry.

'This is ridiculous,' I said to El Hadji, the third time that we stopped to pick up another passenger. 'Where are they going to fit?'

A woman clambered into the truck, and sat with her elbow near my chin and her backside near someone else's chest.

'What can they do about it?' he asked. 'People want to travel, and there aren't enough vehicles.'

I sat looking at the scrum of passengers, and at their limbs and backsides trying to reorganise themselves so that the new addition could be fitted in. I was not sure how much more of this I could put up with.

'What's the fare from Joao Landim to Bula?' I asked El Hadji.

'One hundred and fifty CFA,' he said – about fifteen pence.

I watched the crush with mounting irritation. Predictably, it was this personal discomfort that galvanised me into confronting my fears.

'I could try the gris-gris when we are in that car.'

El Hadji looked at me in surprise.

'Whatever you want,' he murmured.

'What do you think?'

El Hadji agreed that, with the fare so low, I could try out the gris-gris then without guilt.

We reached the port at Joao Landim, where the Mansoa river stretched out like an enormous grey slug in the heat. There was not even a hint of a breeze. The river banks were lined with mangroves which were so still that they seemed dead, as if the heat itself had killed them. Crowds of vehicles and people were awaiting the ferry's arrival from the far side of the river. The lucky ones bought a drink from one of the roadside stalls, and sat in the shade of the awnings.

At a small kiosk, we bought the tickets for the ferry. Then we separated. I told El Hadji that I would conceal myself behind one of the stalls, put on my long-sleeved shirt and then attach the gris-gris.

'I'll wait for you here,' El Hadji said.

'But don't worry if you can't see me,' I replied. 'I'll manifest myself on the far side of the river.'

El Hadji laughed.

I walked across the road, past the stalls and the people and their packets of roasted cashew nuts and groundnuts, and went and stood in the middle of the waste ground near the mangroves.

I looked around, but no one was watching.

So I opened my bag and put on the only long-sleeved shirt that I had brought with me from Europe. I retrieved the gris-gris from my money belt, stretched my arms out behind my back, clenched my teeth, screwed up my eyes and pulled the bracelet up my right arm. As the charm slid upwards, I prayed that this experiment would pass without incident.

Then I straightened, and opened my eyes.

I wondered if the world would appear differently. But the heat, the dust, the flies and the unnerving hubbub of the port were unchanged. The smells of rotting fruit and the acrid smoke of the wood fires had not dispersed.

Then I remembered what Talla Seydi had said about seeing the stars even in the daylight, and I looked upwards. But all I saw was the brilliant blue, fuzzy atmosphere.

So I buttoned up the cuffs of my shirt, picked up my bag and made my way back out into the world.

I realised, of course, that the gris-gris would be the easiest thing in the world to test. It is impossible for a white man in Guinea-Bissau to go unnoticed. As I reappeared from behind the stalls and made my way through the thick crowd of people, it took me about two seconds to realise that I was not invisible.

People still looked at me as they passed. No one called out, for this was Guinea-Bissau. But they knew I was there.

I felt a deep sense of disappointment. I had wanted this charm to work. I did want there to be more to the world than what I saw before my eyes.

El Hadji was standing next to the swampy fringes of the river, talking to an old friend from Bula. I walked towards him, feeling heavy and subdued. As soon as he saw me, he beckoned sharply.

'Oh yes,' he said, looking at me, 'there's a different Toby.'

'What do you mean?'

'Don't you feel it yourself?' he asked in surprise.

'No.'

I felt as if nothing had changed, except for the fact that my illusions had finally been destroyed. I had hoped that there was more to the world than what was visible, but I had been a fool. How had I ever been stupid enough to consider such a thing? Life in Africa was just inordinately harsh, misery was all-encompassing and people lived in their imaginations.

But El Hadji seemed not to notice my disappointment.

'You're a different person,' he said softly. 'You're . . . glowing.'

'Glowing?'

'You won't pay for the journey to Bula.'

Then he turned back to his friend.

But the only thing that I saw glowing was the world about me, which shone so starkly that it seemed as bright and powerful as the sun itself. Everything was silvery: the light on the water, the leaves that hung thickly by the riverside and the glare reflecting from the ferry which was now on the verge of docking.

El Hadji turned to me when his friend had gone.

'Yes,' he said, 'this will work. But what would we have done if you had vanished completely?'

As soon as the ferry was safely ensconced on the quayside, the scene became so chaotic that I temporarily forgot the mystery that I was supposed to be testing. Crowds of people rushed down to push on board before anyone had disembarked. In the midst of the masses, cars and trucks tried to reverse off the ship without running anyone over. A man got off the ferry heaving a recalcitrant pig behind him in the dust. He held onto the rope with a grim sense of purpose, and the rope clasped one of the pig's hind legs with similar determination. The pig, too, was determined, but its resolve consisted in not being hauled up the ramp, and soon the two became engaged in a ludicrous tug-of-war. Eventually the rope caught the man's left leg and he was flipped over. The pig tried to pull him back. A car reversed off the ship at that moment, and nearly ran both of them over. The man picked up the rope, swore and started hauling the pig up the hill. The pig screamed furiously at the torture.

And this was only one of many similar scenes occurring concurrently.

No vehicle could advance because a taxi driver had selfishly driven right down to the boat to await clients for Bissau. The man became involved in an altercation with the driver of one of the cars that was trying to disembark. Insults were exchanged and a fight nearly began.

Higher up the ramp, two touts started to argue over customers for the trip to Bissau, and the inevitable brawl got under way. A score of people settled around the young men and separated them.

And all the while people clambered into the backs of trucks. Their goats were slung like inanimate luggage onto the roofs, their bleats mingling with the noise of the engines, the cries and the arguments. The heat intensified and the concrete seemed to burn. Our skins were frazzled, and almost an hour passed while the chaotic scene sought to resolve itself into some semblance of order.

'*C'est difficile,*' said El Hadji.

Eventually most of the cars were loaded onto the boat, and we picked our way through the throngs onto the ferry. El Hadji saw another group of friends and ran over to greet them, while I squeezed past the cars and found a space next to the ferry's motor. The day was hot, and the motor only made it hotter. I felt the beads of sweat that pimpled my forehead. If I really was glowing, it was probably only because I was so overheated.

As the ship began to pull away from the dock, I sat down on a ledge by the motor. El Hadji was walking back towards where I was sitting. He walked on until he was right in front of me and then stood, staring straight above my head. His eyes dwelt vacantly on the empty space.

But it seemed as though he could not see me.

I sat bemused for perhaps two seconds, wondering whether he was pretending, before El Hadji looked down and saw me.

'There you are!' he exclaimed.

Neither of us said anything. The heat intensified as the motor sputtered us over the river. The ticket collector came and asked aggressively for the scrap of paper that I had been given at the booth in the port.

The gris-gris hadn't worked, I told myself. This question of invisibility was nothing but a myth that had hidden iniquities for centuries. Griffin was a symbol of the atrocities of the colonial enterprise, but there was nothing really invisible about him except for our inability to see.

Nevertheless, as the ship docked on the far side of the river, and we walked slowly up the ramp and found a pick-up truck which would take us the ten kilometres on to Bula, a small doubt persisted in my mind. El Hadji had told me that the gris-gris would not work on the ferry, since we had bought our tickets before I had put it on. Only on the far side of the river, he had said, can we really put it to the test.

There were any number of vehicles waiting to take passengers on to Bula, and I picked one at random. El Hadji and I clambered up with our things. The pick-up truck was lined with twelve people on each side of it, while our luggage was stowed in the space in the middle, together with three bulging sacks of rice. As soon as the vehicle was filled, we set off through the cashew trees and estuarine mud flats. We quickly gathered speed, and the hot wind swept over the cab at the front, enveloping us in cloying warmth.

I sat looking at the other passengers, and some of them returned my gaze. I was not invisible. I had never been invisible. And invisibility was impossible.

The tout progressed along the line of passengers on the far side of the vehicle, collecting the 150-franc fare. He was a young man with broad cheekbones and deep, wide eyes.

Then he came down our side of the car and snapped his fingers for money.

El Hadji located the 500-franc note that I had given him, 150 francs for him, 150 for his invisible friend. He handed the note to the tout, who took it and put it in his pocket.

Then the tout looked sharply at El Hadji.

'No, no,' he said in Kriolu.

He retrieved the note and handed it back to El Hadji.

'Just give me 200 francs.'

El Hadji gave him two silver 100-franc coins, which the tout pocketed, before returning 50 francs in change.

Then he moved on along our side of the truck, ignoring me completely.

El Hadji turned and murmured, 'I've only paid for one of us.'

'I know.'

There was still a little distance between here and Bula, and I was convinced that the tout would recognise his error. The mud flats gradually disappeared and were replaced by thicker groves of trees. The road bore right, and our pick-up truck tore into the centre of Bula.

Still the tout said nothing.

We gathered our bags and I jumped down onto the road. El Hadji prepared to follow suit.

'Wait!'

The tout shouted at us, and I breathed more calmly. He must have realised his mistake, I thought.

Then he said it.

'You've forgotten your change.'

El Hadji started. 'What change?'

'The change I owe you.'

'You don't owe me any change.'

'Yes I do,' said the tout.

He rustled in his money belt and produced some coins.

'You've already given me my change,' said El Hadji, insistently.

'No I haven't,' said the tout. 'Take it!'

El Hadji opened his mouth to argue but, before he could say anything, the tout had pressed the coins into his hand and banged on the roof of the cab.

The pick-up began to drive off.

We looked down at the coins in amazement. The tout had given us 350 francs, which, if El Hadji had been travelling on his own, would have been the correct change to the 500-franc note which the tout had already returned to us.

This sort of thing simply does not happen in Guinea-Bissau.

Further on, the pick-up had stalled amid the crowds in the main street of Bula. Women were proffering trays of fruit and nuts for sale, and the tout was busy rearranging luggage and people so that more passengers could be squeezed in. But he seemed to sense our looks, because he turned in our direction and saw us rooted to the roadside. He straightened and waved so enthusiastically at us that it seemed as if we were the ones who had done him the favour.

Bula!

We stood still for a moment in the heat. This nondescript place of which most of the world is unaware meant a great deal to both of us. For me it symbolised a beginning and an end, in a strange way a complete cycle of life, for it had been here that this voyage into the unknown had begun, and now the events on the pick-up seemed sure to enforce a permanent change in me. Meanwhile, for El Hadji, this place was at once his home and a painful reminder of a past that had so brutally been taken away from him.

Soon, our brief moment of silence was interrupted by the whine of the pick-up truck as it left the market and made its way northwards.

'Come on,' El Hadji said purposefully.

And he led me up the street, through the sleepy town which I recognised as if I had never left it. The centre of the Mancaigne people, Bula also has groups of Pepels and Balantas. This is a place where people sit all day long on porches, gossiping about one another. At the end of the dry season, when the heat becomes most insufferable, they lie beneath mango trees in the afternoons, awaiting the cooler evenings. The back streets are remarkably dusty but, a little way down a hill to the north, the dust gives way to a lush glade, where rice is sown and reaped, and plantations of bananas, onions, tomatoes and sweet potatoes border the grasslands. There are two springs here, gurgling in the shade of towering silk-cotton trees. The men wash themselves in one, the women in the other.

Bula itself possesses one main street, curving in an ellipse from north to east as it makes its way through the town towards Joao Landim. All the stalls line up along this street, with their collections of Chinese electrical goods, packets of rice and tea and sugar, little sachets of coffee and powdered milk, and everything else without which life is unthinkable in West Africa. It was here that El Hadji had run his photographic studio before the civil war.

Friends had told him that his apprentice, Domingos, still ran the business. After being deposited in such extraordinary circumstances in the town, El Hadji and I walked up the street, past two bars and Bula's disco, until we found ourselves in front of the studio. Domingos had painted the front walls a lilac colour, and the words 'Foto' and 'Studio' were emblazoned there in big black letters to attract the clientele. Inside, we could see cloth backdrops of European pastures, snow-capped mountains, a host of skyscrapers and an image of Mike Tyson, against one of which customers could choose to be photographed. People in Bula did not hide their dreams.

We went on in through the front door, where we were greeted by a mangy white mongrel leaping up and barking excitedly.

'Bobby!'

El Hadji wrestled playfully with his pet dog, who licked his hands and then sank down to the floor, hanging on my friend's every move.

'El Hadji.'

Domingos was sitting on one of the wicker chairs, with his friend Lamin next to him. They both looked at us in astonishment and then leapt up, like Bobby, in joy. They could not believe the apparition that had just re-entered their lives, and there was a genuine warmth in the way in which the friends hugged one another. Domingos was a tall and muscular Balanta, lean, with a broad smile and an enthusiastic way of doing things. Lamin was paler and older, and his eyes had developed a shiftiness with the years.

Soon, Malam – another friend – appeared and there were further happy reunions. The two men embraced, and then Malam stood stroking his pointed beard as El Hadji explained his story.

'This man had the luck of God when he left,' said Lamin, when he had heard El Hadji out. 'We thought he was dead.'

I looked at El Hadji, but he did not acknowledge the comment.

Everything seemed so unreal at that moment – the gris-gris, invisibility, my return to Bula and the reunion – that I let it go.

El Hadji led me through into the bedroom that had been his, and we put our things down.

'You'd better take that gris-gris off,' he said to me, softly. 'That's a very powerful thing that you have there.'

I put it in my money belt. Then we went outside to the veranda, which backed onto a yard and several neighbouring compounds in which there were banana plants and papaya trees and children playing in the dust. The skyline was a jumble of luxuriant branches and zinc roofs, on which vultures scrabbled violently, waiting for things to die.

We spent the afternoon drinking tea. In spite of appearances, there was an unhappy domestic situation in this place. A few days later, once we had left Bula, El Hadji told me that Lamin and Domingos were barely on speaking terms, since Lamin refused to pay anything towards the rent of their home, so that they were on the point of being evicted. Nevertheless, they put their differences aside that afternoon, and sat together with El Hadji. They were so delighted to see their former friend that, at the time, I barely noticed the tension.

Instead, I spent those hours watching Domingos busy himself as he arranged everything for his master, fetching the wood, lighting the fire, preparing the rice and the fish, not to mention dusting down the benches and the cracked concrete of the veranda. He even fetched buckets of water with which we could wash. El Hadji accepted it all with the hauteur of the older brother, practised and superior. But nevertheless, he was anxious to do the right thing by Domingos, wanting to pay for his apprentice's clothes and mattress once his own economic situation had improved.

Initially, as Domingos stirred the rice, I followed the conversation – which flitted between Wolof, Kriolu and Mancaigne – as best I could, but inevitably my thoughts drifted back to the events on the pick-up truck.

I had spent long enough here to know that touts were aggressive and exigent when it came to demanding their fares. They were not averse to throwing people off in the middle of the bush if they could not pay. I also knew that, as a white man in Guinea-Bissau, it is impossible to go unnoticed. But the strange thing about the affair had been that the only person who had seemed not to see me had been the tout. Everyone else had been aware of my presence but for him.

And then I remembered the words of Talla Seydi in Kabakunda.

'Only use the gris-gris,' he had said, 'when you want to go about your work without being interfered with.'

When taking public transport, I realised, the person who would interfere with you was the ticket collector. And he had not seen me. In fact, it seemed as if he had been rendered temporarily insane where I was concerned.

I shook my head in incomprehension when I thought of it, and El Hadji caught me at it.

'Today,' he told the others, 'we have seen a miracle.'

But no one seemed to pay much attention. They did not ask us to expand, as if miracles were commonplace and it was the mundane events of real life that required more explanation.

'This man,' Lamin said, gesturing to El Hadji, 'knows a lot about miracles.'

'What do you mean?' I asked.

'He should be dead,' he said again.

'What are they talking about?' I asked my friend in French.

El Hadji looked at me sadly and seemed momentarily unable to speak.

'Things were very bad for me in Bula,' he said eventually. 'During the war, at first, I did well. I did my business between here and Senegal, and made a profit. That was how I was able to lodge so many refugees in my house. But then, after two months, a woman came to see me.'

El Hadji paused.

'She saved his life,' Lamin told me.

She had told him that the army had decided that he was a Senegalese spy. The Senegalese were trying to shore up the regime of President Nino Vieira,* whom the army, led by General Ansumane Mane,† were fighting to overthrow. El Hadji, because of his frequent visits to and from the border with Senegal, was suspected of supplying information to the enemy.

'The night after she visited,' El Hadji said, 'some soldiers came to the door. They asked for El Hadji, and I said that he had gone out. Then they left. The next night, they came again and asked for El Hadji, and I told them that he was out.'

It was Malam who had told him to leave.

'You are trying to sell all your goods and make as big a profit as you can,' he had told El Hadji. 'But your life is worth more than any profit you might gain.'

'But how did you get past the military checkpoints?' I asked.

'I went to the Imam of Bula,' he told me now, 'and he gave me a secret. Every time I saw the soldiers, I recited a verse from the Qu'ran. Then I went unharmed.'

* See Historical Notes, p. 274.
† See Historical Notes, p. 272.

'The day after he left,' Malam said slowly, 'the soldiers hunted for him as if he had been a part of their ration. As if they had wanted to eat him.'

'Toby,' said El Hadji, 'things are difficult here. I was doing well, so I had many enemies in Bula.'

All kinds of things had been said about El Hadji since he had gone. It was said that he was in Portugal. One man claimed to have seen him driving a four-wheel drive Land Cruiser in Dakar. Someone else told Domingos that he had received a letter from El Hadji telling him to leave the studio. Rumours circulated unendingly in this town, moving gently and with subtle persuasiveness from compound to compound, like the people who brought them.

No one had known the truth, which was that El Hadji had been in Dakar, ill and unemployed.

The afternoon came and went. Towards dusk, we washed on the back veranda. El Hadji wanted to wait for the twilight prayer before going on his visiting rounds. So we lay relaxing on his old bed, in the room in which he had lived before he had fled. It was a neat space, containing a cassette player, an urn with drinking water, a mosquito net tied up in a bundle over the elaborate wooden bedstead and many photographs adorning the wall.

'El Hadji,' I said, broaching the subject that we had not mentioned all afternoon, 'what was it that we saw today?'

'Where?'

'On the pick-up.'

'That was African magic,' he said.

'How did it work?'

He laughed. 'Why are you asking me! I'm not the Marabout.'

'No . . .'

But I wanted some answers. I had been taught that the world possessed rational truths that were open to our analysis. But invisibility was not one of these, and it could not be uncovered. I wanted to be able to explain what I had seen. Or rather, I wanted to be able to explain it away.

196

'You were there,' he said eventually. 'You saw the same thing as I did. How do you think it worked?'

I could not explain it. I could possibly have believed that, if I had had complete faith in the gris-gris, my psychic confidence could have influenced the tout. But, at the crucial moment, I had been wondering why I had ever believed that the charm could work. I could also have believed that the whole affair worked through hypnosis, as some people claimed. Hypnotists can, after all, make themselves invisible to those under their spell. But again, I had not had enough faith in the charm to exert this sort of effect over someone else – and Talla Seydi had not been there. Another alternative was that El Hadji had bribed the tout to behave in this way, so that I would see something – but my friend had not had any money other than the 500 francs that I had given him, and he had not had a moment to say anything to the tout when I was not watching.

I thought back to our first morning amid the drab huts of Kabakunda and the moment that Talla Seydi had suddenly appeared behind us, as if out of nothing. I realised that my life could never be the same again.

'*L'Afrique, c'est mystique,*' said El Hadji.

Later, when I returned home, I came across an idiosyncratic work by Steve Richards – *Invisibility: Mastering the Art of Vanishing*. Attempting to synthesise Aristotelian theories of matter, Einstein's theory of relativity, the qualities of light and Yogic philosophy, Richards suggests that invisibility can be induced by calling 'pure matter' out of existence. Pure matter, he writes, is the (usually invisible) physical substance of an object which does not have a definite form. He claims that people with exceptional perception talk of seeing a 'cloud' or 'haze' surrounding objects, and this is a cloud of pure matter, or electrons. These clouds absorb all the light-waves which enter them, thereby reducing the magnitude of their reflected light to zero. Things are only visible when they reflect light, and this cloud – which absorbs it – renders anything that it conceals invisible. Richards claims that, by harnessing Yogic techniques, it is possible to make oneself invisible by drawing this cloud around the body – something that he has done many times himself.

Nevertheless, he notes, it is important to be careful not to show off one's invisible talents, since the possibilities of humiliation are endless, as the Rosicrucian novelist Lord Edward Bulwer-Lytton unwittingly demonstrated in the 1840s. Bulwer-Lytton would pass through a room full of visitors in the morning, arrayed in a dressing-gown, believing himself to be invisble, and then appear later in the day very carefully and elaborately dressed, as if meeting them for the first time.

After my experiences in West Africa, I managed to muster the suspension of disbelief that Richards' explanation required. I wondered whether the glow that El Hadji had talked about had been a manifestation of this cloud. But this method of invisibility still required active participation on the part of the person becoming invisible – you had to will the cloud to form around you – and this was something that I had not exercised. Furthermore, this surprisingly rational explanation did not clarify why it was only the tout who had been unable to see me.

However I looked at it that evening, invisibility did not seem rational.

Outside our room, the colour of the day fell away into dusk. El Hadji left me, and I heard the sporadic splashes of water falling against his body as he washed himself on the veranda. Then he murmured his prayers. After he had finished, we went to see his friend the Imam, together with Lamin.

Although the moon was waxing, the town seemed peculiarly dark that night as we walked through the back streets. We picked our way carefully over the ruts, which scoured the tracks as if they had been canals irrigating a desert. The tracks picked their way between the houses, and people called out to El Hadji as we went by them. We passed an evangelical church, from the inside of which the forced joyousness of the congregation bellowed across the quiet neighbourhood without mercy.

Just beyond the church, the track widened and the moonlight broke through. The sand of the streets glowed like algae in a night sea. Long and crooked shadows emerged from the stands of trees by the roadside and delved profoundly into the shifting piles of dust, which moved with our feet as we turned off the street, negotiated a flimsy wicker gate and walked up towards a lone house where an old man was sitting, contemplating the heavens.

'*Mon fils*,' the man exclaimed when he saw El Hadji, who had taken the Imam as his father in Bula. They embraced, and then El Hadji introduced me. The old man, who was tall and surprisingly solid, shook my hand warmly. The hair of his white beard was fine and crisp, like frosty moss. His gaze was warm and invigorating.

The Imam invited us into his room and we sat on stools, while he lay on the sagging mattress. El Hadji explained what had happened to him since he had left Bula, the machinations of his escape, his illness, his hand, his difficulties and the arrival of his white friend.

The Imam smiled.

He asked El Hadji about me; was I from France, or Portugal? From England, *alhamdoulilah*. But, El Hadji went on, we had travelled to the Imam's own land, to the Fouta Djalon itself.

'The Fouta!'

The man smiled richly, his mouth curving like a crescent moon. He was a Peul from Popodara, near Labé, he said. But it was a long time since he had been back home.

He began to talk with El Hadji about Guinea-Conakry, and El Hadji told him of all the hardships we had suffered while we had been there.

Then Lamin nudged me, and whispered.

'Do you see?' he asked.

'See what?'

Lamin pointed at the bed. 'The cat. Half of Bula would chase it, if they knew it was here.'

There were two cats lying on the bed along with the old man, as he listened to us. I looked closely and saw that the cat that sat beside him, stretched out voluptuously on the rumpled bedclothes and allowing the Imam to scratch its belly, was completely black.

When a black cat is needed to make you invisible, and the night after you have become invisible, you see a black cat; it is difficult not to take it as a sign.

All the fears that had come and gone over the preceding months returned at that moment. That night, once we had eaten and El Hadji and I were alone, brewing tea in the yard, I asked him about the cat.

'I saw it,' he said.

'Aren't you tempted to ask for it yourself?'

'I couldn't do that,' he said, smiling. 'The Imam is like a father to me.'

His grin broadened.

'But,' he said, 'the thought did cross my mind.'

'It seemed to me to be a sign.'

'Toby,' he said, looking at me with utmost seriousness. 'That gris-gris is very powerful. You must only ever use it in an emergency. If you call on the djinns too frequently, they will become angry with you.'

After we had drunk our tea, we paid a visit to Djinaba's family, who lived in one of the back streets of the town. I remembered that, the first time that I had come to Bula, their eldest daughter, Marém, had just been born. El Hadji had taken me to the house where Djinaba had lived with her grandmother, father, mother, brothers and sisters, and I had met her, sitting on a stool in the courtyard, her baby clamped to her breast. This was my only recollection of that event. I did not remember any of the other people I had met.

But they remembered me. Djinaba's sister and eldest brother laughed out loud when they saw me.

'El Hadji's white friend!'

The cry went up. We all agreed that it did not seem such a long time since I had last been there, although much had happened in the intervening years. El Hadji and I were ushered into a bedroom, where we sat on the quilts of the bedspread and El Hadji told them about his plans.

Things had been difficult, as they no doubt knew. He had lost everything, but now he was planning to rebuild and, *insh'allah*, if things went well, everyone would be happy. He spoke with an unusual degree of deference, which was increased when he spoke to Djinaba's mother, a *Fula Preto* with a cheerful smile who doted on him. There was no doubt that his arrival was a source of joy and that, in the exchanges of respect, laughter and stories, there was much love. Of course, everyone was pleased that El Hadji's contact with a white friend might eventually bring some wealth in their direction, but this was by no means the source of their love, which depended on a mixture of responses that was impossible to capture conclusively in the words or images that might have confused it with self-interest or, in other circumstances, for the naked lust whose portrayal has become so commonplace in our world.

Soon the conversation turned to the future, and Djinaba's mother asked El Hadji if he intended to continue working in photography. But he replied that he hoped to travel to Europe, where he would work at whatever came his way. Being a photographer was a good job in Bula, but the competition was very severe in Europe, and it would be harder for him to succeed over there, where images had become of such importance.

After we had sat with his in-laws for an hour, El Hadji said that he had to be getting back, because he had yet to perform his nightly prayer. It was late, and the moon had almost set. We walked through the darkening streets, which echoed to the gentle floundering of our feet in the dust.

After El Hadji had prayed, we tried to settle down and sleep. But we were each of us excited and initially unable to fall into that easy state of tranquillity without which sleep is impossible. El Hadji thought about everything that his years in Bula had meant for him, while I thought about the gris-gris and invisibility.

Eventually, I did manage to get some rest.

Then, at about two o'clock in the morning, Bobby began to bark. Of course, dogs often bark at night-time, and we thought that he would soon be silent. But, to my frightened ears, his barks hinted at a ferocity born of terror. They curdled viciously over the darkness, intensifying their fury sporadically, in seizures.

And Bobby was such a calm little thing, I thought, gentle as the softest creature.

But he barked for half an hour without a pause.

'El Hadji,' I said at last, 'go and sort out your dog.'

He got up reluctantly and stumbled out into the moonlit street.

'Bobby!' he shouted, and his dog whimpered for a moment.

Then he continued to bark.

'Bobby!'

But the animal would not let up. I heard the sound of a stone cracking into the ground. Bobby whimpered, but barked steadfastly. El Hadji cursed.

Then he returned and laid himself out on the mattress.

'I can't see anything,' he said.

'What's he barking at?'

'You know,' he said, 'dogs see things that we cannot see.'

'What sort of things?'

'Djinns. Spirits. Devils. Perhaps there is something out there.'

Bobby continued to bark for another hour and a half.

Twice more El Hadji rose and tried to silence him without success.

But Bobby continued to bark at the unseen world.

My fears became so powerful that they enveloped my consciousness and refused to allow me to sleep. I knew that there were all sorts of rational explanations for what I had heard, but still those barks terrified me. Bobby was an exceptionally placid dog, and was known for being so. Furthermore, before we had even reached Bula, El Hadji had told me how much his dog responded to his every word. But now, faced with an unseen danger, Bobby refused to be quiet, and his yapping seemed to hint at a presence that terrified me: a djinn come to see who it was that had called them down earlier that day, asking them to wreak invisibility.

In the morning, I watched the mongrel panting heavily in the front room. His eyes were closed and flickering in the weak light, as if they could still see the djinns that had circled around us in the night. Then they opened briefly, and I saw that they had become bloodshot. A red stain was spreading across the whites, and covering them with a lingering blindness.

We stayed two more days in Bula. It was only when El Hadji told me how I should treat the gris-gris that my fear began to ebb away.

'If you take that back to Europe with you,' he said, 'everyone is going to ask you to demonstrate it to them.'

'I know.'

'It will be very dangerous. The djinns may become angry.'

So he told me that I would have to leave the gris-gris behind. After the events that had accompanied our arrival, this calmed me. We now decided to search for other examples of African magic. Invisibility, El Hadji told me, was merely the tip of the iceberg. In the Casamance, invulnerability would be ours for the taking.

'There is one thing, though,' I said. 'I would like to see some of the fetishes.'

El Hadji looked at me with annoyance.

'Why?' he aked.

'It is important for my investigations,' I said mysteriously.

I wanted to understand the differences between Islamic magic and what was known as fetishist magic.

'Well,' he said unhappily, 'do what you want.'

I suggested travelling to the heart of the Bijagós Islands as I had done before with Evan but, with his family so nearby in Ziguinchor, this was an unpopular move with El Hadji. So instead we decided that, before returning to the Casamance, we would make for the nearest of the Bijagós Islands, Jeta, which was inhabited by Manjaco people.

But El Hadji was still fed up about it.

'Mystically,' he told me, 'the Manjaco are very bad.'

Nevertheless, we made our way in an open truck along a dusty track towards the port of Caió, through open glades flexing with tall grass and sprinkled with cattle, interspersed with thick groves of palms, cashews and silk-cottons, the branches of which met in arches over the road and threw us into shadows.

At Caió we heaved our baggage along to a cashew grove, where we awaited the high tide and the pirogue that would cross over the channel to Jeta. As we waited, we struck up a conversation with an old man, who stooped as he walked and ran his hand over his tight and whitening curls.

He was the chief of the island.

He was returning from the hospital in Bissau, where he had gone to see if they could cure the unsightly swelling on his ankle. It looked like a tumour, yet the doctors had not been able to help.

'I have spent all my money,' he said, 'but the medicines have not worked.'

'Give him something,' El Hadji whispered to me, and I gave him 500 CFA.

He looked at the note with a hint of disappointment.

'It's not a lot,' he said, 'but it'll do.'

He went off to eat while we waited for the pirogue. Opposite the cashew trees was a house where a social gathering was in full swing. Drinking had begun early in the morning, to judge from the heavy staggers of most of the people. One of the men – tall and bearded, and dressed in a yellow tunic – began to shout at one of the women. A slanging match soon got under way, and El Hadji shook his head at the scene.

'The Manjacos only care about drink and sex,' he said. 'That's it.'

Both seemed to be relevant to the present altercation, which rapidly spiralled out of control. The woman left the compound and walked up the road in high dudgeon. El Hadji shook his head sorrowfully. His Guinea-Bissauan grandmother had been a Manjaco from near Canchungo, so these were his kin.

We waited hungrily for the high tide. At one point, the chief came to sit with us, and accepted a share of the two buns that I had managed to buy in the main square. Then he went into a neighbouring house and devoured a dish of fish and rice.

Two Pepel boys were sitting near us, under the same tree. They looked just as hungry as we were. One of them was tall and broad-shouldered, while the other was squatter and had a curiously shapeless face. They worked as weavers on Jeta, using the fine strands of the raffia palm as their base, and a complex loom which was set up in the shade of a compound. As we waited, they came up to El Hadji and asked him what we were doing. He explained.

But El Hadji whispered in my ear that he did not trust them.

When the pirogue was ready, the Pepel boys accompanied us down to the port, and sat near us on the dank boards of the boat as the loading got under way. Opposite us was a large Manjaco woman clutching a new radio to her chest.

'Hey!'

The smaller Pepel held out his hand for the radio, and the woman gave it up reluctantly. She watched him fiddling with the tuning knob.

'You boys,' she said irritably. 'You come and work, but you don't send any money to your mothers.'

'My mother's got hands,' said the boy. 'She can work for herself.'

The woman eyed him with distaste. El Hadji winked at me.

'Ask these men about work,' said the Pepel, nodding at El Hadji and me. 'They've brought things for the islanders.'

She turned to me. 'So, what have you brought for us?'

El Hadji looked at me knowingly, and I pretended that I had not understood.

We sat, frazzling, in the oppressive heat. The sun burnt everything and turned the brackish water and the air above the swamp into sullen beacons. Eventually, the crew poled the pirogue out along the narrow, muddy tentacle of ocean, and we made our way through the low waters, before motoring out across the wider channel separating the mainland from Jeta. The waves were grey, and dolphins tumbled in the sea. Beyond the haze, the mangroves of the island loomed in ghoulish shapes, rearing up from the shoreline in a macabre and twisted barricade, as if they did not want us to see what lay behind them.

After an hour, we reached one of the island's two ports. The pirogue pitched uncertainly near the jetty and I tried to leap onto dry land, only to sink up to my knees in the thick mud of the channel.

El Hadji roared with laughter.

'Always the same,' he said, as I washed myself down. 'He doesn't care.'

The rest of the passengers looked at me with bemusement. Then the chief told us that we could stay with him. So we followed him across the island. Jeta was green, and sheltered beneath enormous, spiralling silk-cottons, which shaded the cashew trees and the dried-grass fences protecting plantations of beans and onions. A maze of paths criss-crossed over the island, some of them used by people and others carved out by the animals that lived here: hyenas, gazelles and cattle.

We followed the chief for half an hour, through numerous small settlements of thatched huts. Eventually El Hadji asked me to stop.

'Wait,' he said. 'I thought this was an island.'

'It is,' I said.

'Where's the sea?'

'Some islands are quite big,' I explained. 'Britain is an island.'

'Really?'

'It is over a thousand kilometres from top to bottom.'

He shook his head.

'Have you never been to an island?'

No, he said, he had not. He had imagined that you could always see the sea on an island. Now he felt disorientated.

Eventually, we heard the discordant serenades of numerous cockerels, and realised that the main village was nearby. The chief took us down a left fork, and led us past a tumbledown hut to a concrete house, covered with zinc, with a new veranda. There, we deposited our things and waited for him to return with his wife. We sat beside a locked door together with fifty sacks of cement. Nearby, a chicken with a foot infection had been tied to a stake and was hobbling uncertainly over the hot stone.

The veranda looked out on a dried-grass fence and the dense foliage of the island. The sky was grey, and the heavy afternoon echoed with gentle noises – conversations, pestles and mortars, animals rustling in the dust. The sweat clung to the hairs on my legs and beaded El Hadji's forehead. We were surrounded by children, who laughed and giggled as we waited.

The chief shooed them away when he returned, and opened the locked door.

'This is my son's room,' he said, as we looked inside with amazement. 'He's away working in Europe, but he's built this place up for his holidays.'

The room was an extraordinary sight in this remote and impoverished part of the world. The neatly tiled floor was covered with boxes filled with objects – toys, sets of crockery, cutlery and ornaments. To one side, there was a polished wall cabinet, in which were several cut-glass plates and two ornate clocks. As well as two easy chairs, there was an elegant glass table and a sofa bed. The crown jewel, however, of this collection of unused objects was the electric light, which came on in the evening, courtesy of the generator.

We walked inside this cool sanctuary and deposited our bags. The man watched us closely, savouring our surprise.

Then we started to unpack the gifts that we had brought. We gave the chief two litres of rum, five tobacco leaves and three bars of soap. They did not seem quite in keeping with our lodgings. Nevertheless, he warmed to us at once.

'This is good for us,' he said.

Then El Hadji explained that we would like to stay for a few days, and we hoped he would accept 10,000 CFA as a token of our respect and gratitude.

'Stay as long as you like,' he said. 'You can sleep on the sofa bed.'

We eyed the metal contraption which was folded up in the corner of the room. El Hadji had never seen such a thing before, and had not expected that to change on Jeta.

'Your son,' I asked. 'Which country is he in?'

'France.'

'Has he been there long?'

'Many years,' he said. 'Like the other islanders.'

'What other islanders?'

The old man watched us carefully. Then he told us that, out of a total population of around 3000, there were 360 people from the island of Jeta working in Europe – they were in Portugal, France and Spain.

'Where are you from?' he asked me.

'England.'

'Even there we have people,' he said, as if referring to a network of spies.

The first islander had gone on a scholarship to Portugal in the early 1960s and, since that time, each emigrant had paid for a new person to go to Europe. In that way, Jeta had developed a wealth of sorts. Most of the houses had zinc roofs. And the emigrants were paying for the construction of a health post and a school.

'We help each other here. We're not like Pecixe,' the chief said, referring to the neighbouring island.

'What happens on Pecixe?'

'They hurt each other.'

With that cryptic comment, he left us. We placed our bags beneath the table, shut the door to protect ourselves from the prying eyes of the children and then lay down on the bed. As usual, El Hadji seemed to take up more than his fair share of the mattress, and we spent a few minutes nudging one another into place.

Then, when we had settled, I asked him what the chief had meant.

'How do they hurt each other on Pecixe?'

'I told you,' he said, 'but you wouldn't listen. No, no. Toby is headstrong. Toby knows best.'

'What did you tell me?' I asked sharply, tiring of the perennial refrain.

'The Manjaco are mystically very bad. Here on Jeta, they help each other. But on Pecixe, when a person returns from Europe, they kill them mystically.'

'How do they do that?'

'With the fetish,' he said. 'The *irã*.'

El Hadji told me that he had seen such a thing himself in Canchungo. He had been visiting some friends there, and had met an acquaintance who had returned from Europe to see his family. This man had been due to fly back on the following day, but he had died in the night. That's what always happens, he said, when someone comes back. People are jealous, they think they ought to have been given a larger present, and someone gets the fetishist to work for them. The fetishist communicates with the *irã*, and the spirit flies away from its place among the dead, into the orbit of the material world, and wreaks its vengeance on the souls of the living.

On Pecixe, it seemed, when someone returned from Europe, they stayed in Bissau and sent a secret message to their mothers on the island. But no one dared to go there in person. Everyone knew of the dangers of the *irā*. On Jeta, people did not forget them either – the edge of each village had a large, thatched shelter, where offerings of alcohol and animals were left for the spirits. If we stayed here, I thought, we might see something of that.

And then, in my darker moments, I thought of the spirits that were sent to kill people, time and time again, and remembered Bula and the gris-gris. Terror was never far away, neither physical nor mental and, that night, I listened to the gentle sobs of a woman from the porch. Her son had died that morning of malaria. He had only been one year old.

We spent five days on Jeta. We quickly became used to the somnolent atmosphere that clung to the island, as if it had always been dark. In the mornings, we would set off along paths sunken in sand, past stands of palms and snakes and lizards snatching into the undergrowth. Wood pigeons warbled incessantly amid the palm trees, and the thick woods made their calls resonate richly over the island. At dawn, scissor-tailed birds swooped in the gathering light but, with the intensifying of the heat, they, like everything else, crept away into their nests.

The paths linked the settlements, and slid down to the drab green waters of the sea.

At first, El Hadji thought that this was paradise.

'One time, in the future,' he said, 'we'll come here together with our wives. We'll take a hut each. We'll have a proper holiday. There'll be none of this travelling madness.'

'Madness?'

'This job,' El Hadji said, shaking his head. 'If I had known what was going to happen, I would have run a thousand kilometres when you arrived in Dakar.'

At one place there was a curving beach, golden and burning and taut like a bowstring. We found it on our second day.

'They don't maximise the use of the island,' said El Hadji, incredulous at the waste of so much wealth. 'They should bring tourists in. Build a resort down here. Buy a motorboat and bring them in from Bissau. Easy money!'

He looked greedily at the untapped possibilities of so much development.

'Why don't they profit from the island?' he asked the Pepel boys that evening, as they sat drinking rum on the porch.

But the Pepels were both drunk, and they could not think of a reason. Their eyes rolled wildly as they thought it over. Then they bought some more rum from the chief's daughter-in-law, who kept large jerrycans of it in the back of our apartment, and they sat near us, drinking and slipping into the oblivion of the night.

The storing of alcohol appeared to be the only use made of these rooms and their multifarious objects, which spent most of their time gathering dust. Luxuries, and their intimation of an altogether alien world, had no place on this island and were better for being kept under wraps. But nevertheless, the comparative opulence of our lodgings encouraged sluggishness in us, and El Hadji became increasingly unwilling to venture beyond the comfort of the sofa bed, which was infinitely more pleasurable than the cramped quarters he shared in Dakar and Ziguinchor. During the days he would lie there, as if he had been poleaxed, and in the evenings he would retire to sleep soon enough. Wealth bred comfort, which bred laziness. Surrounded as we were by triumphant and disingenuous images of prosperity, we lay inert for much of the time, like sprouting potatoes, loathsome and disregarded amid the pretty tiles.

The next day, the Pepels invited us to come and watch them weave. But, when we reached their loom, they were nowhere to be seen. So we returned and sat on the veranda for much of the afternoon.

El Hadji's initial liking for the island began to dissipate.

'Why did they tell us to come if they weren't planning to be there?' he asked. 'They're not to be trusted.'

I shrugged.

'*Marcher, marcher, marcher dans la brousse.* You walk, and all you find is the sea. You can't escape from here.' He scowled. 'It's a prison.'

'You haven't walked anywhere today,' I pointed out.

'What's the point?' he said. 'What are we going to see? I can tell you right now. Cashews, palms, silk-cottons and snakes. I'm scared of snakes. What are we going to do if one of us is bitten? This place is a death trap.'

He retreated inside and slept.

Nevertheless, that evening, I managed to persuade him to come with me for a swim. We went with the Pepel boys, crunching through the dried cashew leaves which smeared the island. All around, trees loomed above us like mountains. As we passed through the settled areas of the island, we met a few people – women balancing pots of water on their heads and men carrying machetes respectfully before them, like reliquaries, to fend off the dusk.

But then we neared the ocean, and the people fell away, along with the land.

The tide was coming in, and waves curled over onto the beach, lapping the sand and leaving it foaming. Everyone took off their shorts, T-shirts and sandals and prepared to run into the surf.

'Are there sharks?' I asked El Hadji, and he put my question to the Pepels.

'Oh no,' said the smaller one.

But we none of us swam very far out. El Hadji and the Pepels sprayed one another with water, while I dived amid the rollers. The light was fading, and the whole world was clutched by colourlessness, the trees and the beach and the sea and the sky.

I watched the others plunging into the waves and surfacing beneath a sheath of water, like otters.

Then El Hadji cried out.

I thought he was playing until he shouted at me, 'Toby! Go and get your pump.'

'Why?'

'I've been bitten by a snake!'

I ran to my bag. I had brought a suction pump with me from Europe which was capable of removing venom from bites if used at once. I found it and hurried back to El Hadji, my friend, who was staggering like a drunk from the sea.

He fell on the beach, stricken, clutching his ankle. The bite was red with blood and his foot was already swelling. I placed the pump over the bite and began to work. Every time I pumped, El Hadji contorted his face in agony. The Pepels looked on with disinterested concern.

'There aren't any sea snakes here,' one said. 'You've trodden on a crab.'

'It's a snake,' said El Hadji, his face white with determination.

I pumped for ten minutes in the knowledge that, if this had been a sea snake, my friend would soon be dead.

El Hadji's face was, by now, contorted by a perpetual grimace.

'It was a snake,' he said.

'It can't have been a snake,' I said. 'Your leg would be more swollen by now.'

'It was a crab,' said the larger Pepel.

El Hadji gave him a withering look.

Eventually we improvised a crutch, and El Hadji began to hobble up the beach. The Pepels walked in front and I brought up the rear. As we left, there was a silken rustle in the leaves near the path and a black tail shot off into the undergrowth.

'Cobra!' said the smaller Pepel, looking at me with a grin.

We walked on through the palm grove.

Five minutes later, El Hadji started in front of me and pointed out a golden glow, streaked with black, skulking in the shadows.

'Snake,' he said.

'It's not a snake,' said one of the Pepels.

'Yes it is,' said El Hadji angrily. 'I know what a snake looks like.'

He walked on. Every five minutes, he sank down to his knees.

'It was a snake that bit me, Toby,' he said, eventually.

'It can't have been a snake,' I reassured him, remembering our conversation in Guinea-Conakry: always give hope to a person, even when they may be dying.

In fact, I was convinced that he had trodden on a stingray and, when we returned to the village and explained the circumstances to the chief, he agreed. El Hadji doubled up in agony on the veranda, while I checked the treatment of stingray attacks in my health manual.

'Is that fish dangerous?' he asked.

'It hurts,' I said, 'but it won't kill you.'

I did not tell El Hadji that if he had trodden on the body rather than the tail, it was quite possible that he would die. Instead, I asked for some scalding water and we waited for it to be heated up. El Hadji began to murmur and his eyes glazed over. When I saw them roll and the ebony pupils became lost to the whites, I became scared.

'Quickly!' I urged the chief's daughter-in-law, Olga. 'As hot as you can make it.'

She carried in a basin, steaming with vapour, and placed it on the tiles. El Hadji eased his foot off the bed and put it in the water. Almost at once, his expression softened, and the pain vanished from his face and body, as if the two had been one.

'Really,' he said, looking at me, 'you've missed out on your vocation.'

'I should have been a doctor?'

'No,' he said. 'You should have been a murderer. Walking through the bush like that! What are you looking for except snakes and poisonous fish?'

We had intended to leave Jeta the next day. But because of El Hadji's injury we had to stay, since he could not walk to the port. News of his accident spread and, the following morning, we were visited by one of Jeta's emigrants, who had returned from Europe to supervise the construction of a forty-room house on the island.

Louis was a middle-aged man, with a round face, thick glasses and a flourishing paunch. He lived in France, where he ran a haulage firm. At first, we talked of Europe and Africa. In Europe, Louis pointed out, the main aim of a government was to be popular with the people, whereas in Africa, the main aim, all too often, was to be feared by the people. His conversation was sprinkled with perceptive comments such as this, and he had definite opinions on Europe, having lived there for twenty years.

After a time, El Hadji told his story about the stingray.

'Those things are very dangerous,' Louis said. 'We always feared them when I was a child.'

Together with the snakes, of course.

'There are too many snakes here,' said El Hadji.

'It's dangerous,' Louis agreed. 'Although of course,' he went on, removing his glasses and wiping them on his blood-red T-shirt, 'not all the snakes that you see are real snakes. The bad islanders here transform themselves into snakes, and then attack their victims.'

I listened with incredulity to this man, whose opinions and aspirations were largely European, as he talked of the transformation of people into animals. According to Louis, the islanders had learnt the ways of such devils. You could always tell when a victim of snakebite had in fact been killed by witchcraft, for the snake would appear at the funeral on the following day. So, when someone died of a snakebite, all the mourners went to the funeral with a gun, so that they could kill the snake. When the snake died, they transformed themselves back into their human form, and the person responsible for the witchcraft died.

'That happens?'

Louis nodded.

'I have seen it, too,' said El Hadji. 'In Diouparé, there was a man who saw a bird heading for a marriage ceremony, and said that it was a witch. He shot the bird, and a woman died in a neighbouring compound. She had a hole in her heart.'

In Koubia, too, I remembered Sédhiouba had told a tale about his uncle, who had been a soldier in the Guinea-Conakrian army near the border with Liberia. He had been posted with his superior, a man from the forest regions of Guinea-Conakry, to defend the border against the rebels. One night, Sédhiouba's uncle had been attacked by a vicious leopard and he had shot it dead. When the animal had died, it had transformed itself back into the body of his superior.

It was hard to believe that form could be so fluid, and minds so powerful, that what was visible and what existed could be completely separated. But it had been equally hard to believe in invisibility, so now I could only accept that there was a possibility that such things were true. Why did I not believe the stories people told me? El Hadji had once asked me the question, and my dyed-in-the-wool empiricism had answered him then. But now I had glimpsed how much more there might be to the world beyond the images that were brought before me.

'Toby,' said El Hadji, 'you don't believe in this, but it's true.'

It now seemed that everything really might be possible. And that was even more terrifying than the superficially delineated world that I had known before. There was a part of me that wanted to see the Manjaco fetishists at work, but another part just wanted to flee. I felt like the drunk stagecoach driver in *The Invisible Man* who has the misfortune to lodge Griffin in his boarding house. When Mr Hall tried to interview Griffin in his room, he was met, H.G. Wells wrote, with a waving of indecipherable shapes, a blow and a concussion.

There he stood on the dark little landing, wondering what it might be that he had seen.

We spent two more days on Jeta, waiting for the next pirogue back to Caió. After his experience with the stingray and the snakes, El Hadji never stirred from the room, except to go to the latrine and to knock out the spent tobacco from his pipe.

'My whole body hurts,' he would say, lying immobile on the bed.

'Come on,' I would say. 'You'll kill yourself with boredom.'

'I'm scared of this prison.'

And he would lie inert, amid the discarded booty from the West.

'I think it's malaria,' he said to me one evening.

'It can't be malaria,' I said.

'It's malaria,' he said, groaning.

'Well, when we get back to Ziguinchor, if you like, you could rest up with Djinaba and I'll go on with Omar.'

El Hadji sat bolt upright from the bed, moved by anger.

'Do what you want!' he shouted.

'If you're ill . . .'

'As you like it!'

'Don't shout like that!' I snapped. 'I'm only trying to help.'

I stormed off into the dust. When I came back twenty minutes later, El Hadji was smiling.

'There's nothing for it,' he said. 'We'll have to go down to the beach for a fight.'

'We can't,' I said.

'Why not?'

'You won't leave your bed.'

The truth was that three months of travelling, bad diet, illness and fear of the invisible world had drained us completely. We were both exhausted, and verbal sparring was all that we could manage.

While El Hadji waited for us to leave, I walked listlessly about the island. This tranquil and verdant place did not seem to be a home of evil, nor of devils. But, as I walked along the paths, I began to notice that there was a surprisingly large number of people with swellings in their legs. There was the chief, who had gone to Bissau. The morning after my argument with El Hadji, I met a boy who could barely move his leg, limping along a track with a crutch. And then, that same evening, I met a drunken Manjaco at a funeral ceremony.

I heard the drumming from our apartment, and wandered through the groves of papaya and palm trees until I came upon the ceremony in a neighbouring compound. The houses were set in a U-shape around the dusty yard where, in the shade of a silk-cotton tree, a group of women were dancing a slow, rolling rhythm in a circle, while some of their friends thumped out a tune on hollow calabashes. On the far side of the compound, a table suffered under the weight of bottles of rum and palm wine. The men watched the women dance from the shade of a veranda, passing a battered mug around.

Funeral ceremonies are the most important rites in the world of the *irã*. They celebrate the lives of the deceased, so that the dead person's spirit is placated and will do good for the living rather than partake in the ritual cursing of human lives. People can often save up for over a year to finance a funeral ceremony. I was also told that, when a Manjaco died of leprosy, it was forbidden to celebrate a wake until it became apparent that the disease had left the body and dispersed amid the earth in which it had been buried. At this point, the spirit of the deceased would begin to haunt their living relatives, making each of them ill in turn until they remembered that they had not honoured their departed. Then, even five or ten years later, the funeral celebration would be enacted, and the family's troubles would cease.

I had worried that I would not be welcomed to the ceremony, but as soon as people saw the rum and the tobacco leaves that I had brought, a stool was found for me as a guest of honour. The elder of the household proffered an old green bottle, streaming with hardened wax, and I poured my offering of rum inside it. His left eye was clouded with a cataract, a whitening malaise that gave his eyes a curious other-worldly appearance. He moved away and sat on a stool, swigging from the bottle with unabashed greed, before passing it to a younger man sitting near him. The younger man gulped at the burning liquid and wiped his mouth.

Then he turned to me.

'You're from France?' he said.

'No.'

'I was in France for fourteen years.'

His face was long and a scrawny moustache clung to his lips, which were pursed and dribbling. His wide eyes hovered uncertainly over my face as he drank.

'Come to my house,' he said, with an unsteady voice. 'We'll talk about France.'

I wanted to watch the funeral.

'We can come back here later,' he said.

He stood up, and stumbled backwards towards the dancers. When they saw that I was about to leave, two of them ran over to me, thrusting their hands in my face.

'*Tabaco, tabaco,*' they said.

I gave them a tobacco leaf each, which they pocketed carefully. One of them said that she wanted to marry me.

'I'm already married,' I lied.

But this did not matter in Jeta, where, among the Manjaco, men were allowed to have four wives.

'Take me to England,' she said.

'You won't like it there,' I said, 'you don't speak English.'

She laughed and simpered and sidled up to me in a way that suggested that this would not matter.

'Let's go,' I said to my drunken companion.

We walked along a maze of paths. As we left the village, we passed the fetish house, where goat heads and bottles had been left in homage to the spirits of the dead. They seemed lost as they sat in the dust, waiting to be taken away from this world of strangeness and confusion.

The man took me past a plantation of beans, and then we turned into his compound, where his wife and daughters were preparing the evening meal. He sat me down on a stool and swigged from my jerrycan of rum. Then he wiped his lips and swayed.

'My home,' he said, gesturing at the sky, the earth, the trees and the ramshackle huts. He made a grab at one of the younger girls and held her before him.

'My daughter,' he said.

I smiled in embarrassment.

Then he sat down on a stool and rolled up his trousers. I saw that both his legs were covered in festering sores.

'Medicines,' he said, his words swaying in the air. 'Have you brought any medicines?'

'Only rum and tobacco,' I said.

He burped and shrugged. I looked at his wounds, which were poisoned. He waved his hand resignedly in their direction.

'I've had them for three weeks now,' he said.

They had gone to the *irā*.

'You may not know that we are surrounded by spirits here,' he said.

The spirits needed to be propitiated. The world needed to receive gifts, in return for its goodness. The fetishist had told him that he needed to make an offering of several bottles of rum and a goat before the spirits would deign to listen to him. He had made the offering, and now he was waiting for the spirits to do their job and leave him in peace.

He waved his hand at the wounds again, which boiled like miniature volcanoes. The whole island, I realised, was full of these injuries. Poisonous wounds, scars of mystical fear which ate away at a person in the same way as fears of cancer or heart disease prey on people in other parts of the world. The Manjacos, I remembered El Hadji saying, were mystically bad.

When I returned to our apartment, I told El Hadji what I had seen, and he scoffed.

'Toby knows this, Toby knows that! I told you! The Manjaco are bad! Three hundred and sixty people from this tiny island are working in Europe, and why do you think that is? Because they are terrified of being killed by the fetishists when they come back to visit their family!'

'How do you know they don't just poison them?' I asked him.

'Ask my brother Omar about that!'

'What do you mean?'

But he said no more, and turned over to sleep.

On the following morning, we rose before dawn, and walked to the port. The sky was still black as we ghosted over the paths. We passed through a large village, and continued along a narrow track lined by cashew trees. Then, as the darkness began to pale, we saw a young woman stumbling towards us, followed by four older women who were supporting her on the way.

El Hadji stopped.

'Look at that woman,' he said. 'She'll give birth any moment now.'

As we neared her, she sat down on the path, and, to my shock, I saw a baby's head sticking from between her legs like an enormous tuber of cassava. The woman sat there, watching us in horror, as if we had been spirits come to whisk her away to another life. Perhaps she believed this white person to be a figment of her imagination. Then she began to scream. Her eyes circled into a trance and the four elder women shielded her with their wraps, looking at us as if we had been taboos.

'We must go on,' El Hadji murmured to me, sensing the compulsion I felt to remain, and taking me by the hand. So we had to turn our backs on the new burst of life and continue in the pasty half-light towards the port, where we sat on the jetty, waiting for the pirogue to leave. The dawn grew eerily upon the still waters of the inlet. The place gradually filled with women and their bundles, which they would take to sell at Canchungo.

'El Hadji,' I said, as we waited for the boatman to arrive. 'What does Omar know about the fetishists?'

'Ask him yourself!' he said.

So, when we reached Ziguinchor two days later, I mentioned the matter to Omar, who, as always, was delighted to help me. The

Manjaco were very dangerous. There was a fetishist in Dioupare who could get his fetish to kill people almost at once. A woman had once lost some rice from her field nearby, and had gone to the fetishist. She had said that she wanted whoever had stolen the rice to die. Five people from the same family had lost their lives within the next week. The fetish did not stop. It went from one person to the next until it was satisfied.

There had been a time, he told me, when he had developed poisoning in his leg. He had gone to the doctor, and tried every drug they could think of, but the swelling only worsened. Then his grandfather had taken him to see the fetishist at Balimé, who had asked for a litre of rum and palm wine before setting to work. She had drunk both beverages at a stroke, before applying her mouth to his leg and sucking hard.

'She sucked for five minutes,' he said, speaking with surprising coolness, 'and then I felt a sensation of excruciating pain, and saw her with three grains in her hand.'

The grains had been treated by the Manjaco fetishist. The fetishist had propitiated the *irā*, and had the grains blessed. Then they had been thrown at Omar, according to the wishes of his enemy. It was to be hoped that a person was protected against such invisible forces, Omar intimated, and was strong enough to withstand them. Otherwise, their unimaginable power could destroy them, weakening them to nothing. The strength of a person lay in their willingness to confront the invisible world, and in their ability to accept its truth. If the value of our lives was equated only to that which could be seen, it was difficult to say how much of our humanity would remain.

PART IV

'I am invisible, understand, simply because people refuse to see me'

In the dark two-room apartment that I shared with El Hadji's brother Ablai in Ziguinchor, my friend stretched out on a prayer mat and gazed up at the ceiling.

'Everyone thinks that Toby is having a good time,' he muttered, not for the first time. 'But he has only been trying to kill himself and his friend.'

'It's been difficult,' I said.

'I've hated it,' he said.

I sat in a cane chair behind the table where we usually ate together from our bowl. Just outside our front door, women from neighbouring homes went about their eternal business. Their proximity meant that, as always in that part of the world, privacy did not exist. Everything was done communally: people shared the cups from which they drank tea, those who had money helped out the members of their family who did not, and women gave birth on paths.

'Still,' I said, 'at least we have achieved our aim. We have found one gris-gris.'

'Even so, I've hated it,' El Hadji said, looking at me with a determined expression. I decided to ignore him for a moment, and watched the women as they worked outside. They swept out the dust and sprinkled the hardening earth with water, then they chopped the vegetables, sifted the rice and tended to the fire as diligently as if they had been caring for a child. Life had not come to a halt simply because I had, for a moment, become invisible. It poured on unceasingly, as powerful as that terrific waterfall which had once entranced El Hadji in Guinea-Conakry.

'Toby,' he said, reaching forward and touching my arm. 'I'm worn out.'

'I'm sorry.'

'My whole body hurts.'

El Hadji lay with a look of untold suffering on his face.

'We've been travelling like madmen,' he said.

'We've come a long way,' I agreed.

'Madmen,' he murmured. 'If someone comes up to me again and tells me to go to Guinea-Conakry, I'll tell them . . .'

'What will you tell them?'

El Hadji looked at me with a grin.

'*Merde! Merde* to Guinea-Conakry!'

He was of course delighted to be back among his family. We had returned from Kabakunda to get the cat skin, but only very briefly. Now he had the opportunity to talk things through with them. Travelling was interesting to begin with; he had liked meeting people from different civilisations and had hoped that this pastime would continue to be a passion for ever. But after a time, he had tired of the endless journeys and things had become difficult. Both El Hadji and I had stories to tell, but people never really wanted to hear the truth of what had happened – the hours of waiting, the endless days of boredom. They wanted only to hear a nice and sanitised history, which was in any case the version of events that memory always sought to present. So the stories were necessarily flawed and could not really be regarded as objective. They were merely reflections of experience, artistic impressions laced with honesty.

Most of his brothers crowded around. They soon knew our tales almost as well as we did, and could relate our experiences back to us with aplomb: cheated in Guinea-Conakry, ill in Koubia, a chance discovery in Guinea-Bissau, stung on Jeta, back with alacrity to the sanctuary of Ziguinchor. Yes, it was true that El Hadji had travelled a long way with this *tubab*, and it hadn't been easy; in fact it had been *difficile*, not the jaunt that had been envisaged at first. But El Hadji now had high hopes that the effort would prove to have been worthwhile.

Like most other young people in West Africa, he dreamt of escaping. Once I had given him a gift for his troubles, he would use the money to procure a visa and make his way to a part of Europe where he could work peacefully. Time and again, I told him that life there was not as easy as television made out, but, of course, El Hadji preferred to trust the images and his own imagination, instead of my chastening accounts.

Imaginary worlds beckoned at every turn, in El Hadji's future and in both our pasts. The events in the pick-up seemed so surreal that sometimes I wondered what I had really seen: an hallucination of my own making, or a reality so disturbing that the imagination seemed more appealing. But in my heart I knew what I had seen and, after all, it is often a challenge to credit the truth of what is past. It was, for instance, simply hopeless to try to imagine the comings and goings of civilisations across this part of the world, the Peul coming from the north, the Susu retreating from the hills and the Bijagós islanders embarking on slave raids on the coast to feed the European ships which bobbed up and down, without empathy, in the bays. Right at the start of this journey, I remembered, I had stood on the small island of Gorée, near Dakar, which was formerly the centre of the slave trade on this part of the West African coast. The sea had been heaving with white horses, and the froth had given the sweeping bay a white sheen. The tiled roofs of the town had glowed in the sunlight, and I had walked almost as slowly as time itself through the narrow streets lined with acacia trees, past the desolation of old municipal buildings, the fort and the slave prison. I had tried to picture Africans being sold by weight, or attempting to swim to safety on the mainland and being devoured by sharks, but all I had felt was that the still and quiet air here reminded me of the rural villages in France where I had spent my summer holidays as a child, stone-walled sanctuaries in which such gory things had not been easily apparent. And that thought had made me feel ill at ease, and I had turned my attentions elsewhere.

Really, given the enormities of such things, one small experience of invisibility was neither here nor there.

So I told Omar the story of what had happened in the pick-up.

'Then he gave back the 500-franc note to El Hadji,' I said, rehearsing an account that I would soon know all too well, 'and said – "No, just give me 200 francs."' Omar chuckled as he heard this new proof of the strength of African magic. 'Then we got to Bula, and he said – "Wait, you've forgotten your change!" '

Omar stretched out his hand, laughing, and slapped me on the shoulder.

'The old Marabout was very wise,' he said. 'You were right to have faith in him.'

Omar had been busy in our absence, talking with various Marabouts. In Balimé, he told us, he had made a contact with a man who demonstrated the gris-gris for invulnerability against knife attacks in front of you – he was a personal friend, and had agreed to make the charm for us. In Bolana, he had pressed my case with a cousin, Bouabacar, who had studied at a Maraboutic school in The Gambia. Bouabacar was going to make a gris-gris to protect against evil spirits, and that, too, would provide an insight into African magic.

'When we go to Bolana and Balimé,' said Omar, 'you will be amazed.'

But in the meantime, we spent three days recuperating in Ziguinchor before the last leg of our journey. My body felt unusually heavy, and I lay in the room, feeling its weight seeping into the mattress. The bad diet, the growing heat and the profusion of infected cuts that I had suffered since arriving were taking their toll. Even now, I had a poisoned sore on my foot. The skin was red around the cut, which bled with the thick and festering whiteness of the pus.

It was a distasteful sight, which I preferred to ignore, while I pumped myself full of antibiotics.

Illness was so endemic that you gradually forgot about it. Ablai suffered from a chronic cold during our stay. His eyes were dazed and his voice was thick with phlegm. On my last day, I began to feel myself coming down with the same symptoms. My head felt heavy and my sinuses were blocked. I wanted to rest. But then Omar came and knocked on the door of the apartment, and asked if I would accompany him to a funeral. The father of the driver of one of the family's buses had died in the morning, and now, in the late afternoon, it was time for the interment.

We walked up the main street near Ndiayekunda, then made a

couple of turnings and found ourselves in the shade of a mango tree, where several hundred people had gathered. Two large buses sat empty in the dust, waiting to carry the mourners to the graveyard. The implacable heat of the afternoon was just beginning to ebb. This heat had increased imperceptibly, from December, through January and February and now into March, so that the seasons had progressed equally imperceptibly: the piles of oranges that had first greeted me had been replaced by the yellows and reds of the cashews; the mangoes were swelling and, although most of them were still green, some of them had begun to jaundice, like the thick haze which hung in the sky and gave the world a yellow and sickly feel.

At a signal from the Imam, the mourners gathered together on the prayer mats and thought of the deceased. The old men were dressed in *boubous* and skullcaps, and clutched rosaries, while all of the women wore flowering robes and headscarfs. But the younger men were less formal, and sat in their jeans and pirated T-shirts, paying homage to the dead man. A griot rose and began to talk about the life of the man who had died.

Many of us knew him well, intoned the griot, and others not so well, but we are all here to pay respect. The natural thing for us to do would be to lament our loss, but this is not what he would have wanted. He has gone to a new place, and he would prefer for us to wish him well in his new life rather than to bemoan his passing. Those of us who owed him money should come forward and settle their debts with his family. Those who were owed money by him can make their claim, or not, according to their conscience.

The mourners hung their heads, and members of the family came round bearing red kola nuts for us to chew, so that we could immerse ourselves in their bitterness. Then we all stood in serried lines behind the battered Ford Transit van in which the body had been brought from the hospital, in front of the breeze-block wall which rose to the east, and murmured invocations as we faced Mecca.

At the graveyard, the shrouded body was tipped from the coffin into the earth and covered with branches. The branches were then cloaked with a smattering of dust. The body was not set very deep. A few scratches would have revealed it. But the mourners left hurriedly and in silence, returning to their compounds.

Soon, I thought, days would begin to pass, more dust would fall in a flurry from the air, and the body would start to sink until it was lost in oblivion. But then, as I walked away from the graveyard with Omar and his father, I remembered that people here had a different attitude towards the dead. El Hadji would frequently begin to tell the story of someone or other who was doing big things in Dakar or in Europe, and owned so many cars or houses and had so many wives or children. After having regaled me with this person's life history for five or ten minutes, he would tell me with a note of wistfulness that, unfortunately, they were dead.

Dead! Why did you tell me all of this, I would ask, if he is no longer alive?

El Hadji never gave a proper answer, but I realised that the dead were not really gone as far as he was concerned. The spirits of the ancestors still floated around the world, and the gifted could see them and the ways in which they helped and harmed the living. Death only presaged invisibility, after all, if you believed that life was the preserve of that which you could see. But for El Hadji, the dead were still in some sense alive, and past and present constituted a fluid timescale in which all acts were connected, good and bad, and neither guilt nor integrity could be forgotten.

In Bolana, El Hadji, Omar and I made our way to the home of their uncle. Oumi Ndiaye clapped her hands in delight when she saw us approaching, her tresses flowing as she ran towards us.

'Toby!' she exclaimed. *'Nanga def?'*

'Mangi fi.'

Then she said something that I did not understand.

'Dedet,' I guessed.

She collapsed into fits of giggles.

'She says that she's missed you,' Omar explained.

For much of the rest of the afternoon, I was abandoned by El Hadji, who had some serious flirting to do with a nurse at the hospital. My head felt heavier, and my nose began to be gripped by a cold. I sat and watched Maodo working on a new settee that he was making. He squatted in the courtyard and cut up some pieces of foam, preparing the measurements of the cloth that would cover the embryonic cushions.

'Who are you making them for?' I asked.

'The soldiers,' he said.

'How do you stick the cushions together?' I asked, and Oumi, who was listening, pointed to an old Vimto bottle on the floor which was filled with Superglue.

'Your sister's a pain,' I informed Maodo. 'She understands everything that I say. Her French is much better than my Wolof.'

Maodo smiled.

'*Dedet*,' said Oumi, shaking her finger at me and grinning. '*Wolof rek.*'

'Really,' Maodo agreed, 'she's a pain.'

As the afternoon wore on, I retired to the room in which I had slept before and lay on the bed. I felt slightly feverish, my whole body ached and, in the morning, my throat was sticky and sore. This was, I remembered, how my malaria had begun in Koubia, and I told El Hadji as much.

'You're a hypochondriac,' he said. 'All you've got is a cold.'

'My whole body hurts,' I said, mimicking him.

He left me to rest.

On my own, as I sweated, it was impossible not to suspect that one of the mosquitoes of this fever coast had penetrated the defences of my Lariam yet again. I sniffled and worried and felt once more how powerless I was here.

At lunchtime, El Hadji and Omar came to check on my progress.

'It's malaria,' I told them.

'It's not,' said El Hadji. 'It's just a cold.'

I looked doubtful.

'You don't know the colds we suffer from here,' El Hadji said. 'They're awful. You think it's malaria, but they go quite quickly.'

'Have they always been this bad?'

'No,' said Omar. 'We didn't use to have such bad colds in the past as we do now. And people weren't as ill then.'

Omar said that, when they had been growing up, none of those infectious diseases – malaria, diarrhoea and colds – had been as widespread or as damaging as they were now. It was only in the last twenty years or so that, while so many technologies had progressed with great speed, their lives had become so difficult.

I slept all afternoon and, towards evening, I began to feel better. The heaviness of my head cold was passing and my throat had ceased to sting. On this occasion, El Hadji had been right – it had just been a bad cold, but I had been on the edge of genuine panic.

The following morning, I accompanied El Hadji and Omar to see their cousin Bouabacar and talk to him about the charm that would protect me against evil spirits. Bouabacar lived with his mother, sisters, wife and young son in a small compound a little way from where we were staying. He was a very thin man, with a broad face, high cheekbones and an eternally eager expression. His speech was handicapped by a severe stutter, which interfered with even the most basic utterances.

I had met him briefly when we had been in Bolana before. Now he greeted me warmly.

'Toby!' he exclaimed with a broad smile, and we embraced. He was wearing the same blue trousers, white singlet and battered flip-flops that he always wore.

He invited El Hadji, Omar and me to sit in his room, where we were offered the chairs while he sat on the mattress. There was a clock on the wall and a picture of the former Khalif of the Tijanniya brotherhood, Abdul Asis Sy. In the corner of the room was a new stereo.

'One of Bouabacar's clients gave him that,' Omar whispered in my ear, 'after his gris-gris worked perfectly.'

'You have travelled a long way!' Bouabacar exclaimed with a broad smile. His teeth were gleaming white.

'We have suffered a great deal,' El Hadji told him, and he recounted some of his favourite stories. When he told Bouabacar the story of the pick-up truck, Bouabacar clicked his tongue in wonder at the wisdom of the Marabout in Kabakunda.

'There are very few like him,' he said.

El Hadji explained to Bouabacar that now I was seeking to experience as many examples of African magic as possible, and that we knew he could perform miracles where evil spirits were concerned.

'That's easy!' Bouabacar exclaimed in a rare burst of fluency.

All we needed was a red cockerel.

'Why do we need that?' I asked El Hadji.

'He'll bury it,' he said, nodding at his cousin.

'The cockerel is protected by a gris-gris,' Bouabacar explained. 'With that gris-gris . . .' His eyes twinkled. 'Anything is possible!'

It seemed that the cockerel would be buried for seven days in the earth, protected by a gris-gris which would be its substitute for food, water and oxygen. On re-emerging, the cockerel would be healthier than it had been when it had been buried. The gris-gris would be sanctified through its protection of the bird, and would be used to ward off evil spirits.

'You have to be protected,' Bouabacar asserted, looking at me. 'These days, anything is possible.'

His eyes darkened.

'The rebels,' he explained.

'They're very bad,' I agreed.

A haze drew over his eyes as he thought about it.

'I will go to Dioupare tomorrow.'

In Dioupare, Bouabacar told us, he would be able to locate a red cockerel. We rose, all smiles, and Bouabacar led us outside to a mango tree, where young children were hurling stones into the highest branches of the tree in an attempt to dislodge those fruits that had begun to ripen. The stones hurtled back down to the ground, falling about us like shrivelled meteors.

Since Bouabacar was a relative of El Hadji and Omar, I decided to ask him a little more about how he worked.

'This is a secret from the Qu'ran, isn't it?' I asked.

'Yes.'

'But the red cockerel,' I said, 'that can't be in the Qu'ran.'

'That's a secret,' he said.

I looked disappointed.

'There are ninety-nine known names for God in the Qu'ran,' Bouabacar said, then. 'But there is a hundredth name, which is a secret. He who knows that name has many powers.'

This sounded like a very similar code to the Cabbala of Judaism, whose most mystical practitioners in the Middle Ages also wrote out supposedly magical passages from their holy books. The secrets of God were hidden in His word, Bouabacar explained, looking at me with the sincerity of genuine faith, so that all the powers of the world could be held by those who had the fortune to access them.

So we waited for the whole of the next day while Bouabacar walked to Diouparé to get the cockerel. I had wanted to accompany him, but El Hadji talked me out of it.

'That cold can come back at any time,' he told me.

So we waited in the compound as the morning progressed, and boys whipped their donkeys down to the port to collect goods that had just been brought in. Pirogues lay overturned like strands of dismembered jungle on the beach. Fishermen pegged out their nets at the port side so that they could dry in the sun, which intensified with every minute so that, in the afternoon, after the empty dishes had been cleared away and the women had put them to soak, no one did anything except lie beneath mango trees and brew tea.

Once the worst of the heat had subsided, we all sat outside on the veranda, watching the sky beginning to blush as the sun fell away. One of the cousins of El Hadji and Omar came to visit, nursing her baby and suckling her unselfconsciously as we sat and talked. She put a cassette of *m'balax* into the stereo, and rose, before swinging gracefully around the compound's cracked central area, in time to the music. After a minute, she decided that the baby was an encumbrance and passed him to me. I cradled him and cooed in his ear, and he started to cry, perhaps at the tuneless sounds reverberating in his eardrum, perhaps at the colour of my skin.

El Hadji took the child from me and began to play expertly with him.

He held him by the armpits and swung him in time to the aggressive syncopated rhythms of the music, and then lay on his back and allowed the baby to kneel on his chest, goggling as he stared deep into my friend's eyes.

'You're a born father,' I told him.

'I like children,' he acknowledged. 'I'd like to have as many as possible.'

'That will be hard work for Djinaba.'

El Hadji smiled.

'If things go well for me,' he said, 'I will have several wives. Like my father.'

'*Insh'allah.*'

'If I stay five years in Europe, and save some money...'

El Hadji's eyes gleamed with a faraway look as he talked about his dream. Arriving in Paris, Madrid, London or Rome, he would meet a girl. She might be rich. He would tell her that he wanted to go out with her. But he had a family back in Senegal – a wife and children. He was in Europe for them. He could only go out with her if she would help him. Find him work, good work, well-paid work, perhaps he could send back four or five thousand pounds a year. Save up. Buy some bush taxis...

He looked at me sharply.

'Perhaps I'd better not mention Djinaba,' he said.

'Perhaps not.'

'Things are different over there,' he said.

'Very different.'

He sighed and thought of Europe. This adventure seemed to be increasingly imminent to him. And naturally, I wanted to help my friend. He had been through a lot. And the immoral differences in wealth between my home and his – simple accidents of birth – would make me uneasy for ever if I did not do something for him. But I was not sure if going to Europe was his best plan. Perhaps he ought to invest the money that I was giving him in Africa.

'What can I do with it here?' he said. 'There is nothing.'

'Things are not easy in Europe. It's not like television. You will not have any papers. Unless you are very lucky, people will take advantage of you.'

'I will fight,' he said. 'I will succeed.'

'It will be difficult.'

'Not as difficult as Guinea-Conakry.'

El Hadji had always dreamt of going to Europe, and now that journey seemed within touching distance. He was not alone. The overwhelming majority of the young people I met dreamt of escaping to Europe and North America, unaware that, if they did reach those distant places, they would be as likely to become enslaved by the unscrupulous as to make their fortunes. And meanwhile, in those rich parts of the world, barricades were raised and differences were accentuated until it was not entirely clear whether the walls were raised higher to keep the immigrants out, or whether they were there to prevent us from seeing what we and others like us had done to the world.

'Toby,' El Hadji said, looking at me earnestly from beneath the baby, 'if I go to Europe, I will work hard. You'll see. I'll save every month and come back here a different person.'

Night was approaching and, along with it, the evening prayer. El Hadji performed his ablutions near the tubs in which washing had been put to soak, and then he went to pray. His square, imposing figure rose and fell like a clockwork toy in the fading light. Then, the prayers finished, he unwound.

Once darkness had fallen, we walked to Bouabacar's compound and discovered that he had found the cockerel that he had been looking for. He would bury it at eight o'clock the following morning, in our presence.

By now I was experienced in such matters, and the prospect of burying a cockerel in the earth and keeping it starving, thirsty and deprived of oxygen for one week did not seem abominably cruel to me. Had I been in Europe, this would have seemed complete madness. But I now had faith that this would work. Omar told me that he had seen it done five times in front of his eyes. The gris-gris was also used for holy men who wanted to immerse themselves with God for a week, and likewise took no food or drink, protected by this simple prayer. Maodo's father, who had saved Omar's life when he had been bitten by the snake, was said to do this from time to time. I was no longer scared, or sceptical, as I went to sleep that night. In the morning, I believed, the beginnings of a miracle would be set in place.

El Hadji and I woke early and were at Bouabacar's compound well before the appointed time. The greyness of early mornings in Africa was already being dispelled by the orb of the sun, low and orange and flaring. Many cockerels were crowing, but the bird which Bouabacar had procured was mute and tied with a string to one of the walls of the house.

Bouabacar was washing his face near the dusty road when he saw us approach.

'Toby!' he said in greeting.

'Bouabacar.'

'Now we are ready.'

The red bird was adorned with a vermilion crown. Bouabacar's wife untied it and picked it up, ignoring its squawks and claws, and brought it over to her husband, who handed it to El Hadji. El Hadji held the cockerel while Bouabacar wrapped a small gris-gris around its neck and tied it securely with some string.

'The gris-gris protects it,' I said.

'*Insh'allah*,' Bouabacar replied.

The bird began to shake in fear as El Hadji moved towards the corner of the veranda, in which Bouabacar had dug a hole that was almost a metre deep. Once the bird had been placed within the hole, Bouabacar covered the opening with cardboard, on top of which he scraped great mounds of dust.

'It's a long way down,' I said to Bouabacar.

'*Allahu akbar*,' he said.

Even though I now had faith in these processes, I still devised some sort of test. I could not spend the next week surveying this hole to check that the cockerel was not surreptitiously removed, and so, as we were leaving the site, I pretended to have dropped something, bent down and made a knuckle mark in the earth. If anyone removed the bird, they would have to disturb the mark.

'You must come back in seven days,' Bouabacar said, smiling. 'If we are lucky . . .'

This time he did not finish the sentence. We all knew that if we were lucky, and the miracle took place, the earth would be undisturbed and the buried cockerel would, against all odds, have survived the cruelty that it had been forced to endure.

There were seven days left until we could move on to Balimé. El Hadji soon caught the cold from which I was recovering, and lay on his prayer mat in the compound for much of the time.

It took him two days to get better. I still felt as though I should explore the town. But each time that I suggested some exercise, El Hadji blanched.

'*Tu veux me tuer,*' he said once. 'You want to kill me.'

'Don't be silly.'

'You've made me catch malaria and be bitten by the fish. Now you've given me your cold.'

'I'm sorry. I just want to get out a little.'

'What are you going to do?' he asked.

'Just go for a walk.'

'Where to?'

I shrugged, and he extended himself with even more finality on the prayer mat.

'Now you know what there is out there,' he said. 'You know it as well as I do. Haven't you seen enough?'

This was his perennial refrain and, during his illness, I gave in. We would lie together on the mat, reminiscing about the events that had brought us together. Sometimes we argued, and then El Hadji would raise himself up on his elbow and look at me with a twinkle in his eyes.

'If you were going to stay here any longer,' he said once, 'it's certain that we would end up having a huge fight.'

Then I rose and left him to grumble, going outside to the veranda, where Omar was brewing tea and poking the herbs with a twig.

'El Hadji can be difficult,' I said to him, and Omar chuckled.

'You should have known him when he was a kid,' he said.

But we were disturbed by the miniature green volcano of herbs and water which now erupted, spending itself and sticking to the blue enamel of the teapot and to the wood burner. Omar lifted the pot from the coals with difficulty, balancing the handles between two twigs. Then he started to pick off the clods of moist tea, wiping them onto the floor.

'El Hadji,' he said, chuckling to himself.

Once the pot was clean, he replaced it on the coals and began to pay more attention to the tea. While I watched him, I thought of the cockerel. Perhaps, I thought, fleetingly, birds could survive this sort of thing naturally. After all, they did not eat very much. But then I considered the heat, the lack of air, water and food, and decided that such a thing was impossible. I tried to imagine the conditions that the bird was experiencing and realised that, if they did not kill it, hopelessness normally would. It did not know that it would be retrieved, nor that it was being kept alive by faith.

But I had no doubt that the bird would be living when we dug it up.

'Just the gris-gris,' I said to Omar now.

'What gris-gris?'

'The cockerel,' I said. 'The gris-gris is the only thing that keeps it alive?'

'Insh'allah,' he said, pouring the tea, and watching the bubbles as carefully as if they themselves had been magical.

On the third day after burying the gris-gris, El Hadji began to recover from his cold. But as soon as he improved, Omar came down with the same illness. We transferred to Omar the medicines that we ourselves had been using, and began to look after him. But he wouldn't have it.

'You've only got a little while left here,' he said to me. 'Go out into the town.'

So El Hadji accompanied me on morning and afternoon walks. We would go listlessly through the streets of Bolana, nodding at acquaintances, stopping for short conversations, and then heaving our weight off through the heat. Sometimes we stopped at Bouabacar's compound, and Bouabacar would take me to look at the place where the cockerel had been buried. The sand showed no signs of having been touched, and the knuckle mark was still there.

Bouabacar would look at me with a broad smile.

Invariably, on these walks, El Hadji would end by leading me to the house of his cousin, Astu Fall, a tall and elegant woman with a sharp face and an effervescent sense of humour who always welcomed us to her compound. Astu Fall spent her day organising the household, shopping in the market, cooking lunch, washing up, watching television, washing clothes, cooking dinner, washing up and retiring to her bedroom.

Toby Fall, she called me – whenever her husband, Massalia, was out.

Massalia was the headmaster of one of Bolana's three primary schools. He was a broad, squat man, with a gentle face and much historical knowledge. When I had first met him, more than two months before, I had told him about my project, and he had been enthusiastic.

'It's about time that someone came over from Europe to look into that,' he had said.

So he had been especially pleased to hear the story from the pick-up truck. 'Although,' he had added, 'you haven't really seen anything. There are people around here who can perform miracles that are even more remarkable than that.'

We were often invited to eat with him, together with other teachers from the primary school. They did their best with the students, who came from the surrounding bush to Bolana for fear of the growing threat posed by the rebels. In the previous few days, they had held up three buses on the main road and ambushed a village only forty minutes' walk away. Women were raped and livestock stolen. Recently they had even attacked Bolana itself. In the months following my visit, the situation became even more severe, and the frontier between Senegal and Guinea-Bissau – where the rebels were alleged to be hiding – was closed. Sometimes, we heard the army planes growling in the sky, looking in vain for the rebels so that they could swoop like mechanical vultures amid the bush.

'Do you want to know why I am worried about going for walks?' El Hadji asked me, one afternoon.

'Yes.'

'You don't know what the rebels are like,' he said. 'If they see you, that will be the end. And what will I tell the British Embassy?'

'What do you mean?'

'They will say that I did not look after you. You were my friend, and I allowed you to be killed.'

'Don't be ridiculous.'

'Toby!' El Hadji would look at me, full of anger. 'I know the rebels.' But he never said any more than that.

Secretly, I shared these fears. Every day, there were further stories of attacks in the nearby bush. So, now that the dry season was progressing and the heat of each day was more insufferable than the one preceding it, we spent the afternoons with Massalia, listening to music under the yellow flowers of the acacia tree outside his house.

Massalia was very proud of his music collection. His tastes ranged from *m'balax* to jazz to kora music, from Elton John to Celine Dion. Once the afternoon had set in and there was no hope of activity, he would lie on the prayer mat, playing with his baby son, who was swathed in gris-gris, and toying with the tapes that lay discarded beside him. Elton John, he told me, had a wonderful voice, and Celine Dion's emotional range could not be matched. When pressed, however, he agreed that his favourite sounds were the harmonies of the kora.

The kora is the West African harp, originating in a large and bulbous gourd and then rising in a straight wooden stem, along which twenty-one strings are finely strung, capable of producing music of seamless beauty. There is something so natural about the transparent sounds of kora music that it often seems as though the music could wash over you for ever. This is the classical music of West Africa. It was with the kora that griots told the tales of the heroism of their leaders, in which legend and magic and history and musical virtuosity were intertwined. And so, in the epic of Sunjata Keita,* founder of the Mali empire, it

* See Historical Notes, p. 275.

was of course sorcery that was the principal weapon in the war between Sunjata, a Mandinga leader, and Sumanguru Kante,* who was Susu, as the two men fought each other with mysterious and unknowable arts, until Sunjata finally defeated Sumanguru.

Usually, the intense heat of the afternoons forced Massalia, El Hadji and me into silence, and we would sit watching the tea boil and feeling the percussion of our hearts. But one afternoon, after listening to some kora music, we discussed the Mali empire.

'I once listened to a recording of griots singing the epic of Sunjata Keita,' Massalia told me. 'When you listened to that music, you felt as if history was happening to you.'

He paused.

'Of course, it was the sorcerers who won the empire for Sunjata,' he said.

'We are preparing a miracle just now,' I said. 'We have to wait for seven days.'

'The cockerel!' Massalia's eyes lit up. 'When will it be ready?'

'Saturday.'

That was a great miracle, he said, well worth the wait we were enduring. But, even though there were still powerful people, no one was as capable as the sorcerers of old. In those times, he said, people had extraordinary mystical powers. If you offended a person, they turned you into a tree or a stone just as they wished. Only if you yourself had significant powers would you have been protected.

'Are there no people who still have those powers?'

'There are some,' he said. 'But they keep themselves to themselves.'

'There's the Kankoran,' said El Hadji.

'Who is that?'

'The Kankoran!' Astu Fall, who was listening to us, huddled over in mock terror. 'Watch out – the Kankoran is coming!'

The Kankoran accompanied boys to the circumcision ritual. Dressed in red leaves, wielding knives and uttering strange spells, the Kankoran would ward off devils as they made their journey. Sometimes, said Massalia, he will vanish from one place and appear in another, or he

* See Historical Notes, p. 275.

will shoot out of a well, or appear on several roofs all at once. Sometimes he will seem to be many people, sometimes an ordinary person.

'You may see him this weekend,' said Massalia. 'There is a circumcision ritual on Saturday.'

It was already Thursday, I realised. We had been waiting for five days. On Saturday, too, the gris-gris would be ready.

'Does the Kankoran use gris-gris?' I asked.

'Yes,' Massalia agreed. 'Although the Kankoran has nothing to do with Islam.'

'It's a Mandinga thing,' El Hadji said.

'The gris-gris just enhance their powers,' said Massalia. 'Some people are born with so many powers that they don't even need gris-gris. Gris-gris and knowledge of the Qu'ran only develop their strengths for them.'

'What I don't understand,' I said now to Massalia, 'is why the first Europeans to come here never took such things seriously.'

'They were always prejudiced against us.'

It was often said to me that Europeans had always been prejudiced against Africans and against African beliefs. While in West Africa, I attributed the incapacity of early European visitors to deal with African magic to the different belief systems. But later I remembered that, at the time of the first European contact with West Africa and for at least two centuries afterwards, Europe had been just as much a hotbed of magic as Africa. This was the era of the witch hunts, a time when people were executed for being in communion with the devil. So the prejudice of Europeans against African magic cannot have been because they thought such things were impossible. It must have been due to a baser prejudice than that: the belief that African magicians were not sophisticated and intelligent enough to rival their European counterparts.

'That's one of the greatest evils in history,' Massalia said to me that afternoon, as we awaited the dusk. 'Racism.'

'But it will be impossible to eradicate,' said El Hadji. 'People are too used to fighting and enslaving each other.'

'A great wrong has been done to us,' said Massalia. 'We need money now, so that we can begin to rebuild our lives. But all people do is talk.'

Now that I had spent many months living with people in Senegal, Guinea-Conakry and Guinea-Bissau, I saw no difference between myself and the people around me. I sat happily together with El Hadji's brothers in Ziguinchor – my friends. We were all the same for, as they said to me, we all of us had red blood in our veins. Racism, some people said, was a natural human characteristic. And yet, when Marco Polo* referred to the Africans living on Zanzibar in the thirteenth century, racism and the sense of the white man's superiority were largely absent from his account. Although he wrote that the people there were very ugly, his main sociological concern – as in all of his writings – was religion: the Zanzibaris were neither Christians nor Muslims, but idolaters.

While there were black slaves in Europe from the decline of the Roman empire onwards, there was also a substantial trade in white Christians captured by the Moors along the North African coast. It was only with the discovery of the Americas and the commercialisation of the Atlantic slave trade at the beginning of the sixteenth century, and the dwindling of the trade in Christians in North Africa, that slavery became essentially a racial issue. Many subsequent factors helped in developing the Europeans' sense of innate superiority, such as the industrial and intellectual revolutions, but these themselves depended on the wealth forged in the Americas, which could not have been created had it not been for the labour of African slaves and the trade in human beings. The simple fact, wrote the brilliant Guyanese historian, Walter Rodney, before his assassination, is that no people can enslave another for centuries without coming out with a notion of superiority, and when colour and other physical traits were quite different it was inevitable that the prejudice should take a racist form.

'The white men who came here to buy our ancestors did not even look at us,' said Massalia, in the gloaming. 'They just saw us as commodities.'

* See Historical Notes, p. 273.

The light continued to ebb, mingling with the rising dust and the growing obscurity of the world beyond the acacia tree.

'But this is not Toby's fault,' El Hadji said at length. 'Toby is not a slaver, and El Hadji is not enslaved. That is why it is better to forget.'

It was almost dusk. The evening prayer heralded a sudden stilling in the town, as if everyone needed a hiatus in their lives before being able to continue. After El Hadji and Massalia had done their duty by Mecca, we settled down to dinner and television. Astu Fall brought a dish of rice and fish, laced with palm oil and lemons, and we squatted around the bowl and stared entranced at the screen, at the humourless newsreader and the endless stream of words that issued, apparently disconnected, from his mouth: a web of noise and image that allowed all conscious thought to evaporate from our minds. This activity was the perfect tool for oblivion. The day had been long and hot, and this was such a powerful mechanism for forgetting that for the first time I wondered whether technology shaped society, or only responded to its needs.

The presidential campaign, the newsreader said, was over. The *Parti Socialiste*, which had been in power for forty years, had for the first time been beaten; and the opposition coalition, led by the *Parti Démocratique Sénégalaise*, whose principal policy seemed to me to be that they were not the government, now issued an endless stream of statements about jobs, education, health, the young, and their growing anger and sense of disenfranchisement.

'You will see, Toby,' El Hadji said loudly, as he listened to the broadcast. 'Things will change in Senegal now. We will be a big country.'

We have got to work for the young, said the president elect, Abdoulaye Wade,* and somehow create a world in which they can genuinely feel optimistic.

Massalia smiled and looked cynical.

'They'll see,' he murmured into my ear. 'Give them two years, and people will begin to realise that nothing has changed.'

* See Historical Notes, p. 271.

243

Both he and Omar were supporters of the *Parti Socialiste*, but they had taken their defeat well. People had talked of civil war if the opposition did not win. Many had thought that the *Parti Socialiste* would try to rig the result. But everything had passed off peacefully, and the outcome was accepted by everyone.

'The best thing,' Omar said to me later, 'is that democracy has won.'

After the news was over, we returned to the compound to see how Omar was feeling. During our enforced wait in Bolana, he had been hoping to go to Dioupare to work on the family's mango plantations. But his illness had rendered him immobile. Nevertheless, that evening, when we returned, he was up and about on the veranda for the first time in two days.

'It's a bad illness,' he said to us now. 'But I'm beating it.'

The evening was surprisingly cold. A breeze blew in from the wide creek beyond the port, and chilled us as we sat watching the darkness. As yet there was no moon, and shadows glided effortlessly along the nearby track, almost unseen, parodies of the people whose presence they betrayed.

'It's on nights like these,' said El Hadji, 'that I worry about the rebels.'

Twenty minutes later, a tank jolted along the street, flaring its headlights at the darkness.

'What are they looking for?' I asked El Hadji.

'Rebels,' he said.

'Here? I thought they were out in the bush.'

'They've got their spies here too,' said El Hadji.

'Why didn't you tell me that before?'

'You don't listen.'

Omar chuckled as he heard us arguing.

'You two are terrible,' he said.

'You don't listen,' El Hadji went on, ignoring his elder brother. 'You've got a death wish. You don't take the rebels seriously, but you don't know anything. Ask Omar about them, if you want.'

Omar placed the blue teapot down on the coals, and raised himself up.

'The rebels,' he murmured. He chuckled again, without humour, and there was a deep and unshakeable sadness in that sound.

I asked what had happened.

'You see,' Omar said, as a preamble, 'after those events in Diouparé, I have given thanks to God. Every day that I am alive is only thanks to God.'

That was then he had learnt the true value of gris-gris. Several years ago, he had obtained one almost by chance, taking a bush taxi from Dakar to Ziguinchor. An old man had not had all the money for his fare, and had been on the point of being thrown out, so Omar had paid the difference. When they had reached Ziguinchor, the elder had told Omar to visit his village, when he would be given something important. He had gone a year later, and been presented with a gris-gris, which the old man had said would protect Omar from all danger.

'Shortly afterwards,' said Omar, 'I noticed a strange pattern. I would be bicycling along the road, and people would tell me that, almost as soon as I had left a place, the rebels had attacked. But they always missed me.'

He had kept the gris-gris safe.

'Then I lent it to a friend who was in the army. He was based in the Casamance. One night, the rebels attacked his base and everyone was killed except for him. He did not want to return the gris-gris,' said Omar, 'but eventually he accepted that it was not his. I kept it safe.'

Omar paused, and we all felt the sharp sensation of the wind on our skins.

'About eighteen months ago,' he went on, speaking quietly, 'the rebels attacked Diouparé. I was sleeping with my wife when I heard them come, and I helped her out to hide in the mango plantation before creeping back to the house. The rebels were everywhere. The noise of gunfire echoed viciously through the village, and I heard the sounds of their voices. They were near. Then they burst into my parents' house and I heard bullets rattling against the back wall. If I had had a gun I would have killed them. But I did not have any weapon with me.'

'Omar,' said El Hadji, 'was protected by a miracle.'

245

'I put my gris-gris on,' Omar said quietly. 'I heard them shooting in the house, and I went to confront them. They saw me, and were less than five metres away. They raised their Kalashnikovs and fired, and I ran away. I heard the guns fire, but none of the bullets touched me. I climbed a tree and looked at the rebels, who were still very near. "Where is he?" I heard one of them ask.'

But they had not been able to see him, and had assumed that he was dead, for no one could have survived that.

Omar smiled.

'No one could have survived,' he said, 'unless they had been protected by magic. My father was killed instantly. My mother died a week later.'

There was a long pause after he had finished talking. The far east was lightened by the waning moon, which skulked below the skyline like an invisible star. The wind came in gusts, unsure whether or not to allow itself to die.

'I did not want to tell you that,' El Hadji said now, softly. 'Not when you arrived.'

Omar coughed, and I patted him on the shoulder.

'You don't know these rebels,' El Hadji said again bitterly. 'I have tried to tell you, but it's impossible. Toby is headstrong.'

That night, I found it difficult to sleep. At about three in the morning, the door blew open several times. On each occasion, El Hadji went outside to see what was there, but came back and reported nothing. Nevertheless, in the morning he said that he had been terrified of the rebels.

'I thought that they had tracked you down,' he said, 'and were coming to get you. So I crouched behind the door, ready to punch one of them in the face.'

We rested on the next day, waiting for Saturday and the ceremony with the cockerel. In the evening we went to see Bouabacar, and he told us to be ready at eight o'clock in the morning.

All that night, the compounds of the boys who were to be circumcised kept up dances and violent rhythms on percussion sticks. The sounds were vivid, loud and bore a hint of fear, a sense that something would come and split the music asunder. Even when I slept, the sticks cracked in my dreams.

El Hadji and I rose early, and headed for Bouabacar's household. Already, the dancers had gathered in the compounds of those who were to be circumcised. They huddled in a circle and stamped their feet and raised dust which rose with their voices as they cried out to the Kankoran for the safety of the boys' rite of passage.

We walked through the town, and came across four women running towards us waving branches of an acacia tree and looking behind them.

'The Kankoran!' they cried. 'The Kankoran!'

We turned a corner of a street, and El Hadji cried out: 'There he is!'

A tall man loomed out of the morning, wreathed in red leaves that flowed like streamers in the air. He was about fifty metres away, feinting at compounds with his machete as he passed them. In front of them, a man ran with a *tama*, drumming violently and shattering the morning peace.

The Kankoran was shouting.

'What does he say?' I asked El Hadji.

'Kill,' he said. 'Kill.'

He was fighting the devils. A group of women watched him and started an impromptu dance around their compound.

'The Kankoran! The Kankoran!'

We reached Bouabacar's compound, where the Marabout was waiting for us.

'Everyone is very excited,' I said.

'The Kankoran!'

He beamed.

'Come on,' he said.

And we followed him to the place where he had buried the cockerel a week before. We had not seen the bird in all that time, and there was no apparent reason why we should not simply have uncovered a heap of bones. But we all had faith that the unseen creature would still be there when we set to work. Bending down quickly to have a look, I saw that the knuckle mark had not been disturbed.

Bouabacar knelt down and scooped away the sand. The earth had hardened, and he dug at some of it with a knife. Then he removed the cardboard, delved into the hole and came up with the bird, which was still wearing the gris-gris. The cockerel squawked and fluttered its wings, and cried out. It showed no signs of having been weakened by its ordeal.

'The bird can only survive for seven days,' Bouabacar explained, 'because God said that the week was seven days long and the seventh was for rest.'

The whole affair took less than two minutes. There was no ostentation, no gasp of astonishment, no shock from any of those present. This was, I realised, because we all of us had known that the bird would be alive. Miracles seemed everyday to me now, just as they did to everyone I had talked to.

It was possible to suppose that the cockerel would have survived anyway. But I believed Bouabacar's explanation – and when someone does inexplicable things before your eyes and you trust their integrity, it is natural to credit their explanations.

'Let's have some breakfast,' said El Hadji.

He sent a young boy to buy bread and butter. Then we sat with him and Bouabacar, eating the food and drinking sweet milky coffee.

'Now do you believe it?' asked El Hadji.

'Yes.'

Bouabacar smiled. 'You have seen a miracle of God.'

He looked very happy.

'Now we can look for the Kankoran,' said El Hadji.

Bouabacar accompanied us to the edge of his compound and saw us off. The cockerel had been tied up again, next to the washing area. From the way the children were eyeing it, I sensed that it was not long for this world.

'I am very happy,' he said.

'So am I.'

He insisted on shaking me with his left hand, which meant that, at some future point, I would return. From the town, we heard the shrieks and the drumming that accompanied the progress of the Kankoran.

Then there came a roar, and a gasp of astonishment.

El Hadji smiled at me.

'Come on,' he said.

And we made for the magic.

In Balimé, we stayed with Cheikh and Fatu, as we had done during our previous visit. Their life seemed to have progressed happily in the intervening time – that is to say, without incident. Everyone in the household was slightly more corpulent than before, for this was the season of plenty, a time to ensure a goodly supply of body fat for the hard times at the end of the rainy season. The baby in particular was larger. He had swollen so that his face had almost disappeared amid folds of flab and his arms seemed like giant puffballs.

In this contented home, the same rituals were played out as before.

'Toby, you must eat,' Fatu said, as we sat down to our first meal.

But I was not overly hungry, and I put my spoon down before I had devoured every last morsel of food. She looked at me with an expression of disgust.

'What's the matter?'

'I'm full.'

'Eat!' she commanded.

'*Doi na doi na. Fes na fes na*,' I said, having learnt the Wolof words which were most important to me: I was full.

'Full?'

'*Bibi fes na torop!*'

'Omar! Tell your friend to eat.'

As so often, Omar laughed.

But Omar did not have much to be happy about. Although he was recovering from the cold, he now had an agonising toothache which rendered him immobile in the afternoon. He had also developed a festering sore on his leg.

'*C'est difficile*,' said El Hadji.

Nevertheless, in spite of his illnesses, Omar tried to make arrangements. As he had told me in Ziguinchor, he had organised things here with a friend of his who possessed the secret for the gris-gris against knife attacks, and demonstrated it before your eyes. On our first evening in Balimé, Omar went to look for the man, and returned with the news that the gris-gris would be ready in two days.

'He would have had it ready before,' he said. 'But someone else came to beg it from him, and he did not have the heart to refuse.'

El Hadji was upset. Time was progressing rapidly, and I was supposed to be leaving Dakar in five days. If the charm was not ready for two more days, we would be cutting things very fine to make it back for my flight.

'Tell him that he has to hurry,' he said.

But Omar could not really understand our worries.

'This man is my friend,' he told me. 'He will not let us down.'

So that night we ate a meal of sweet peanut butter pudding, enriched with juice from baobab fruit, and slept in a spare room in the house of one of Omar's friends.

In the morning we rose and washed and went to eat a breakfast of gruel and yoghurt, before lying beneath the mango trees and looking up into their crowns. But Omar was ill, and El Hadji was decidedly unwilling to move. Although I went for one walk through Balimé in the morning, along the dancing heat of the eastward road, which dived through a glade and stretched like an arrow into the palm trees, I soon tired of this senseless wander into nowhere. So I retired to lie with them in the shade and dream of everything that we had seen.

After lunch, Omar switched on his radio and listened to the news in French. The grating crackle of the noise emanating from the frequency soon cast its interference over the village. El Hadji seemed to find this tiresome, and he took the radio from his brother and twiddled with the knob. He passed through a succession of frequencies, one of which, I heard, was the BBC World Service. El Hadji tried to find a programme that interested him, but without success.

It was, quite literally, a stunning afternoon. The heat poured out of the sky, and drenched us in sloth. The sibilance of the radio hissed like a snake.

Before long I stretched out my hand and took it, playing around with the frequency until I had found the World Service again. The announcer was telling listeners all around the world that, in London, it was almost three o'clock and time to go over to the Thames where the University Boat Race between Oxford and Cambridge was about to get under way. Entranced, I listened to the sense of controlled panic that rose in the commentators' voices as they talked us through the beginning of the race: the inevitable clash of oars, the inevitable battle between the coxes, the inevitable strain of the oarsmen, the inevitable roars of the crowd, which peaked and ebbed with the strength of the signal to this remote village in the Casamance. Each year, the scene was the same, each year the excitement mounted and fell, like the oars dipping in and out of the water. But nevertheless, the commentators managed to sound as if they were genuinely excited, which was no mean feat, I thought, sitting beneath the mango tree, when they saw so many similar events every year.

The continuity was reassuring, and I clamped the radio to my ear. But then the signal was lost and we were greeted by a whining hiss once again.

I switched the radio off, and was startled by the sudden gentleness of the silence that returned with that simple action. Although there were always many sounds in the village – the sounds associated with daily routines – they belonged to this place in a way that the dissonant whine of the radio did not. That brief visit to the Thames had transported me back home, and I had remembered how impossible it was to live there without a bombardment of artificial noise. Sometimes it seemed to me as if my life had been accompanied by an incremental increase in this aural and visual noise, year on year, so that now it was almost impossible to experience any moment of quiet.

Silence is for prayer, said the Bosnian Nobel laureate Ivo Andric, in *The Bridge over the Drina*, a novel that he wrote in Belgrade amid the mounting cacophony of the Second World War, perhaps aware that those years foreshadowed a world in which many people would soon find themselves incapable of prayer, happy instead to surround themselves with aural confusion, an instinctive armour against the world's hidden magic. If, indeed, it is possible to judge our awareness, our sense of ourselves, from the amount of time made available for quiet reflection, it is probably quite safe to pronounce ourselves brain-dead.

But in Balimé, once I had switched off the radio, silence returned to us. Magic seemed thick in the air.

We sat in the heat for some time. When the oppressiveness began to show some signs of lifting, Omar raised himself on his elbow and spoke to El Hadji.

'You should take him to see the griot,' he said.

El Hadji turned his head from where it lay, lolling on the prayer mat, and blinked rapidly as he surveyed his brother.

'Griot?'

'Melamin Jobarteh.'

Omar looked to me, his pain temporarily forgotten. His face was shining with enthusiasm.

'That griot knows a lot of history.'

But El Hadji lay sluggishly on the prayer mat, reluctant to move.

'I'm tired,' he said.

'My whole body hurts,' I moaned.

My friend sat up and grilled me with his eyes.

'You know what I want now?' he asked. 'I want us to go down to the beach and have a fight. But no gris-gris!'

We looked at one another and laughed.

He stood up and kicked the dust off his sandals.

'Come on then,' he said, smiling. 'Let's go and see the old man.'

We walked through the village, shifting the sands as we went. The thatched roofs of the huts drooped down towards the road like wilting flowers. People sat listlessly in the shade, tending their stores and watching the world. Outside one of the shops, a shoemaker hailed Omar and shouted something out to him.

'That's my friend,' Omar murmured to me.

'Which friend?'

'The one with the secret. He told me to go and see him this evening.'

We passed the market, then turned off the track and entered a compound where an old man with white stubble and a flabby chest sat in a gold-brocaded *boubou*, staring at his daughters and granddaughters pounding millet in the sun. One of them was the Moorish woman who had been El Hadji's first girlfriend.

They held hands while Omar introduced me to the griot.

'Come on,' said the old man. 'Let's go and sit behind the house.'

He shuffled around the corner of his home, into the shade of a small mango tree to which a goat was tied and spinning itself into knots. One of the women emerged with a deckchair, into which the griot settled himself. Already he seemed to be drifting off into the stories of battles and betrayals that revolved around his mind.

El Hadji, Omar and I sat in the shade as the old man began to strum his kora, which emerged, tumescent, from between his thighs. Soon a fly settled on my cheek, and El Hadji swiped it away with force.

'Don't hit me,' I said.

'Toby is headstrong. Toby knows everything.'

I sighed.

'That was a tsetse fly,' my friend told me.

'What shall I tell you?' the griot sang, interrupting our argument. His chords milked the early evening light.

'A story of the Bainungs?'

'No, no,' said El Hadji, 'tell us something else.'

'What shall I tell you?' sang the griot. 'A story of Samory Touré?'

He looked down at the strings of fishing wire that criss-crossed his instrument, and the sounds tinkled like crystal in the silence.

'Samory,' he sang, strumming, and tapping the wooden frame of his kora to develop a rhythm. Then he interrupted the tune with a knock, and looked at us.

'He was a great man,' he sang. 'Samory fought the French. He ruled Guinea-Conakry. And the griots told Samory – "You have a very beautiful daughter, called Mahawa."

'Samory,' he sang, strumming, and tapping the wood. Then he paused, and chuckled.

'He had so many daughters,' he sang, 'that he did not know them all. So he summoned them all to inspect them, and see if what the griots told him was true.

'Samory,' he sang.

'All the Marabouts came for a three-day feast. Samory faced the east, and told his daughters to come out one by one. He had them sit in gold chains.

'Ah, Samory,' he sang, and caressed his kora for two minutes at a time, in a stream of melodious beauty.

'The first daughter came out, covered in gold jewellery. "Is that Mahawa?" Samory asked the griots. But they said that she was not. "Mahawa must be beautiful," said Samory.

'Many daughters came out, but only when the sun was hot did Mahawa emerge. All the griots cried out, "Mahawa!" And Samory stood up and saw that indeed she was beautiful. So he ordered his men to lay down gold and silver for her to walk on, all the way to his throne.

'Ah, Samory,' he sang, together with his kora.

'Samory spoke to the griots. He told them to play a rhythm that matched her pace up to his throne. "If not," he said, "I'll kill you all." Mahawa began to walk. The killer raised his machete. The griots looked at each other in terror.

'Ah, Samory.

'And then,' sang the griot, knocking the frame of his instrument, 'the griots began to play – like this.'

His fingers stroked the strings in a rhythm that we had not heard before, working a sound and a particular form of the beauty that fell into the evening as naturally as birdsong.

'Mahawa walked, and the griots played like this,' he sang, playing the timeless rhythm.

'Ah, Samory. He smiled. He embraced his daughter. He wanted to marry her, but it was forbidden. So he showered the griots with gifts, for he was truly happy.'

Melamin Jobarteh extemporised on his kora again, and then slowly allowed his fingers to ease their peregrinations over the strings. The chords drifted into the silence of the twilight, together with the brilliance of the day.

'You see,' said El Hadji, as we walked slowly back towards the compound, once we had taken our leave, 'the Europeans only tell the story of Samory's wars. They tell you nothing about the man.'

'He knows many stories,' said Omar, of Melamin Jobarteh.

'That's why we say that when an old man dies, it is as if a library has gone up in smoke,' said El Hadji.

'What was that other story?' I asked. 'The one about the Bainungs?'

'The Bainungs were the first people in the Casamance,' Omar told me. 'But they betrayed their most powerful king, and buried him alive. As they were filling in the earth, he told them that they would be cursed from then on and cease to dominate the territory. That's why the Bainungs have fallen so greatly in numbers. Their court was not so far from here,' he said, 'in the village of Brucama.'

'Brucama?' I asked astonished.

'It was once a great place,' said Omar. 'Our elders have told us all about it.'

Brucama was a small village between Balimé and Bolana. It clung to the road without anything to draw attention to itself other than a lush glade to its west, where men hauled themselves up palm trees with calabashes in hand to collect palm wine. Yet, at one time, Brucama had been the centre of this area. As well as being the home of the Bainungs, it had held the royal residence of the kings of the Cassangas – a place of nobility and riches. Later, when I returned to London, I discovered that Portuguese traders had cut into the interior from an early period, to win the allegiance of the kings. By the end of the sixteenth century, there were *lançados* living in Brucama – many more Europeans than live in the region today – and the king, Masatamba,* ate at a high table covered with an ornate cloth, in the Portuguese style. The Portuguese brought wealth and prestige to the king. So much did Masatamba appreciate these newcomers, wrote André Donelha in the sixteenth century, that the Portuguese had more security at Brucama than anywhere else in the world. Donelha knew of one European who had dropped his dagger on the road to Brucama. The next day, an African came in the early morning with the dagger and gave it to the king, who asked the man when he had found it. The man replied that he had found the dagger the previous day, but that since he had not

* See Historical Notes, p. 273.

arrived at Brucama until late at night, he had not brought it immediately to His Majesty. Whereupon, says Donelha, Masatamba said that the man ought to have awakened him; it was wrong to sleep with anything belonging to a white man, and so he put him to death.

Of course, it had appeared to be in the king's interest to please the Portuguese, since the slave trade brought him so much apparent wealth. Yet the future prosperity of the region was mortgaged on this decision. The gold and silver in which the courts of Masatamba and Samory Touré had been steeped were in the past, and there was now not a vestige of the grandeur of these kingdoms left in this dusty place. People coughed and wheezed. They died of malaria, AIDS and gangrene. Diseases were on the increase, everyone agreed, and often it seemed to me that the standard of living in this part of the world must in fact have declined since the time of the first European contact. As Walter Rodney noted, referring to the standards of life in Europe and Africa, what was a slight difference when the Portuguese sailed to West Africa in 1444 was a huge gap by the time that the European robber statesmen sat down in Berlin 440 years later.

After dinner and the evening prayers, Omar went to see his friend the shoemaker. I wanted to go with him, but Omar could not permit it.

'My friend is only doing this as a special favour to me,' he said.

'I thought he was a Marabout.'

'No,' said Omar. 'He does not call himself a Marabout. There are very few people who know that he has these powers.'

It seemed that his friend's father had been a well-known Marabout, but he himself had not widely advertised his own knowledge. There were many Marabouts in Balimé, and he feared that it would irk them to have another competitor in the village. This was why he did not want to be seen with us in public. What else could a white man be doing in Balimé, if not searching for magic?

El Hadji and I waited in the compound, staring up at the glittering sky. I always preferred it when the moon was not out, because the stars shone more brightly on those nights, and the blackness was illuminated by the subtler glow of silver. But the moonlight was too bright. It wanted everything to be naked, stripped of the protection of secrecy.

After half an hour, Omar returned. He seemed subdued as he sat down beside us on the prayer mat.

'Everything is fine,' he told us. 'The gris-gris will be ready in the morning.'

'Has he finished it?' El Hadji asked him.

'Not yet,' said Omar. 'But he will come early for the test.'

I no longer felt scared by the prospect of testing the charm. I thought back to the beginning of my journey, when I had walked out into the bush around Balimé and tested the gris-gris against gunfire. I had felt terrified of this world. It was a measure of how much I had changed that I slept easily that night, and did not doubt what I would see on the following day. It was only later, when I returned home, that the strangeness of this attitude struck me, for in Balimé I had already been aware of the numerous African peoples who had mistakenly believed themselves invulnerable before being slaughtered by Europeans. If so many people had died because of their blind faith, it was difficult to see how such a thing as invulnerability could possibly exist.

Then it occurred to me that, in a society where stories are the source of history, if there really are some people with extraordinary magical skills and someone appears claiming to be endowed with these powers, it would be very hard not to believe them. But if only a small proportion of the mystics were actually authentic – and as I had seen, there were charlatans as well as genuine people – the results, far from protecting Africans, would have been catastrophic. The fact that so many Africans had been massacred as a result of a mistaken belief in their own invulnerability did not mean that such a thing did not exist.

I read up on the subject when I returned home. And, tucked away in a book written by the Scot Alexander Gordon Laing in 1825, I came across a story that seemed to confirm this interpretation of faith, miracles and African history. In his *Travels in the Timannee, Kooranko and Soolima Countries in Western Africa*, Laing describes arriving at the court of the king of the Soolima, who, he noted, had been a very successful king for his people, and greatly expanded his dominions. After being greeted by war songs, said Laing, the king stepped forward with sword in hand and opposed himself to twelve musketeers, who made repeated attempts to fire at him, but in vain, the priming always burning in the pan. Yarradee [the king] laughed and shook his gris-gris in defiance, and at length overcame them all, before commanding them to discharge their muskets in the air.

To Laing's great surprise, not a single musket missed fire.

I, of course, wrote Laing, with a superior tone, knew that they had some sleight-of-hand method of stopping and opening the touch-hole at pleasure. But, he concluded, although I witnessed the same performance repeatedly, I could never detect them.

Early next morning, before the sun had properly risen, I rose and accompanied Cheikh to Balimé's port. There we found several precarious dugout canoes beached amid the sandy roots. We stood at opposite ends of one of them, flipped it over and scooped out the worst of the sand. We rolled the vessel out into the shallow brine. Then we climbed in, balanced ourselves and paddled in the direction of some of Cheikh's nets. We circumvented a sandbank and then headed out towards the fringes of the lagoon, with the greyness of the dawn gradually beginning to break into colour. The water was as still as the air that hung invisibly above it, drifting off into the shadows of the glades and the palm trees which struggled to emerge from the recent darkness.

After ten minutes we arrived at the nets. Cheikh reached into the waters and hauled the patched white squares through his hands. Every so often, the work would reveal the squirming body of a fish, which he dislodged into the canoe so that it could lie there twitching away with dismal thuds. The fish piled up among us, until this unsteady hollow of wood was gradually enveloped by the chastening spectacle of so much life draining away.

When the nets had been exhausted, Cheikh turned to me and smiled.

'Alhamdoulilah,' he said, gesturing at the bottom of the boat and his family's food.

I smiled in reply, feeling a brief moment of happiness that I had been able to live with so many people and understand something of their lives. When I had arrived in Dakar, I remembered, I had wanted this journey to bring me a proper understanding of this place, something much deeper than the cursory knowledge that I had gathered on my first visit. Perhaps, I thought now, watching the blues and yellows break the stillness above the marshes, if I had not been ill, I could not really have understood the nature of life here. And if I had not felt hungry and listless, I would have understood even less. While, if I had had no experience of magic, perhaps I would have understood nothing at all.

It's not a lot, I said to myself, thinking of the magic I had seen, but it'll do.

Then Cheikh swept his oar through the water with swift, powerful strokes, and the boat turned in the eddies. We were heading inexorably back towards the village and the test of the gris-gris.

We beached the canoe and I helped Cheikh slip the fish into the buckets and carry them back to the compound. By this time, El Hadji and Omar were both awake, and we sat watching the light gathering as we waited for the shoemaker.

He arrived quite early. He was a short, stocky man with a square face and an expression that seemed to betoken gentle suspicion.

He knocked on the door of Cheikh and Fatu's home, removed his sandals before entering, and then advanced towards us dressed in dead men's clothes and brandishing a plastic bag.

Omar greeted him. Then the shoemaker shook hands with El Hadji and me.

'Let's go somewhere quiet,' Omar said, and we followed him into the room at the back of the house where Cheikh and Fatu slept – a dark, rectangular space festooned with fishing nets. They spread out across the floor, their tiny white boundaries standing out amid the morning darkness. They sandwiched the bed and the table, which clung to each end of the room like wreckage to a shipwreck.

Omar bent down and scooped up handfuls of netting, which he bundled onto the mattress. Then the shoemaker searched around in his bag and emerged with a long gris-gris, designed to fit around the waist. It was wrapped in dark fur, which tapered into two leather buttons at one end and into a small leather noose at the other.

'What sort of skin are they wrapped in?' I murmured to Omar.

'It's the rat,' he said.

The shoemaker held the gris-gris up to the weak light, showing it off to El Hadji and me. If we liked, he would demonstrate it now before proceeding any further.

I nodded in agreement. The shoemaker wrapped the mixture of dead animal and prayer around his waist and tightened the small nooses around each of the two buttons so that the charm was completely fastened. Then he looked inside his plastic bag once again and found a smaller charm which he wrapped around his right arm and tightened securely.

He picked a long knife out of the bag and handed it to me.

'Test it,' he said, and I poked the point of the knife – which was probably twenty centimetres long – into my finger. It was sharp, I agreed.

He took hold of the knife, rolled up his right sleeve and then began to attack himself with it. He did not jab at his arm, but instead he raised his hand high in the air, like a man with an axe, and jammed it down into his skin as hard as he could. I saw his stabbing arm flex and thrust, like a piston, and watched, with something approaching fatalism, as the knife bounced off his skin, leaving no trace except for some tiny marks which looked as if they had been made by a blunt pinhead.

The shoemaker attacked himself seven or eight times in this way before stopping.

'You see,' he said, and we crowded around to stare at the minute indentations that had surfaced reluctantly on his skin, and were barely visible against the brilliance of his blackness.

We said nothing.

Then he started to explain the gris-gris to Omar. The charm was especially powerful. In general, he said, slipping the buttons out of their nooses and unravelling the skin from around his waist, it was advisable to wear it at all times, for one never knew when an enemy might present themselves. However, what was also true was that it was better to keep one button only fastened, and to be ready to fasten the second if necessary. The securing of one button provided a measure of protection, but when it was accompanied by the second button, the wearer became exceptionally powerful and proof against all assaults. It might be that a friend would greet you in the street and clap you on the back as a gesture of friendship – but if you had both buttons fastened, he would fall down onto the ground and writhe in an unspeakable agony until you had unfastened one of them.

We nodded in understanding.

The powers of the gris-gris could only be detroyed if we did not take it off when having sex. In that case its capacities would be lost. But at all other times it was advisable to wear it. Remember Samory Touré, said the shoemaker, and how he was betrayed by one of his wives, so that the French knew the time at which he would not be wearing his gris-gris! Remember Samory, and wear the gris-gris at all times.

'Now you try it,' he said to El Hadji.

El Hadji stepped forward, keen to show that he was braver than I was. He slipped the long gris-gris around his waist and the smaller one around his arm, and the shoemaker began to attack him with the knife.

'Agh!' El Hadji screamed, and backed away as he was assaulted.

'Enough,' he said. 'Enough!'

He pulled his arm away after two or three thrusts. The skin remained unbroken, but that was not to say that the knife was not painful. The force of it being driven down bruised his skin and made it hurt but, the shoemaker explained, as he wrapped the charm around me and fastened the buttons, the magic of the charm protected the skin and made sure that it could not be cut. He wrapped the smaller gris-gris around my right arm and then I held it out before me like a sacrificial offering, which the man touched briefly with his left hand, before standing back.

If the charm were to fail now, I thought, after having witnessed its success for the other two, I would be very unlucky.

Then the shoemaker began to attack me.

He raised his arm and hammered it down like an axe murderer. The knife rose and fell almost as if it had borne a will of its own. I felt it hit my skin and saw it retire into the air, watching the brutal event repeatedly, like a succession of still frames frozen on a video screen, flickering before my alienated eyes so that it seemed as if what they represented was unreal.

The attack was painful, but very quickly I saw that the knife could not cut me. Again and again the shoemaker struck, while El Hadji squatted down in the corner of the room and tried to capture the image for ever with the flashing eye of my camera, so that, in times to come, when this event seemed like nothing but a dream, and I could not believe that there had been a moment when I had been invulnerable, I would stare at the image and try to decipher whether or not it told a true story.

Eventually, the man took his knife back, and placed it on the table. We examined my arm. It was laced with eleven small marks, which looked like stitches and lined my flesh in a jagged and uneven pattern above the elbow. The flesh was already beginning to bruise, but the skin was unbroken and there was no blood.

'It is a very strong gris-gris,' said Omar and I nodded, looking at my appendage with wonder and finding it difficult to believe that it belonged to me.

It was time to pay the man. He had asked for 16,660 CFA, a precise figure which his father had told him was the correct charge for such a gris-gris. It seemed a small price to pay for invulnerability.

Then the shoemaker left us for a time and returned in a long white *boubou* and rosary, asking if we could have our photograph taken together: the Marabout and his *talibe*. I stood together with him in the centre of the living space, watched over by the bats and the murmurs of the creaking roof, and El Hadji took the picture, which disappeared into the memory of the inanimate black box of my camera and would shortly return with me to Europe.

The man told El Hadji that he was very proud to have done a successful piece of work. 'But,' he said, 'I doubt that I will ever see that photograph.'

I protested.

'Of course I will send it,' I told El Hadji, and the man seemed reassured.

He left us, and we saw him later that morning in the main street of Balimé, hunched over a pair of shoes and stabbing away at the leather with a needle and thread, his scissors placed beside him. He raised his head briefly and acknowledged us, before returning to his humdrum work, as if everything that had occurred that morning belonged to some illusory and now vanished corner of the imagination.

We now had little time to lose. We decided to have lunch with Cheikh, Fatu and Omar, before catching an afternoon bus back to Ziguinchor and travelling on to Dakar the following morning. On hearing that we had to leave that day, Fatu threw up her arms in mock protest and berated me.

'Everyone is going to say I am very bad,' she told me.

'No they won't,' I said.

'Yes they will. They will say that the *tubab* left my house thinner than he was when he arrived.'

This did not seem likely. Fatu prepared an enormous dish of rice, fish, groundnut sauce, onions and tomatoes, and watched over me like a doting mother as she ensured that I finished every last morsel.

Feeling that I was likely to explode at any moment, I waddled through the heat towards the mango tree under which we usually lay in the afternoons. The prayer mats were already there, and El Hadji was reclining, stroking his belly and turning his head to one side.

I lay down beside him.

'Toby has seen a lot,' he said.

'Yes.'

'He has seen what he wanted to see. And now he believes.'

El Hadji picked his red baseball cap off his head and began to play with it.

'But I won't return home with the gris-gris,' I said to him.

'It could be very dangerous for you.'

I now believed that this was true.

He sighed.

'Now El Hadji is going to travel,' he said.

'I know,' I said. 'Don't think that I am unaware that although my adventure is ending, yours has only just begun.'

263

'It's true.'

He sighed, and dreamt of Europe.

However much I had told him that he was likely to be exploited, and that he might well end up in a difficult position, El Hadji maintained that he would go. He wanted to see for himself.

'Now you understand why I had to see the gris-gris work with my own eyes,' I told him. 'Sometimes a story is not enough.'

'It's true.'

He watched the leaves of the mango tree, still as death in the afternoon heaviness.

'But,' he said, 'it is only difficult for Africans in Europe because the *tubabs* do not like us.'

'That's not true,' I said.

'It is.'

I did not want to get drawn into this argument once again, and so I allowed the comment to pass. But what neither of us knew was that, although I would give him as much money as he thought was necessary, getting hold of the right papers would prove impossible, and he would have to buy a taxi and remain in Dakar. Even after all that we had seen, the true extent of the chasm in opportunities between my world and his was not yet clear to us in Balimé. We had been through so much together that, at that moment, our differences appeared not to stand between us. The unexpectedly intimate essence of the relationship that we had built during our journey is perhaps expressed in the letter that El Hadji later wrote to me from Dakar, explaining to my shock that, had I been a woman, he would have taken me for his second wife.

'It is of no matter,' El Hadji went on now, thinking over what had been said. 'Everything will turn out for the best, *insh'allah.*'

And we sat in silence for a time in Balimé, where the sounds of the afternoon rang like musical chimes, solid and resonant, across the village.

Then I heard the hissing of a radio, and Omar appeared beside us, clutching the machine to his chest and then sitting on the prayer mat, with the noise clamped like a leech to his ear.

He smiled softly and listened to the poor reception.

'The stations don't have good enough transmitters to reach here,' I said.

He smiled.

'We are too far away,' he said. 'But I like to keep up with the news as best I can.'

He listened to the hiss.

'What about you?' he said. 'You don't seem to care.'

Other than the previous day, when I had listened to my own country's programme, he said, he had never seen me interested in radio and television.

'No,' I agreed. 'That's because in my own country we are now constantly bombarded by news and information. I don't care to listen to it here, since I know I will have no peace when I return.'

Omar nodded, and returned his attention to the radio.

Immersed in the hubbub of the world, I had longed only to escape from it for a while. But for Omar, who was so far removed from those unimaginable places where there was a disturbing surfeit of information and technology, the news was an object of fascination. I looked at his earnest expression as he tried to catch the announcer's words amid the crackles of the storms that were no doubt gathering over the Atlantic, and remembered how impossible I found it to live in silence at home. Soon I would be there, I thought, amid the ceaseless cultural noise.

For the first time I thought of the sorts of things that I would hear, and of the widespread complaints about a society that was becoming increasingly superficial, where things were only taken at their face value, and images or soundbites or headlines were what mattered most. This was thought by many to be a dreadful thing, a dangerous collapse into banality. This alarm now reminded me of the first wave of immigrants from francophone Africa, who had been similarly dismayed on coming to France in the first decades of the twentieth century. Arriving as students picked out for their promise from mission schools, they appeared in Europe full of hope that a true African intellectualism would emerge and that they could be equals with the French – this was, after all, a central *raison d'être* of French colonial policy, and African art and culture was all the rage in fashionable Parisian circles. How shocking it was for them to discover, on arriving in Paris, that while they saw themselves as symbols of hope, with important ideas and brains alive with intellectual ferment, the vast majority of people saw nothing more than the fact that they were black. It had not taken long, Léopold Sédar Senghor said at a lecture at Oxford University in October 1961, to be convinced of the failure of assimilation. The Africans had been able to assimilate the French language and mathematics, but they were not able to change the fact that they were black. Instead of being judged for the people they felt they were, the new African intellectuals in Paris were judged by something as superficial as the colour of their skin.

One of the books that I had brought with me from Europe was Ralph Ellison's *Invisible Man*. I had read it in Guinea-Conakry, and struggled to put myself in the position of the protagonist, a brilliant African American whom none of the characters will see for what he is, only for what they want him to be. Some want him to be a brilliant student, others a leading race campaigner, but their concern for him lasts only as long as his actions suit their own interests and prejudices. When he understands this, the man realises that he himself might as well not exist, since no one sees anything beyond the colour of his skin.

'I am invisible, understand,' he says, 'simply because people refuse to see me.'

Even when white men claimed to be trying to integrate African Americans into North American power structures and Africans into French cultural structures, the essential superficiality of racism was so deep-seated that no amount of liberal idealism could shake it off. And this was hardly surprising, since the phenomenon had been afforded four centuries of slaving history to develop. At the outset of the Atlantic slave trade, the whole world had believed in the existence of invisible worlds, in the existence of the supernatural and in the truth that there was much of reality that could never be seen. But, as the next centuries unravelled, an increasingly empirical way of thinking began to hold sway in Europe, particularly in Britain in the eighteenth century, when, coincidentally, British ships dominated the slave trade. By the time the trade eventually died in the second half of the nineteenth century, the world had been altered by these new ideas. In the twentieth century, the intellectual descendants of empiricists were the Vienna School of philosophers, one of whom was A.J. Ayer, who claimed that nothing was true unless it could be verified through experiment, almost as if all that mattered was the bare evidence of the eyes. This philosophy could be construed as progressive and liberal, but it had murky roots – the ubiquity of slavery, perhaps, which had given birth to a similar ubiquity of racism, a phenomenon that, like the elements of contemporary culture that some people find disquieting, depended on a predominant superficiality.

A sudden spurt of noise from the radio made us all sit to attention. The airwaves were now filled with the headlines of the three o'clock news, which was to be followed by a programme promising a full discussion of all the latest events. We were soon mesmerised by the information that circled about us.

The newsreader announced that, on the morrow, at the *Stade de l'Amitié* in Dakar, the formal transfer of power from the outgoing President Diouf* to the incoming President Wade would be made. It would be an historic event, at which dignitaries from many West African states would be present. The president of The Gambia would attend, as would the leaders of Guinea-Bissau, Mauritania, Mali, Burkina Faso, and representatives from Morocco and Niger. This was the start of a new era in Senegalese history, which, it was hoped, would prove to be auspicious.

'Dakar will be heaving tomorrow,' said El Hadji, snapping out of the apathy that had engulfed us as we had listened. 'Everyone will want to go.'

This meant that our journey back from Ziguinchor would be even longer and more time-consuming than usual.

He sighed.

'*C'est difficile.*'

Omar smiled.

'Travelling is not easy,' he said. 'I would not have wanted to do what

---

* See Historical Notes, p. 271.

El Hadji has done. Last night, when I spoke to the shoemaker and explained what you two had undertaken, he could not believe it.'

Sometimes it seemed difficult for me to credit. Even that morning seemed like a dream. Thinking over the knife attack, I wondered whether, perhaps, if you clenched your arm hard enough, you could withstand that sort of assault. Or perhaps the man had a method of withdrawing his hand at the last moment so that he barely touched you. But then I looked down at the bruises on my arm, proof that he really had hit me. And I remembered the length of the blade – no amount of muscle-clenching should have been able to withstand that.

Omar was chuckling.

'What is it?' I asked.

'I didn't tell you last night,' he said.

'What?'

'When I went to see the shoemaker, he had already finished the charms. He said that he would demonstrate them to me. But one of them did not work.'

'What do you mean?'

It seemed that the shoemaker had struck himself with the knife and that he had instantly started to bleed. They had washed the wound and then the man had examined the prayer that he had written. There had been a verse missing, and he had had to work on it overnight.

Any last doubt that I had vanished. It could not have been a trick of the knife, if he had cut himself with it once. Neither was the shoemaker trying to spread word of his skills, since we had done everything clandestinely.

He simply happened to possess a magical secret.

'Come on,' said El Hadji, interrupting my thoughts. 'We'd better get going. Otherwise we'll miss the last bus back to Ziguinchor.'

We rose and brushed the dust off our bodies, which fell from us like small and opaque clouds. Then we went to gather our things, which we laid against the wall of the house. We entered the room where Cheikh and Fatu lay side by side on the prayer mats, and told them that we had to say farewell. Cheikh raised himself on one elbow and shook me warmly by the hand.

'*Nyungi dem,*' I said. 'We are going.'

'*Demna wa fofo? Are you going home?*'

'*Wow.*'

'*Alhamdoulilah.*'

He lay down again.

'Toby,' said Fatu.

'Yes.'

'You're going?'

'Yes.

'You won't eat food like this at home, will you?'

'No,' I said, 'we eat differently over there.'

She sighed.

'Come back,' she said.

Then we walked through the changeless sands to the road. Omar insisted on carrying my bag, which he bore on his shoulders as lightly as if it had been empty.

We reached the tarmac, and waited in the heat for the next bus. A group of people had gathered under palm trees near the edge of the village, watching with tireless hope across the glade to the east.

They greeted us gently as we arrived, and we sat with them, awaiting the bus.

Soon it came. Omar passed my bag up to the tout, who strapped it down to the roof and then told us to get inside. I shook hands with Omar and he smiled.

'Look,' he said.

He pointed at my arm and the scars that still stood out boldly from the morning's knife attack.

'It will take a long time for those to heal,' he said.

'Yes,' I agreed.

'Whenever you look at them, you can think of me.'

He smiled, before looking away.

El Hadji and I squeezed through the crush of arms and legs that enveloped the interior of the bus as if it had been a cage. We sat down and watched Balimé roll past us like a dream.

Then the vehicle accelerated, and we left the village and the miracle behind us.

Historical Notes

The history of the Guinea Coast is extraordinarily rich and complex, and this book contains references to people and events that may be unknown to some readers. For this reason, I have included notes on some of the more important of those appearing in the narrative.

Abdou Diouf The second president of Senegal. Groomed from an early age by Léopold Sédar Senghor, Diouf, of the *Parti Socialiste*, became president in 1981. He led Senegal until his defeat by Abdoulaye Wade in the election of March 2000.

Abdoulaye Wade An international lawyer and veteran opposition politician, Wade became the third president of Senegal after a resounding victory in the election of March 2000. Leading the opposition, Wade polled almost 60 per cent of the vote in the run-off against Abdou Diouf. Wade's support came from the young, and from Dakar and Rufisque, while the rural areas and areas to the north of Senegal tended to support Diouf. As in all previous Senegalese elections, some Marabouts instructed their followers to vote for the *Parti Socialiste* and for Diouf, but for the first time many disregarded the orders – a sign that the old chain of command is beginning to fragment.

Alfa Yaya The last ruler of the Fouta Djalon empire, Alfa Yaya was the fifth son of the king of Labé. He was strikingly mature from a young age, and led a campaign near Buba, in modern Guinea-Bissau, before deposing a cousin and an elder brother to become Almamy in 1892. He justified this through the need to take a strong line against the French, but his disregard for the traditional rules of succession caused widespread resentment. In 1896, the region became a French protectorate, which Alfa Yaya saw as a power-sharing arrangement, but which led inevitably to French control.

Ansumane Mane   A veteran of Guinea-Bissau's war of independence, and commander-in-chief for years of Guinea-Bissau's armed forces, Ansumane Mane led the coup against President Nino Vieira – a former comrade from the independence war – in 1998, which led to civil war. Fighting with widespread popular support, Ansumane Mane's rebels overthrew Vieira and paved the way for the country's first genuinely democratic elections in January 2000, won by Kumba Yala. However, Mane then led a failed coup against Yala's government in November 2000 and was killed in a shoot-out with forces loyal to Kumba Yala.

Cadamosto   An Italian navigator who worked for the Portuguese, Cadamosto led the first European ships to reach Guinea-Bissau in 1456. This may also have been the first European expedition to set eyes on the archipelago of Cape Verde.

Felix Houphouët-Boigny   The first president of Côte d'Ivoire after independence, Houphouët-Boigny led the country to relative prosperity, ruling uninterrupted from 1960 until 1993.

Karamoko Alfa   The first Almamy of the Fouta Djalon, Karamoko Alfa was elected by popular assent at Timbi-Touni after the victorious jihad of the Peul against the Djalonke in 1726. He was succeeded by his cousin Ibrahima Sori-Mawdo in 1770, but this led to a rift in the Peul elite between the Alfaya (followers of Karamoko Alfa) and the Soriya (followers of Ibrahima Sori-Mawdo). Uniquely in Africa, the rift was resolved through the leader of the empire alternating between the two factions, each giving way to the other every two years.

Koli Tenguela   A Peul leader who originated in the region of the Fouta Toro, near the River Senegal, and led a group of followers to colonise the Fouta Djalon region. This migration took place c.1530.

Lansana Conté   The second president of Guinea-Conakry, Lansana Conté succeeded Sékou Touré in 1984. Susu by origin, Conté was a colonel in the army before seizing power on Touré's death. Originally he tried to work with some of Touré's ministers but, in 1985, Malinké army officers attempted a coup which Conté brutally suppressed. Although making some token moves towards democracy in the 1990s, opponents accused him of maintaining an autocratic style of government.

Léopold Sédar Senghor   Poet and politician, Senghor is a member of the *Académie Française*. Born in 1906 near Joal, south of Dakar, Senghor was educated at a mission school and went to study in Paris in 1928. During the Second World War he fought as a member of the *Tirailleurs Sénégalais*, and became the first president of Senegal on independence in 1960, ruling until 1981.

Mansa Mohammed   Emperor of Mali at the turn of the fourteenth century, Mansa Mohammed is supposed to have equipped two fleets to cross the Atlantic. His rule was part of the golden age of the Mali empire, when their control was unchecked throughout the region and news of their power had even reached some European cartographers.

Mansa Musa   Emperor of Mali from around 1320 to 1340, Mansa Musa made a famous hadj to Mecca in 1324, taking so much gold with him that it took thirty years for the price of gold to recover in Egypt.

Marco Polo   In recent years, some scholars have cast doubt as to whether Marco Polo (*c.*1254–1324) ever visited China at all, pointing out that his failure to recount some of the more elementary customs of the area (such as drinking tea) is – to say the least – surprising. Nevertheless, his historical accounts do tally broadly with other sources from the time. But while he may have visited Burma and India, it is unlikely that Polo ever went to Zanzibar, and his description of the island is probably based on hearsay. This makes his account even more noteworthy since, writing without any first-hand knowledge, Polo would have been most likely to tell stories which confirmed the prejudices of his age.

Masatamba   King of the Cassangas in the latter half of the sixteenth century, Masatamba had his court at Brucama. He conquered the Bainung people and took over the running of their chief slave port, Buguendo (the forerunner of the modern town of São Domingos, in Guinea-Bissau). Masatamba was a friend of the Portuguese and appears to have been receptive to Christianity – there are reports of the local people at Buguendo performing the Christian mass with as much devotion as Europeans. The most important kingdom in the area, however, was the neighbouring one of Cacheu (between Buguendo and Bissau). The Portuguese courted the king of Cacheu, and *lançados* lived among the local people in the sixteenth century. The relationship was so well-established that the king of Cacheu in 1585 was said to speak Portuguese. The first fortified settlement in this part of Africa was founded in Cacheu in 1591.

Nino Vieira Nino Vieira was leader of the 'people's army' in the last years of Guinea-Bissau's war of independence. He became Commissioner of the Armed Forces after independence in 1974, and then led a coup in 1980 against the first president of Guinea-Bissau, Luiz Cabral, capitalising on widespread resentment at perceived preferential treatment given by Cabral to Guinea-Bissauans of Capverdian origin. Vieira became president and ruled uninterrupted until civil war broke out in 1998. By this time, Vieira was suspected by many of massive corruption, and was greatly unpopular in his home country. He was granted political exile in Portugal in May 1999.

Samory Touré Samory Touré was a Malinké warlord in the region of modern Guinea-Conakry, and provided some of the fiercest resistance that the French came across in West Africa in the nineteenth century. Samory's army was well organised, and is thought to have had 400 gunsmiths working at the height of their campaigns. With his stronghold in the plains of *Haute Guinée*, Samory proved a thorn in the side of the French from the early 1880s until his eventual capture and deportation to Gabon in 1898. After his arrest the revolt fizzled out, and Samory died in exile.

Sékou Touré Sékou Touré was the first president of Guinea-Conakry, ruling from independence in 1958 to his death in 1984. Like Samory Touré (whom he tried, unsuccessfully, to claim as an ancestor), Touré was a Malinké. He became Mayor of Conakry in 1955 and vice-president in 1957. Discounting compromise of any sort, Touré said that 'we prefer poverty in freedom to riches in slavery'. Guinea-Conakry was the first francophone country to achieve independence, in 1958, and the French responded by banning

Guinea-Conakry from the francophone monetary system and withdrawing all aid from the country. Sékou Touré persisted in an isolationist policy by which he alienated Guinea-Conakry from both the Russians and the Americans. The late 1970s saw a rapprochement with the West, but by that time Touré had terrified his people by a succession of programmes of terror, inspired by the threat of 'external aggression' and what became known as the 'permanent plot'.

Sumanguru Kante The Susu warlord defeated, according to legend, by Sunjata Keita, in a battle which paved the way for the foundation of the Mali empire. Like the Saraholé, the Susu of this time are thought to have descenced from the Soninké. After the defeat, the Susu migrated to the hills of the Fouta Djalon, where they lived in relative peace until the migrations of the Peul from the north.

Sunjata Keita The Mandinga leader whose heroics against Sumanguru Kante are still an important part of the oral tradition of the region. This battle probably took plate in the mid-thirteenth century, and Sunjata Keita then founded the seat of the Mali empire at Niani (on the border between modern Mali and Guinea-Conakry).

Glossary

alhamdoulilah   Arabic phrase meaning 'I thank God', widely used in West Africa.

Almamy   The title of the rulers of the theocracy of the Fouta Djalon.

Azande   Central African people located from the Upper Nile basin in Southern Sudan to the semitropical forests of the Democratic Rebublic of Congo. Until 1858, the Azande had no contact with European or African traders, but subsequent expeditions sought to inveigle them into the business of slaving. Their king Gbudwe attacked Arab caravans in the late 19th century, describing both Arabs and Europeans as 'dirty little crop-headed barbarians'.

baobab   The oldest trees in Africa, many of them over a thousand years old. Their fruits – white pulp enclosed in a hard green shell – can be mashed, mixed with water and sugar, and turned into a delicious juice.

Bainung   Once the most powerful people in the Casamance, now much reduced in number.

bairro   Portuguese name given to neighbourhoods in Bissau.

Balanta   The most numerous ethnic group in Guinea-Bissau, originating, according to oral history, from the highlands of the Fouta Djalon.

bissap   Widely cultivated plant in West Africa, producing a sweet nut which can be crushed and used in sauces.

boubou   Kaftan or robe worn as formal wear by Muslim men. Pronounced 'booboo'.

branco   Portuguese for 'white person'.

bush taxi   The most widely used form of public transport in West Africa. In francophone countries, bush taxis are generally Peugeot estate cars in which an extra seat has been added to the boot. In Senegal, these cars transport seven passengers; in Guinea-Conakry, they can be used to transport anything up to fifteen people.

CFA   The currency of most of francophone Africa and Guinea-Bissau. 1000 CFA = 10 French francs, or about £1. Pronounced 'Sayfa'.

Casamance   Senegalese region between The Gambia and Guinea-Bissau. From the fifteenth to the nineteenth centuries, the Portuguese were the only Europeans to have significant dealings in this area, and there are many similarities – ethnic and historical – between the Casamance and Guinea-Bissau.

Djalonke   The original inhabitants of the mountains of the Fouta Djalon.

Djola   An important coastal people in the Casamance, and – together with the Balanta – the only people of the region to shun the slave trade.

fetishist   A generic European term (*fétisheur* in French, *feiticeiro* in Portuguese) for people who make offerings to ancestral spirits.

Fouta Djalon   The mountains of north and north-eastern Guinea-Conakry, and the name of a theocratic Islamic state of the eighteenth and nineteenth centuries.

Franc Guinéen   Guinea-Conakry's currency: 1 CFA = 2.5 *francs Guinéens* (approx.).

Fula Preto   Literally, a 'black Fula'. The Portuguese in Guinea-Bissau recognised three types of Fula, or Peul: the *Fulas Forros*, the descendants of the Peul who accompanied Koli Tenguela in the sixteenth century; the *Futa Fulas*, a mixed race of Peul and Susu–Djalonké; and the *Fulas Pretos*, whose ancestors had been the slaves of these two castes, and were probably descendants of the original peoples of the area who had been thrown into upheaval by the arrival of the Peul.

griot   The praise singers of the old West African empires. Still very much used as guardians of oral history and to accompany ceremonies. Pronounced 'gree-oh'.

gris-gris   Charm, amulet. Pronounced 'gree-gree'.

Imam   A leader of a mosque.

insh'allah   'If God wills it.' Or, 'hopefully'.

irã   The ancestral spirits of many peoples in Guinea-Bissau.

jihad   Islamic holy war.

ju-ju   A disparaging term coined by British colonists to describe African magic. Derives from *joujou*, the French for plaything.

Kaabu   One of the most important centres of the Mali empire, receiving tribute from coastal peoples around Bissau, and the origin of the modern city of Gabú in Guinea-Bissau. Some rebels in the Casamance claim to be seeking the rebirth of the kingdom, and this movement has some support in The Gambia and Guinea-Bissau.

Kankoran   A mystical figure who accompanies young boys to be circumcised in the Casamance.

Khalif   A leader of an Islamic religious movement.

kola   Very bitter nuts containing light traces of amphetamines – formerly a currency in West Africa and still used as gifts on ceremonial occasions.

kora   A West African harp with twenty-one strings.

Koriteh   The Islamic festival marking the end of Ramadan. More commonly known as Id al-Fitr.

Kriolu   A hybrid of Portuguese and local languages, spoken as a lingua franca in Guinea-Bissau and the Cape Verde Islands, and understood by many in the Casamance.

kunda   A generic Mandinga term for 'compound' (as in Ndiayekunda, Kabakunda).

Labé   The main seat of learning in the theocracy of the Fouta Djalon – now Guinea-Conakry's second city.

lançado   A term coined by the Portuguese for their traders who settled on the West African coast.

laterite   The red clay that is common in West Africa.

Layen   Islamic brotherhood based in Yof, near Dakar.

Lebu   The people who originated from Cap Vert, Senegal.

m'balax   Senegalese music, heavy on aggressive rhythms from *tamas*.

Mancaigne   Also known as the Brahmas, this people are based around Bula, Guinea-Bissau.

Mandinga   Also known as Mandingo and Mande, this is one of the largest ethnic groups of West Africa, spreading from The Gambia to Mali and Guinea-Conakry, the heartland of the old Mali empire.

Manjaco   An important ethnic group of Guinea-Bissau's northern coastal regions.

Marabout   A holy man with magical powers and a connection to Islam. Pronounced 'Maraboo'.

meistizo   A Guinea-Bissauan of mixed Portuguese and African origin.

Mouride   The most influential Islamic brotherhood in Senegal, founded by Ahmadou Bamba at the beginning of the twentieth century.

Pepel   The people of the coastal heartland of Guinea-Bissau. The first Portuguese sailors made treaties with the Pepel kings in the area around the slaving post of Cacheu, which was the first European city on this part of the West African mainland.

Peul   Also known as Fula and Peuhl, this nomadic people populate a wide region of West Africa, from southern Senegal to Niger, via Guinea-Conakry and northern Nigeria. Notably lighter skinned than other peoples in West Africa, they are believed to have migrated from the Nile Valley. The Peul ruled the Islamic theocracy of the Fouta Djalon in Guinea-Conakry from the early eighteenth century to the end of the nineteenth century.

pirogue   A dugout canoe.

Qu'ran   The holy book of Islam.

Ramadan   The holy month of Islam, a time of fasting to commemorate the month during which the Qu'ran was revealed to Mohammed. The fasting takes place from dawn until dusk only.

Saraholé   People originating from southern Mauritania and northern Senegal, believed to descend from the Soninke, who ruled the empire of Ghana in the eleventh century.

soukouss   Pop music dominated by complicated electric guitars from Kinshasa, Democratic Republic of the Congo.

Sufi   Mystical movement of Islam, whence the brotherhoods in Senegal all derive.

Susu   A large ethnic group in Guinea-Conakry, driven out of the Fouta Djalon to the coast of Guinea-Conakry by the Peul during the foundation of the Islamic theocracy.

talibe   A disciple of a holy man.

tama   A narrow, elongated Senegalese drum – the 'talking drum'.

Tijanniya   The largest Islamic brotherhood in Senegal.

Tirailleurs Sénégalais   A regiment of soldiers from francophone Africa which fought in the First and Second World Wars, in Algeria and in Indochina.

tsetse   A large fly responsible for transmitting the lethal disease of sleeping sickness.

tubab   A white person. The term is used mainly by the Wolof.

Tukulor   People from the north of Senegal, deriving their name from 'Tekrur', the first Wolof state.

Wolof   The predominant ethnic group of Senegal, the Wolof descend from the Jolof empire that was in place at the time of the first Portuguese visitors to West Africa in the fifteenth century. The Jolof empire was by far the largest kingdom on this part of the West African coast, although it later split into the sub-kingdoms of Cayor, Waalo, Baol, Sîne and Saloûm.

wrakadiang   Susu term for 'bad' sorcery.

Acknowledgements

It will be clear to anyone who reads this book that none of this would have been possible without the help of El Hadji Mamadou Kabir Ndiaye and all of his family, especially Tidiane and Omar. In Labé I would like to thank Tal for his restorative and delicious cooking, and in Bissau I owe a great deal to Aruna Diallo.

I am enormously indebted to Ian Rakoff, who went through the draft of this book line by line and was far too generous in sharing the huge benefit of his experience with me – he has saved me from many disasters. Emily Fowke and Janak Jani also read early drafts of this book and made countless useful suggestions, while Mark Leonard gave me crucial support right at the outset. Thanks are also due to Tamsin Todd for a very helpful suggestion, Rachel Holmes for a book and Danny Hahn for looking over my Portuguese. Simon Trewin and Sarah Ballard were always encouraging, and helped me to see the funny side when I needed to. Once again I have been fortunate with my editor at Weidenfeld, Alison Provan, whose enthusiasm and hard work in every aspect of the editorial process have been a great help. I am very grateful to Ion Trewin, Katie White and Emma Finnegan for their ongoing encouragement, and to Celia Levett for again providing such thorough and indispensable copy-editing. I would also like to give a big thank you to Evan Jones, who travelled with me on my first visit to West Africa and helped to inspire me to return.

Finally, I have been greatly helped by Carmen Neto at the Guinea-Bissau British Trust. The situation in Guinea-Bissau continues to be critical, and Carmen does sterling voluntary work in supporting political exiles in this country and in trying to get development projects started in Guinea-Bissau. Funding is short, and interested parties can e-mail carmeneto@hotmail.com if they wish to help.

Many readers may be sceptical of the events recounted in this book. Every magical happening that I have described occurred as I have written it – I have tried to be as faithful as possible to those events.

I hope that most people will be open-minded. I would welcome any queries and doubts that they may have, and will do my best to answer them. I can be contacted at toby_green@hotmail.com

In order to protect communities, I have changed the names of some individuals and places.

Bibliography

Adamolekon, Ladipo, *Sékou Touré's Guinea* (London, Methuen, 1976)

Adanson, M., *A Voyage to Senegal, the Isle of Gorée and the River Gambia* (London, Nurse & Johnston, 1759)

Almada, André Alvares d', *Tratado Breve dos Rios de Guiné do Cabo Verde* (Porto, Typographia Commercial Portuense, 1841; first published 1594)

Al-Umari, *Masalik al-absar fi 'mamalik al-amsar*, translated as *L'Afrique moins l'Égypte* by Gaudfroy-Demombynes (Paris, n.p., 1927)

Anonymous, *Establecimentos e resgates Portuguezes Na Costa Occidental de Africa* (Lisboa, Imprensa Nacional, 1881; first published 1607)

Arberry, A.J., *Sufism: an Account of the Mystics of Islam* (London, George Allen & Unwin, 1950)

Arcin, André, *Guinée Française* (Paris, Éditions Augustin Challamel, 1911)

Article 19 International Centre on Censorship, *Freedom of Information and Expression in Guinea* (London, Article 19 International Centre on Censorship, 1989)

Ba, Oumar, *Cheikh Amadou Bamba et la France* (Dakar, Archives du Sénégal, 197?)

Barbot, Jean, *A Description of the Coasts of North and South Guinea* (London, Henry Linton & John Osborne, 1746; first published 1732)

Beaver, Philip, *African Memoranda Relative to an Attempt to Establish a British Settlement on the Island of Bulama* (London, Dawson, 1968; first published 1805)

Behrman, Lucy C., *Muslim Brotherhoods and Politics in Senegal* (Cambridge, Mass., Harvard University Press, 1970)

Besant, Annie, *The Reality of the Invisible and the Actuality of the Unseen Worlds* (Madras, Theosophical Publishing House, 1914)

Biddlecombe, Peter, *French Lessons in Africa* (London, Little, Brown, 1993)

Bigman Laura, *History and Hunger in West Africa* (Westport, Greenwood Press, 1993)

Blavatsky, H.P., *Isis Unveiled* (Pasadena, Theosophical University Press, 1972; first published 1877)

Boahen, Adu, with Ade Adayi, Jacob F., and Tidy, Michael, *Topics in West African History* (Harlow, Longman, 1965)

Boulègue, Jean, *Les Anciens Royaumes Wolof* (Blois, Éditions Façades, 1987)

— *Les Luso-Africains de Sénégambie* (Lisboa, Ministério da Educação, 1989)

Boxer, C.R., *Race Relations in the Portuguese Colonial Empire 1415–1825* (Oxford, Clarendon Press, 1963)

Brévié, J., *Islamisme contre 'Naturisme' au Soudan Français* (Paris, Éditions Ernest Leroux, 1923)

Carreira, Antonio, *Vida Social dos Manjacos* (Bissau, Centro de Estudos da Guiné Portuguesa, 1947)

Coelho, Francisco de Azevedo, *Descrição da Costa de Guiné* (Lisboa, Emprêsa da revista Diogo-Caão, 1937; first published 1669)

Correia Lopes, Edmundo, *A Escravatura: Subsidios Para a Sua Historia* (Lisboa, Agência Geral das Colónias, 1944)

Crone, G.R. *The Voyages of Cadamosto*, translated and edited by G.R. Crone (London, Hakluyt Society, 1937)

Cruise O'Brien, Donal, *The Mourides of Senegal* (Oxford, Clarendon Press, 1971)

Davila, Julio, *Shelter, Poverty and African Revolutionary Socialism* (London, International Institute for Environment and Development, 1987)

Diallo, Thierno, *Alfa Yaya – Roi du Labé (Fouta Djallon)* (Paris, ABC, 1976)

Diop, Abdoulaye-Bara, *La Famille Wolof* (Paris, Éditions Karthala, 1985)

Donelha, André, *An Account of Sierra Leone and the Rivers of Guinea and Cape Verde* (Lisboa, Junta de Investigações Ciéntificas do Ultramar, 1977)

Duquesne, *A New Voyage to the East Indies* (London, Daniel Dring, 1696)

Eanes de Zurara, Gomes, *Cronica de Guynee* (Lisboa, Emprêsa da revista Diogo-Caão, 1937; first published 1506)

Ellison, Ralph, *Invisible Man* (Harmondsworth, Penguin, 1965; first published 1952)

Evans-Pritchard, E.E., *Witchcraft, Oracles and Magic among the Azande* (Oxford, Clarendon Press, 1976; first published 1937)

Fernandes, Valentim, *Description de la Côte Occidentale d'Afrique* (Bissau, Centro de Estudos da Guiné Portuguesa, 1951; first published 1510)

Field, M.J., *Religion and Medicine of the Gâ People* (London, Oxford University Press, 1937)

Galli, Rosemary E., and Jones, Jocelyn, *Guinea-Bissau: Politics, Economics and Society* (London, Frances Pinter, 1987)

Gellar, Sheldon, *Senegal: an African Nation between Islam and the West* (Boulder, Co., Westview Press, 1995)

Gomes, Diogo, *De la Première Découverte de la Guinée, récit par Diogo Gomes*, translated by Th. Monod (Bissau, Centro de Estudos da Guiné Portuguesa, 1959)

Gray, William, *Travels in Western Africa* (London, John Murray, 1825)

Guibert, Armand, *Léopold Sédar Senghor: l'Homme et l'Oeuvre* (Paris, Présence Africaine, 1962)

Hiskett, Mervyn, *The Development of Islam in West Africa* (London, Longman, 1984)

Hopkins, A.G., *An Economic History of West Africa* (London, Longman, 1973)

Hudgens, Jim, and Trillo, Richard, *Rough Guide to West Africa* (London, Rough Guides, 1999; first published 1990)

Hudson, Mark, *Our Grandmothers' Drums* (London, Secker & Warburg, 1989)

Humbaraci, Arslan, and Muchnik, Nicole, *Portugal's African Wars* (Dar-es-Salaam, Tanzania Publishing House, 1974)

Hymans, Jacques-Louis, *Léopold Sédar Senghor: an Intellectual Biography* (Edinburgh, Edinburgh University Press, 1971)

Joris, Lième, *Mali Blues* (London, Lonely Planet, 1997)

Kesteloot, Lilyan, and Mbodj, Chérif, *Contes et Mythes Wolof* (n.p., Nouvelles Éditions Africaines, 1983)

Kipp, Eva, *Guiné-Bissau: Aspectos da Vida de um Povo* (Lisboa, Editorial Inquérito, 1994)

Labat, Jean-Baptiste, *Nouvelle Rélation de l'Afrique Occidentale* (Paris, Théodore le Gras, 1728)

Laing, Alexander Gordon, *Travels in the Timannee, Koorankoo and Soolima Countries in West Africa* (London, John Murray, 1825)

Laye, Camara, *The African Child* (London, Collins, 1970; first published 1954)

Lemos, Francisco de, *Descrição da Costa de Guiné* (Lisboa, Emprêsa da revista Diogo-Caão, 1937; first published 1684)

Lespinay, Charles de, 'La Disparition de la Langue Baynunk', in *Contributions à l'Histoire du Sénégal*, edited by Jean Boulègue (Paris, Éditions Karthala, 1989)

Lindqvist, Sven, *'Exterminate All the Brutes'* (London, Granta Books, 1997)

Lobban Jr., Richard Andrew, and Karibe Mendy, Peter, *Historical Dictionary of the Republic of Guinea-Bissau* (London, Scarecrow Press, 1997)

Lyall, Archibald, *Black and White Make Brown: a Journey to the Cape Verde Islands and Portuguese Guinea* (London, W.H. Heinemann, 1938)

McNaughton, Patrick R., *The Mande Blacksmiths* (Bloomington and Indianapolis, Indiana University Press, 1988)

Manning, Patrick, *Francophone Sub-Saharan Africa 1880–1985* (Cambridge, Cambridge University Press, 1988)

Mapunda, O.B., and Mpangan, G.P., *The Maji-Maji War in Ungoni* (Dar-es-Salaam, East African Publishing House, 1969)

Markovitz, Irving, *Léopold Sédar Senghor and the Politics of Negritude* (London, W.H. Heinemann, 1969)

Marty, Paul, *Études sur l'Islam au Sénégal* (Paris, Éditions Ernest Leroux, 2 vols, 1917)

Mbiti, John S., *African Religions and Philosophies* (Oxford, W.H. Heinemann, 1989; first published 1969)

Mendelsohn, Jack, *God, Allah and Ju-Ju* (New York, Thomas Nelson, 1962)

Mendes Moreira, José, *Fulas do Gabú* (Bissau, Centro de Estudos da Guiné Portuguesa, 1948)

Mollien, Gaspard, *Travels in the Interior of Africa* (London, Henry Colburn, 1820)

Montefiore, Joshua, *An Authentic Account of the Late Expedition to Bulam* (London, J. Johnson, 1794)

Monteil, Charles, *Les Empires du Mali* (Paris, Maisonneuve et Larose, 1929)

Neal, James H., *Ju-Ju in My Life* (London, Harrap, 1966)

Okechukwu Mezu, S., *The Poetry of Léopold Sédar Senghor* (London, W.H. Heinemann, 1973)

O'Toole, Thomas, with Bah-Layla, Ibrahim, *Historical Dictionary of Guinea* (Lanham, Mass. Scarecrow Press, 1995; first published 1977)

Park, Mungo, *Travels into the Interior of Africa* (London, Eland, 1983; first published 1799)

Parrinder, Geoffrey, *Witchcraft* (Harmondsworth, Penguin, 1958)

Richards, Steve, *Invisibility: Mastering the Art of Vanishing* (London, HarperCollins, 1992; first published 1982)

Rivière, Claude, *Guinea: the Mobilisation of a People* (Ithaca, Cornell University Press, 1977)

Rodney, Walter, *A History of the Upper Guinea Coast: 1545–1800* (Oxford, Clarendon Press, 1970)

— *How Europe Underdeveloped Africa* (Dar-es-Salaam, Tanzania Publishing House, 1972)

— *West Africa and the Atlantic Slave-Trade* (Dar-es-Salaam, East African Publishing House, 1969; first published 1967)

Rogado Quintino, Fernando, 'A Habitação das Balantas', in *A Habitação Indígena na Guiné Portuguesa*, edited by A. Teixeira da Mota and G. Ventim Neves (Bissau, Centro de Estudos da Guiné Portuguesa, 1948)

Salverte, Eusebe, *The Philosophy of the Occult Sciences* (London, Richard Bentley, 1846)

Schoelcher, Victor, *L'Esclavage au Sénegal en 1880* (Paris, Librairie Centrale des Publications Populaires, 1880)

Sédar Senghor, Léopold, *Poèmes* (Paris, Éditions du Seuil, 1964)

— *Nation et Voie Africaine du Socialisme* (Paris, Présence Africaine, 1961)

Snelgrave, William, *An Account of Some Parts of Guinea and the Slave Trade* (London, James Knapton, 1734)

Sow, Alfâ Ibrâhîm, *Chroniques et Récits du Foûta Djalon* (Paris, Librairie C. Klincksieck, 1968)

Suret-Canale, Jean, *French Colonialism in Tropical Africa 1900–1945* (London, W.H. Heinemann, 1976; first published 1971)

— *La République de Guinée* (Paris, Éditions Sociales, 1970)

Suso, Bamba, and Kanute, Banna, *Sunjata: Gambian Versions of the Mande Epic* (London, Penguin, 1999; first published 1974)

Sy, Cheikh Tidiane, *La Confrérie Sénégalaise des Mourides* (Paris, Présence Africaine, 1969)

Sylla, Assane, *La Philosophie Morale des Wolof* (Dakar, Sankoré, 1978)

Teixeira, Candido da Silva, *Companhia de Cacheu e Comércio da Guiné* (Lisboa, Boletim do Arquivo Histórico Colonial, 1950)

Teixiera da Mota, A., 'Classificação e Evolução da Casa e Povoamento Indígena', in *A Habitação Indígena na Guiné Portuguesa*, edited by A. Teixeira da Mota and G. Ventim Neves (Bissau, Centro de Estudos da Guiné Portuguesa, 1948)

— *Guiné Portuguesa* (Lisboa, Agência Geral do Ultramar, 1954)

Thomas, Hugh, *The Slave Trade* (London, Picador, 1997)

Touré, Sékou, *Texte des Interviews Accordées aux Représentantes de la Presse* (Boston, Mass., Boston University African Documents Centre, 1959)

— *Poèmes Militants* (Conakry, Parti Démocratique de la Guinée, 1969)

Vellez Caroço, Jorge, *Monjur, o Gabú e a Sua História* (Bissau, Centro de Estudos da Guiné Portuguesa, 1948)

Vieillard, Gilbert, *Notes sur les Peuls du Fouta-Diallon* (Paris, Bulletin de l'Institut Français de l'Afrique Noir, 1940)

Villalón, Leonardo A., *Islamic Society and State Power in Senegal* (Cambridge, Cambridge University Press, 1995)

Wells, H.G., *The Invisible Man* (London, Fontana, 1966; first published 1897)